GILBERT SHELDON,
ARCHITECT OF ANGLICAN SURVIVAL,
1640–1675

ARCHIVES INTERNATIONALES D'HISTOIRE DES IDEES

INTERNATIONAL ARCHIVES OF THE HISTORY OF IDEAS

Series Minor

12

VICTOR D. SUTCH

GILBERT SHELDON,
ARCHITECT OF ANGLICAN SURVIVAL,
1640–1675

Directors: P. Dibon (Paris) and R. Popkin (Univ. of California, La Jolla)
Editorial board: J. Aubin (Paris); J. Collins (St. Louis Univ.); P. Costabel (Paris); A. Crombie (Oxford); I. Dambska (Cracow); H. de la Fontaine-Verwey (Amsterdam); H. Gadamer (Heidelberg); H. Gouhier (Paris); T. Gregory (Rome); T. E. Jessop (Hull); P. O. Kristeller (Columbia Univ.); Elisabeth Labrousse (Paris); S. Lindroth (Upsala); A. Lossky (Los Angeles); J. Orcibal (Paris); I. S. Révah† (Paris); J. Roger (Paris); H. Rowen (Rutgers Univ., N.J.); G. Sebba (Emory Univ., Atlanta); R. Shackleton (Oxford); J. Tans (Groningen); G. Tonelli (Binghamton, N.Y.).

GILBERT SHELDON

Architect of Anglican Survival, 1640-1675

by

VICTOR D. SUTCH

MARTINUS NIJHOFF / THE HAGUE / 1973

© *1973 by Martinus Nijhoff, The Hague, Netherlands*
All rights reserved, including the right to translate or to reproduce this book or parts thereof in any form

ISBN 90 247 1567 9

PRINTED IN THE NETHERLANDS

TABLE OF CONTENTS

Preface	VII
CHAPTER I: EARLY LIFE	1
CHAPTER II. THE CIVIL WAR	13
CHAPTER III. SHELDON DURING THE INTERREGNUM	32
CHAPTER IV. THE RESTORATION	61
CHAPTER V. ARCHBISHOP VS. KING I	91
CHAPTER VI. ARCHBISHOP VS. KING II	107
CHAPTER VII. SHELDON AND PARLIAMENT	130
CHAPTER VIII. SHELDON, PASTOR AND HIS PEOPLE	148
Conclusions	167
Bibliography	176

PREFACE

The place of Gilbert Sheldon in seventeenth century history and his influence upon the events of the period have long presented a tantalizing problem. A historian exploring the archives of the time cannot help but be impressed by the ubiquitous appearances of the archbishop. Yet the frequent references too often provide little detail, so that what emerges is a wraith-like picture of the man and a very uncertain account of his activities.

As a result it is difficult to know what to think of Sheldon. He has been termed a "Laudian," but Mathew Wren, Laud's loyal assistant and sharer of his imprisonment, was completely baffled by the initials "G. Sh." which appeared in a letter sent to him in the early 1650's. Also labeled a staunch Tory and a firm believer in the institution of monarchy, Sheldon showed no compunction whatever about lecturing the king on his duties or in boldly opposing the royal wishes when his lectures were ignored. He has been described as a man of "iron character," yet he was invariably soft-spoken and gentle to those in his immediate presence. He is pictured as a ruthless persecutor, but he often offered assistance, material and otherwise, to those who had been his opponents. Supposedly he was avaricious, yet the record suggests that during the Interregnum he impoverished himself to assist needy friends and church acquaintances, some of whom he barely knew.

These apparent paradoxes are the result of two problems pertaining to the archbishop. One has to do with the times in which he lived and the other the meagerness of the sources which have come down to us concerning his life.

The seventeenth century was a battle-riven period. Feelings ran high, and politics were bitter. There was little inclination on the part of most people to be either generous or forgiving to the foe. Consequently, the records of Sheldon vary dramatically depending on whether one is reading accounts written by the Puritans and Low Churchmen (his enemies usually), or those recorded by Anglicans and High Churchmen (usually his friends and followers).

The scanty sources, on the other hand, were the result of several factors. During the 1650's, when Sheldon, assisted by Henry Hammond, virtually commanded the Church both at home and abroad, records are particularly sparse. This was because the powerful Sheldon had ordered that no written records be kept by anyone for fear that a sudden government raid upon some suspected Anglican might uncover and implicate numbers of other people. So succesfully did he impose this rule that few records of the Anglican achievements in those years have survived. Because of this paucity, some historians have scornfully concluded that Anglican activities in this period were negligible and have labeled the Church's leadership as almost universally craven.

In the period of the Restoration Sheldon himself carefully collected and filed his correspondence, records, and other memorabilia, intending to write a history of his own time. Unfortunately, the archbishop was engaged in political activity almost to the time of his death, and when surcease finally came, he was too ill to carry out the projected work. Subsequently much of his data was lost or destroyed, although some still remains in manuscript form.

Finally Sheldon's own temperament and character work against the historian. He was a terse, self-contained individual who seldom bothered to discuss his thoughts, plans, or feelings. All of his official correspondence, even that sent to intimate friends, is brief, straight to the point, almost curt in tone. Only rarely is one given a glimpse into the workings of the inner mind.

For all of these reasons Gilbert Sheldon remains, and perhaps will always remain, something of an enigma. This work is an attempt to reclaim a part of the man at least.

If this book has value, it is mostly to be attributed to Professor Walter G. Simon of the University of Colorado. It began under his direction, and he continually offered much-needed encouragement and consistently wise advice. Colonel Alfred F. Hurley, Professor and Head, Department of History, United States Air Force Academy, assisted greatly at one point by arranging a few weeks of free time. My wife, Rebecca, patiently suffered much over several years to make it possible.

CHAPTER I

EARLY LIFE

Gilbert Sheldon was born at Ashbourne in Derbyshire on July 19, 1598. Very little is known of his family background.[1] His father, Roger Sheldon, is listed simply as a "menial servant" of Gilbert Talbot, the earl of Shrewsbury. But the term "menial" cannot have been used here in its modern sense. There is evidence that both Sheldon and his older brother Ralph inherited a considerable amount of property;[2] and the earl himself, along with the father of Bishop Sanderson, stood godfather at Sheldon's christening. These facts seem to indicate that Roger Sheldon was no ordinary servant. Perhaps it would be safe to surmise that the elder Sheldon was either a trusted bailiff who managed the earl's estates, or he may have been a Shrewsbury client – a neighbor of some standing – who served in the earl's interest.

Sheldon's own story begins in 1614 when he matriculated at Oxford University at the age of sixteen.[3] Robert Sanderson, ten years his senior and soon to become a lifelong friend and supporter, was already a

[1] V. Staley, Sheldon's only biographer, says that the Sheldon family was an old and respected one in the county. See V. Staley, *The Life and Times of Gilbert Sheldon* (London, 1913), p. 7. While pastoring at Ickford in the 1880's, Staley saw Sheldon's entries in the parish register, became interested in him, and attempted a short biography. This work is of very little value to the student. Apparently Staley was unaware of the manuscript sources available at the British Museum and the Bodleian library.

[2] Ralph Sheldon, who had the reputation of being a spendthrift, still left some property to his sons upon his death. In the fifties, Sheldon was involved on more than one occasion in suits at law aimed at protecting his nephew's holdings. See W. N. Clarke, "Illustrations of the State of the Church During the Great Rebellion." *The Theologian and Ecclesiastic,* (1851), XIII, 328, where Henry Hammond is assisting Sheldon in protecting some land belonging to his nephews. One of these, Sir Joseph Sheldon, was Lord Mayor of London in the 1670's. (This work is hereafter referred to as *Theologian and Ecclesiastic*.)

[3] Sheldon did not enter the University as a servitor as was usually the custom for very poor scholars, again indicating that his parents possessed some financial means.

proctor at Trinity College, and it was there that Sheldon embarked upon his academic career. He passed through the university at an average rate, taking the B. A. degree in 1617 and an M. A. in 1620. The two years following this latter accomplishment composed one of the few periods in his life when Sheldon was ruled by indecision. What was his life's work to be? Should he continue his studies at Oxford? Enter the Church? Turn to some secular activity? Whether he remained at the university or returned to Ashbourne during this period is not known. However, the year 1622 saw these problems resolved. Three events of that year profoundly influenced the remainder of his life: He was ordained into holy orders, he was elected a fellow of All Souls College, and he became chaplain to the family of Sir Thomas Coventry.

It is unlikely that the young Sheldon was impelled to enter the Church as a result of any powerful religious experience. He was later described as always "placing the chief point in religion in a good life" rather than in prayer and contemplation.[4] His reasons were problaby much more prosaic. He had ambitions of becoming a scholar, and scholarship and the clerical life were still inextricably bound together in the early seventeenth century as they had been for centuries past. Then too he was ambitious in other ways. In the event that scholarship proved not to be his forte, then the Church could provide an avenue to rank, perhaps wealth, and even to positions of national influence and prestige. Indeed in that aristocratic age the Church was almost the only institution in which his low birth would not prove an insuperable handicap.[5] At twenty-four Sheldon would have been well aware of all these factors.

This is not to say, of course, that his religious profession was in any sense hypocritical. As a citizen of the seventeenth century, Sheldon believed profoundly in the mission and importance of the Church. In his view society could not exist without it. It was a vital aid to the individual as he sought security in this life and the next, and it was equally vital to the preservation of a proper civil order within the kingdom. Sheldon was no time-server, merely seeking the main chance. To him the priestly vocation was sacred. He took his vows seriously, never married, and only one item of scandal ever arose concerning his private life – and that was probably manufactured from whole cloth by

---

[4] Samuel Parker, *History of His Own Times* (London, 1777), p. 41.
[5] To some extent the Church offered a career open to talent – one of the few areas of endeavor where that was true in the seventeenth century. After all Laud was the son of a linen draper, Jeremy Taylor the son of a Cambridge barber, Sheldon was the son of a "menial" servant, and William Sancroft, his successor at Lambeth, was also of obscure parentage.

a malicious enemy.⁶ In 1622 Sheldon took his vows to the Church, and his devotion and highest loyalty were to her and to her alone throughout his life.

In the seventeenth century, even as now, election to an All Souls' fellowship was recognition that one possessed scholarly potential. It provided quarters and an income and permitted Sheldon to continue his studies, thus opening the way to the fulfillment of his academic ambitions. With his election, Sheldon began a quarter century of daily activity centered at the Oxford college. Upon Warden Astley's death in 1636, he was elected to the wardenship and served in that capacity until evicted by the Presbyterians in 1648. In 1659, as the Restoration approached, he boldly re-occupied the warden's quarters but remained there only a few months until he was summoned to London to assume larger responsibilities. Upon being promoted to archbishop of Canterbury, Sheldon became All Souls visitor and was again intimately involved in that college's affairs. His love for All Souls and for Oxford University, and his interest in the progress of both, never flagged to the day of his death.⁷

The third event of the year 1622 – appointment as chaplain to the family of Sir Thomas Coventry – was perhaps the most significant in its immediate impact upon the young scholar's future. Coventry was a rising favorite at the court of Charles I. Upon Charles' accession to the throne in 1625, he appointed Coventry Lord Keeper of the Great Seal, and three years later raised him to the rank of baron. The new lord was active in court affairs, had a great deal of pressing business to transact, and delegated some of it to his chaplain – with astonishing results. He found that the young divine combined a sound business sense with meticulous attention to detail and a truly astounding capacity for work. The result was an administrator of the first rank. Employing Sheldon in a number of enterprises, both religious and secular, Coventry became steadily more impressed with his protegé's abilities.⁸ He obtained a prebendship for Sheldon at Gloucester Cathedral, and sometime in 1630 he recommended him to the king as "one well versed in politics and business." ⁹ There followed an invitation to preach at court, and

---

⁶ H. B. Wheatley (ed.), *The Diary of Samuel Pepys* (New York, 1948), II, 612. Pepys reports gossip to the effect that Sheldon was a "wencher."
⁷ For a summary of Sheldon's activities as warden of All Souls see Montagu Burrows, *Worthies of All Souls* (London, 1874), pp. 247-250.
⁸ Clarendon says that Coventry employed his services "not only in all matters relating to the Church, but in many other businesses of importance" as well. Clarendon, Edward, earl of, *Life* (Oxford, 1759), pp. 25-26.
⁹ Staley, p. 9, and *Dictionary of National Biography*, Sheldon's life.

the Oxford scholar was shortly installed as a royal chaplain. In a very short time the king too came to have a high regard for Sheldon's practical abilities. Rising steadily in his monarch's esteem, by the time of Charles' execution in 1649, the warden of All Souls had become one of the king's most trusted spiritual and political advisors.[10]

With such highly placed patrons, Sheldon shortly began to accumulate church livings on a grand scale. Besides the Gloucester prebendship and the royal chaplaincy – he was installed in both positions in 1633 – he was presented the vicarage of Hackney by Archbishop Laud when William Roberts, the former holder of that benefice, was promoted to Bangor. In 1636 he resigned Hackney when Charles presented him with two wealthier livings – those of Ickford and Oddington – both within easy range of Oxford so that he could properly supervise them. The warden subsequently resigned Oddington in 1639 when Laud granted him the even more lucrative benefice of Newington. The latter holding was only nine miles from Ickford, thus further simplifying his supervisory problems. In that same year Sheldon became Clerk of the Closet, and in 1641 the king increased his emoluments once again by bestowing upon him the mastership of Savoy hospital with its handsome London quarters and equally handsome income.[11] All of these, of course, were in addition to the wardenship of All Souls where he continued to reside and to which he devoted most of his energies throughout this period. All told, by 1641 Sheldon must have commanded a very satisfactory income.[12]

Throughout these years of steady advancement and growing prosperity, Sheldon was also achieving a reputation among his peers at Oxford. Unfortunately this was not, as he had hoped, the result of scholarly thought and productivity. It was rather for his courageous espousal of unpopular causes and intellectual positions.

Sheldon's independent judgment first became evident in the contro-

[10] The partnership between Sheldon and the king is described in Chapter II.

[11] Staley details all of these preferments, pp. 8, 9, 20, and 28. He seems to have the facts generally correct, although he does not make allowances for the change in the calendar. Thus he has Sheldon elected warden of All Souls in early 1635, when, in keeping with the modern reckoning of the year, it was actually March, 1636. Sheldon was prevented from occupying the Savoy quarters by the Civil War and only succeeded to that lucrative preferment in 1660. Besides the London residence, it probably brought him £ 400 to £ 500 per year.

[12] Apparently, with the single exception of Ickford, Sheldon served none of the above parishes himself – employing in every case a curate to serve in his stead. Ickford alone has entries in its parish register in Sheldon's handwriting. However, all of these are from the period of the early 1650's when Sheldon was dispossessed of all of his other livings but, through an oversight on the part of parliament, retained Ickford for several years.

versy over Arminianism. In the 1620's Arminian theology with its emphasis upon freedom of the will in religious matters – a position in direct opposition to the older predestinarian views of the Calvinists – was imported into Oxford and became a popular topic of conversation and debate. Encouraged by Laud and a few other university leaders, and also intrigued by Arminius' thought, a group of young scholars met regularly to discuss and forward the new doctrine. Sheldon, we are told, strongly opposed the new theology and was publicly counted as one of its chief antagonists.[13] Of course in the 1620's this was not a particularly unpopular position to take. But by the 1630's, with Laud firmly ensconced in the seats of power and pushing Arminianism vigorously and imperiously upon the Church and the country, it was a different story. Yet Sheldon never retracted his position. To the contrary, his membership in the Great Tew Circle accentuated his opposition to Laudian Arminianism and its accompanying ceremonial innovations.

The Great Tew Circle was composed of a group of congenial scholars, poets, wits, and friends who frequented Lord Falkland's manor house at Great Tew not far from Oxford. Besides the scholarly and open-handed Lord Falkland and the warden of All Souls, members of the circle included Sir Francis Wenman, Edward Hyde, William Chillingworth, George Morley, Robert Sanderson, John Hales, John Earle, and several other Oxford leaders.[14] The tenor of this group was notoriously pro-Calvinist and low church in sentiment. Falkland himself is described as having "such a latitude of opinion, he believed nothing in the Church could not be dispensed with," and both Sanderson and Morley were later to be on good terms with Presbyterians during the Interregnum and Restoration periods.[15] The story is told that on one occasion a lord, sincerely seeking information, asked Morley "what the Arminians held." Pleasantly the latter replied, "All the best Bishoprics and Deaneries in England" – a response which, when repeated to Laud, earned him the enmity of that humorless prelate.[16] It was with this group who gathered around Lord Falkland at Great Tew that the later Latitudinarian or Low Church Party originated, and of course this placed them in direct op-

---

[13] See DNB, Sheldon's biography, for Anthony Wood's emphatic statement concerning Sheldon's anti-Arminianism.

[14] It is reported that Falkland kept such constant open house that on any given day he never knew who was partaking of his hospitality until his guests gathered for dinner. Clarendon, *Life*, pp. 20-22.

[15] See *ibid.*, for a description of Falkland's position.

[16] *Ibid.*, p. 26. Laud was down on Morley for some time as a result of this remark, says Clarendon.

position to Laud and his supporters who have been described as the progenitors of the High Church Party.[17]

Although he would not have been in complete agreement with all the views expressed at Great Tew, Sheldon was in sympathy with most of them. An urbane, handsome man whose ready wit and quick repartee delighted all who gathered at the Falkland residence,[18] Sheldon regularly attended the Circle's sessions and took an active part in its discussions.[19] Robert Sanderson and George Morley were his closest and oldest friends, and Falkland appointed him executor of his will and guardian of his young son.[20] There can be no question but that Sheldon, along with the other members of the Great Tew Circle, was anti-Laudian and anti-Arminian in the 1630's.

Surprisingly, however, this did not place Sheldon solidly in the Calvinist camp. This became evident during the academic exercises held at Oxford in 1633. The All Souls fellow was standing for the degree Doctor of Divinity, and during the course of his examination, he emphatically denied that the Pope was anti-Christ. This peculiar belief was practically an article of faith among Oxford Calvinists, and everyone expressed surprise at Sheldon's stand. Dr. John Prideaux, who was presiding, refused to believe his ears.

"What, my son," he questioned Sheldon sharply, "is the Pope not anti-Christ?"

"*Etiam nego*," the young scholar firmly answered.

"*Profectò multum tibi debet Pontifex Romanus, et nullus dubito quin pileo cardinalitio te donabit*," Prideaux returned sarcastically.[21] Very shortly after this exchange Sheldon was joined in his enlightened position by a young scholar named Henry Hammond. But apparently for some years these two alone maintained their heretical position against the solid phalanx of Oxford opinion.

Not only did Sheldon oppose Laud's theology, at least on one occasion, he also boldly opposed the archbishop's actions. This was the celebrated Jeremy Taylor incident at All Souls. A graduate of Cambridge, Taylor came to Laud's attention in 1635 as the result of a brilliant sermon he

---

[17] George Every, *The High Church Party, 1688-1718* (London, 1956), Chapter I.

[18] During the Interregnum, Hyde could write to Sheldon from the continent and recall with nostalgia those pleasant days at Great Tew and could hope that "the time is drawing on that we may [again] enjoy each other." Peter Barwick, *Life of John Barwick* (London, 1724), p. 398.

[19] Clarendon reports that Sheldon was "frequently" at Great Tew. *Life*, p. 25.

[20] See *Theologian and Ecclesiastic*, VII, 147 and 285, where Sheldon and Hammond are supervising the Falkland holdings in the early fifties. There are numerous other entries in this series pertaining to Falkland business matters.

[21] This exchange is reported by Brian Walton. See H. J. Todd (ed.) *Memoirs of the Life and Times of Rt. Reverend Brian Walton* (London, 1821), I, 291.

preached while temporarily filling a London pulpit. Impressed by his abilities, Laud determined to arrange a fellowship for Taylor at Oxford. The opportunity came shortly after when a fellow at All Souls resigned his position and delegated to the archbishop the right to nominate his successor. Laud suggested Taylor, and the fellows compliantly voted to install him as one of their colleagues. As acting head of the college – Warden Astley was ill and shortly to die – Sheldon interposed the warden's veto.

To Sheldon, Taylor's election was fraudulent in every sense of the word. The custom by which the All Souls fellows nominated their own successors was itself a violation of the statutes under which the college was founded and was supposed to operate. As visitor, Laud had railed against the practice and had labored to reform it. (This apparently was one reason the fellows were so quick to accept Taylor. They wished to insure that this illegal practice would continue, and that they would in the future be permitted to nominate their successors.) Now the archbishop was making use of, and in the process confirming, the very evil he had previously denounced. Furthermore, Taylor could not qualify for a place at All Souls under any pretext. The statutes clearly declared that three years' study at Oxford was a prerequisite for an All Souls fellowship. Thus Taylor's Cambridge training barred him from entering the college at all. To overcome this objection and to lend "colour" to what he was doing, Laud hurriedly had Taylor enrolled at Oxford's University College just ten days prior to nominating him for All Souls. Such open and flagrant violations of the college statutes, by one who, he thought, ought to have known better and to have acted more honestly, was more than the warden could stomach. He denounced the whole unsavory business – in letters to Laud and by his veto – and fought to bar Taylor's admission.[22]

But Sheldon's was a lone voice, and as acting warden he had not the power to halt the illegal intrusion. In his customary, headlong way Laud rode roughshod over his subordinate's opposition and as All Souls visitor ordered Taylor's immediate installation. Very reluctantly Sheldon complied, and the Cambridge scholar was finally admitted to the fellowship.[23]

---

[22] This controversy between Laud and Sheldon is detailed in R. Heber (ed.), *The Works of Jeremy Taylor* (London, 1828), I, XIII, and Montagu Burrows, *Worthies*, pp. 144-148.

[23] Taylor remained at All Souls only for a year or two and then resigned his place. Perhaps he could not face the daily hostility of the warden, for Sheldon could be implacable in his hatreds. Later, during the Interregnum, Sheldon rescued Taylor and supported him with periodic financial contributions (see Chapter III). Taylor was deeply appreciative, but the two never became close friends.

These incidents from Sheldon's early life highlight certain traits of character which were to mark his activities throughout a long career. He possessed an independent cast of mind, and he had proved himself by 1640 to be a man who could stand stubbornly against all opposition, no matter how popular nor how high placed. He had the courage of his convictions. When examined, however, those convictions prove to be static, fixed opinions received from the past. There is no evidence in all of his life of a deepening intellectual growth nor of increased spiritual insight and understanding. He invariably looked to the past for guidance. Prescriptive right, tradition, common law – it was to these that he always turned to buttress his opinions, just as he turned to the founders' statutes in his controversy with Laud. When he found a basis for his actions in the past, he would cling stubbornly to that position, sometimes at great cost to himself both materially and otherwise.

In theology what he had received was the *via media* of the Elizabethan compromise, and he grimly opposed innovation in that religious position from the right or the left. In his early life Calvinism appealed to him more than Arminianism, not because of the intellectual attractiveness of either system, but simply because the former was ninety years older than the latter and hence possessed a longer tradition. But he is on record as opposing both Arminianism and Calvinism because both represented threats to the Elizabethan settlement. It was that illogical compromise that he had grown up in and which he loved and to which he would cling all his life. The only change one can see in Sheldon's views over a lifetime concerns the priorities of his opposition. Prior to 1640, his chief enmity was directed at Laud and the Arminians. They had the power, and they were busily engaged in revamping the Church of England into a new image that seemed to them more logical and proper. But these Laudian innovations represented a decided change from the Church which Sheldon had known in his youth. After 1660, when he had witnessed the terrible chaos and trouble which the Calvinists visited upon both Church and State during the Civil Wars, Sheldon reversed his position. From then on for the remainder of his life, he reserved his deepest hatred for the latter group. By that time, in comparison, the Arminians seemed an insignificant danger indeed.

From the foregoing analysis it would seem that the All Souls warden was hardly a *bona fide* intellectual. Nor was he. Although he worked hard and earned the scholar's professional credentials, yet he produced no original work. He read omnivorously all his life, appreciated scholars and their works, but was unable himself to produce anything of publishable value. Even sermons – that standby of almost every aspiring clerical scholar of the period – were for him a failure as a medium by which he might get his ideas before the public. Only three ever reached the light of day, and those were printed simply because they were preached before the king and were ordered published by royal proclamation. All three are lengthy, logically wrought works, with very little fire, and no imaginative flair at all; they would seem to offer conclusive proof that Sheldon's success as a churchman was in no way connected with outstanding oratorical or intellectual abilities.[24] (This would explain why, as far as we know, Sheldon preached only once before Charles I and just twice for Charles II. About the only thing these two monarchs had in common was a keen appreciation of good sermons.) To some extent it was this very lack of intellectual depth which made Sheldon what he was. Ideas seldom excited him, and therefore the lack of a cohesive theology inherent in the Elizabethan compromise bothered him not at all. In short, Gilbert Sheldon was an unimaginative, but totally convinced, conservative. He never doubted. For him the track of the past *always* provided the safest, surest, and most satisfactory path to the future. This was the secret of his great strength.

Since he was such a complete conservative in religious matters, one could safely predict that in politics Sheldon would also be firmly wedded to the past and just as firmly opposed to innovation, as indeed he was. We have already noted the Falkland Circle's opposition to the Laudian reforms. As a group they were equally opposed to the king's eleven-year experiment in personal rule. He was violating the basic tenets of the traditional English constitution, and they were certain – and Sheldon was firmly with them here – that things would never go well in England until parliament was recalled.

Edward Hyde and Lord Falkland have been aptly labelled "constitutional royalists," with the emphasis on the first word.[25] Thus it was with great relief that they welcomed the events which forced Charles to call parliament again in 1640. In the Short Parliament both men opposed the king and supported all efforts to insure that Charles would in the future recognize the legislature's rights and privileges. Both were decidedly upset when that parliament was abruptly dismissed, and they returned for the opening sessions of the Long Parliament in much the same temper.[26]

[24] For Sheldon's sermon before Charles I in 1630, see MS. Eng. Th., f. 14, Bodleian Library.
[25] I. Coltman, *Private Men and Public Causes* (London, 1962), p. 22.
[26] Hyde considered this abrupt dismissal of the Short Parliament as the most short sighted action of the reign. The members of that body, he was sure, wanted some reform, but they were basically loyal monarchists whereas the new parlia-

Upon his arrival in London in November of 1640, however, Hyde began to have some doubts about the new legislature. He wrote to Sheldon describing the makeup of the Long Parliament and expressing some concern over the increased radicalism of many of its members. He was apprehensive as to where they might lead the country and was bitterly critical of the royal ministers who had advised the dissolution of the earlier body – a much more loyal group to his way of thinking. Sheldon's answer shows him in complete agreement. He wrote:

> I am sorry matters do not move hopefully with you. The best service my meanness can contribute is my prayers, which I hope will be heard at this distance as well as if I were with you. If any good success happen, next under God, we are to thank men of your prudence and temper for it.[27]

Sheldon's opposition to the throne continued into 1641. In early spring of that year John Pym uncovered a plot in the London pubs to enlist men in a force that was to serve in "Portugal." Since the Portuguese ambassador knew nothing of any such army, Pym and his followers assumed that the military force was intended by the king for use at home, and they proceeded to expose the royal plot in the House of Commons. When they did so, several English officers who were apparently in charge of the recruiting fled to France, thus lending credence to the charges.[28] Pym and his colleagues then proceeded to make good use of the ensuing hysteria in order to force through the lower house a bill requiring all members to subscribe to an oath disavowing the desire for any kind of popish innovation in religion. This pledge reads:

> I, A. B., in the presence of Almighty God, promise, vow, and protest to maintain and defend, so far as lawfully I may, with my life, power, and estate, the true reformed Protestant religion, expressed in the Church of England against all poperie and popish innovations.[29]

Every member of the House of Commons took the vow, and it was then ordered sent to the country to be administered to all persons of significance everywhere. Later in the spring, Sheldon signed and accepted the

---

ment which met in November– the Long Parliament – was composed of rebellious, factious members whose loyalty to monarchy was suspect from the beginning. W. Dunn Macray, (ed.), *Clarendon's History of the Rebellion* (London, 1888, reprinted 1958), I, 183.

[27] F. J. Routledge, et al, (eds.), *Calendar of State Papers, Clarendon* (Oxford, 1872-1928), I, 209. (Hereafter referred to as CSP, Clarendon.)

[28] Hyde gives the details of this "plot" in *History of the Rebellion*, p. 198.

[29] See *The Parliamentary and Constitutional History of England from the Earliest Times to the Restoration of Charles II* (London, 1763), IX, 291.

oath at Oxford.³⁰ Since he never in his life signed anything under duress, and since the vow was clearly aimed at Laud and the court, it places Sheldon squarely in opposition to both at that time.

Yet curiously, none of this – Sheldon's active opposition to Arminianism, his membership in the Great Tew Circle, and his open support of Hyde and Falkland in their political opposition – seemed to affect Sheldon's standing with either the archbishop or the king. Both apparently were favorably disposed toward him, and in the period 1639 to 1641 the All Souls Warden, as has been noted, received promotion and rich benefices from the hands of both. However, the paradox here is more apparent than real.

Partly at least Laud's interest in and lenience toward Sheldon stemmed from the latter's part in reconverting William Chillingworth to the Anglican communion. Laud's godson, Chillingworth was a brilliant student who had defected to Romanism and had gone to the Jesuit training school at Douai. He quickly had second thoughts on the matter but was loath to return to England and his old faith. Both Laud and Sheldon labored mightily to rewin the errant cleric, but it was Sheldon's persuasive voice which finally convinced Chillingworth that the Church of England's discipline was broad enough to encompass his beliefs and that it was his proper spiritual home.³¹ It was with great relief that Laud welcomed his godson back into England and into the Anglican fold.

In addition, for all his angry intolerance, the archbishop was capable of appreciating and rewarding outstanding talent even when it resided in one who firmly disagreed with him. He is on record, for instance, of pressing a prebendary at Windsor upon John Hales, another member of the Falkland group who vigorously opposed the archbishop's religious policies, simply because he wished to reward Hale's superior scholarly attainments.³² So it was with Sheldon. Both the king and the archbishop appreciated his shrewd business sense and his superior administrative talents.³³ Both probably also correctly assessed the prevailing sentiment among the members of the Great Tew Circle. Fundamentally all were loyal to the throne and most were loyal to the Church. When the moment

---

³⁰ For Sheldon's signed pledge, see *Historical Manuscripts Commission Reports*, 5th Report, p. 131.
³¹ When he was dying in prison, Chillingworth wrote to his "spiritual" godfather, Sheldon, to inform him that he was still strong in the faith. Staley, p. 10.
³² Clarendon's *Life*, p. 27.
³³ For a glowing reference to Sheldon's administrative abilities, see a letter from Laud to Warden Astley, in William Laud, *The Works of Archbishop William Laud* (Oxford, 1860), VI, Part II, 444.

of decision came, all would flock to the royal standards.[34] For all of these reasons, Sheldon's career continued in its upward arc through the whole period of the thirties and early forties.

In early 1641 Sheldon's future appeared bright indeed. His livings gave him a magnificent income. He was an acknowledged leader in university affairs, and his advice was sought and valued by both archbishop and king. In proof of the latter he had just been made Clerk of the Closet – the closest personal religious advisor to the king – and had been awarded also the mastership of Savoy hospital. It was further rumored that he was shortly to be made dean of Westminster.[35] In modern terminology he would certainly be described as a "comer." Hyde felt that the warden's "learning, gravity, and prudence" made him "very equal to any preferment the Church could yield." [36] His Great Tew friends unanimously agreed. Sir Francis Wenman was often heard to declare that "Dr. Sheldon was born and bred to be Archbishop of Canterbury." [37] Unfortunately those fair prospects were soon to be hopelessly blasted.

---

[34] Nor were they mistaken. Every member of the Great Tew Circle supported the king. Clarendon and Sheldon became his closest advisors, Sir Francis Wenman and Falkland both died fighting for the royalist cause on the battlefield, William Chillingworth died in a Parliamentary prison after being captured on a battlefield where he was serving as royal chaplain, and Morley and John Earle shared Charles II's exile in the fifties and served as his court chaplains.

[35] Barwick, p. 280, n.
[36] Clarendon's *Life*, p. 25.
[37] *Ibid.*

CHAPTER II

THE CIVIL WAR

When it became evident early in 1642 that accomodation between king and parliament was impossible, Edward Hyde secured permission from the House of Commons to retire to his family estates in Wiltshire. He pleaded ill-health and the need of country air. He fully intended, however, to join the king and the court at York but did not dare let his purpose become known for fear that parliament's leaders might attempt to detain him in London. On his way north he stopped at Oxford where he stayed overnight with his friend, the warden of All Souls College.

Hyde and Sheldon must have spent several hours that May evening discussing the political situation and the grim outlook for the future. As Chancellor of the Exchequer, Hyde was particularly concerned about the king's lack of money. Parliament had moved immediately to block the crown's main sources of revenue and without some supply of ready cash, he could foresee little hope for the royal cause. Sheldon offered a suggestion. There was, he said, in every college treasury in Oxford – and he thought the same was true of Cambridge – a vast store of valuable plate which was seldom used and which could be melted down to produce a sizable sum of money. He was sure that whenever the king saw fit to send for it the colleges would loyally hand their treasure over, and he urged Hyde to relay this information to Charles.[1]

The king and his advisors eagerly grasped at Sheldon's suggestion. On July 7, 1642, letters were dispatched to both universities requesting loans of money from the fellows as well as the college plate, all of which was to be loaned to the crown at eight per cent per annum. The Oxford colleges ransacked their treasuries and shortly had several wagon loads of plate rumbling north toward York, 253 pounds of it coming out of the All Souls treasury alone.[2] All told Charles received over ten thousand

---

[1] Clarendon, *History of the Rebellion*, II, 330, n.
[2] Burrows, *Worthies*, p. 165.

pounds from Oxford in the summer of 1642 and probably an equal amount from Cambridge – although at the latter institution some of Sheldon's future bishops had to out-wit the vigilant Cromwell who attempted to ambush the university's wagon train and appropriate the treasure for parliament.[3]

Temporarily at least, the plate and money relieved the king's financial distress. After paying his most pressing debts, he still had plate left over which the royal treasury proceeded to mint into gold and silver coins.[4] There was no question as to the value of the warden's advice in this instance, and his standing at court increased perceptibly. When, late in 1642, Charles chose to move his headquarters to Oxford, Hyde made his home at All Souls and the two friends were deep in the royal counsels.[5] Over the next two and one-half years a good percentage of the royalist political planning was accomplished in the warden's quarters at All Souls.

Sheldon was soon joined also by another friend whose presence injected a large measure of buoyant, confident faith into the scholarly community at Oxford. This was his old acquaintance Henry Hammond. Since their anti-Christ controversy with the Calvinists back in the early thirties, Hammond's career had taken some extraordinary twists. A noted Latin, Greek, and Hebrew scholar, he had been invited to preach at court to replace the ailing Dr. Accepted Frewen. His sermon so impressed the earl of Leicester that he bestowed upon Hammond the living of Penshurst in Kent, and the devout scholar forthwith resigned his Magdalen College fellowship in order to devote himself to the cure of souls. His household at Penshurt included his mother, who acted as housekeeper and confidante, and his nephew, the later renowned diplomat, Sir William Temple, who came to further his education under Hammond's supervision. Thus the years passed in a quiet round of parish routine and scholarly activity.

When war broke out, the determined curate vigorously began to recruit a troop of horse on behalf of the king. To attempt such an action so close to London, practically under the nose of parliament, was at best foolhardy. Hammond's company of cavalry was run to the ground and defeated before it was even at full strength, and the doughty clergy-

---

[3] See Barwick, p. 24, where he reports that St. John's College, Cambridge, supplied plate in excess of £ 2000. Barwick, who was at St. John's at the time, relates the Cromwell incident.

[4] Another loan from the same source, attempted after Edgehill in January, 1643, was not nearly so successful. Cromwell was not to be outwitted a second time, and Oxford was able to give very little. Burrows, *Worthies*, p. 165.

[5] See DNB, Hyde's biography, for his residence in those years.

man shortly found himself a fugitive with a price on his head. Eluding his pursuers, Hammond escaped to Oxford where he was re-admitted to his old Magdalen College quarters. Having failed with the sword, he now tried the pen, and to his amazement, his first published work, *Practical Catechism*, proved an instant success and brought with it a train of honors. The university chose him as its public orator, the king made him a royal chaplain and gave him a canonry at Christ Church, and he was admitted fully into the royal counsels where both Clarendon and Sheldon came to value him highly. Within a very short time the two chaplains had become fast friends and co-workers, thus forming a partnership which was to last for years and was to bear much fruit for the royalist and Anglican cause in the future.[6]

In those first years of the war Sheldon left Oxford only once – to attend the ill-fated treaty of Uxbridge which was attempted in February of 1645. He was appointed one of the clerical commissioners for this task, along with Richard Steward, an All Souls fellow who seems to have borne the main burden of the ecclesiastical debates held there. Assisting these two were Hammond, Benjamin Laney, Henry Ferne, and Edward Potter. The secular commissioners were led by Hyde himself who was assisted by the earls of Hertford and Southampton. Since the king remained adamant in his preference for Episcopacy over Presbyterianism, the negotiations ran fruitlessly for twenty-one days; whereupon the argument was transferred once more to the battlefield. Sheldon's part in the treaty discussions seems to have been negligible. On one occasion he warmly seconded Steward's arguments, drawing upon himself, as Hyde reports, the ire of the parliamentarians for his vehement defense of the Anglican position.[7]

By early 1646 the New Model Army had swept the royalist forces from the field. As a result Charles' headquarters at Oxford became untenable, and a move in some direction became mandatory. In April the king spent long hours with Sheldon, Hammond, Sanderson, and Morley trying to decide how far he might "with good conscience comply with the proposals of parliament for a peace in Church and State." [8] He and his clerical advisors recognized that some compromise arrangement was probably now inevitable, and it was possible of course that the complete Presbyterian system would have to be accepted for the whole realm. However, they were not yet willing to surrender on this issue, and

---

[6] For these details of Hammond's life, see his biography in the DNB and J. Fell, *Life of Henry Hammond* (Oxford, 1847), Introduction.
[7] Clarendon, *History of the Rebellion*, II, 583.
[8] I. Walton, *Lives* (London, 1678), p. 451.

even if they did, they were certain in their own minds that the Anglican cause would, at some future time, triumph. Furthermore when that glorious day arrived the Church must be restored in all of its splendor and with all of its lands and wealth intact. As proof of his firm intentions in this matter – and perhaps also as proof of his full commitment to the Church of England – during the course of a long discussion with his Clerk of the Closet, Charles wrote out the following vow:

> I do here promise and solemnly vow, in the presence and for the service of Almighty God, that if it shall please his divine Majesty of his infinite goodness to restore me to my just kingly rights and re-establish me in my throne, I will wholly give back to his Church all those impropriations which are now held by the Crown, any land so ever I now do or should enjoy which hath been taken away, either from any Episcopal see or any Cathedral, or Collegiate Church, from any Abbey, or other religious house. I likewise promise for hereafter to hold them from the Church, under such reasonable fines and rents as shall be set down by some conscientious persons, whom I shall choose with all uprightness of heart to direct me in this particular, and I most humbly beseech God to accept of this my vow and to bless me in my designs I have now in hand.[9]

Charles signed this pledge April 13, 1646, and gave it into Sheldon's keeping. Two weeks later, accompanied by only two retainers, he rode out of Oxford to make peace with his enemies.

Sheldon's leadership of the Church of England begins here. Laud was dead, many of the bishops were imprisoned, and many others were dispossessed and unwilling or unable to provide effective leadership. As one who possessed the king's full confidence in religious matters, Sheldon's standing with Anglican leaders was already high. News of the king's vow must have soon circulated among loyal Anglicans, and the fact that the All Souls' warden had been entrusted with that paper, and with it the key to the Church's future, enhanced his prestige and standing immeasurably. From this point on Sheldon's counsel and advice in church matters was regularly sought by bishops and college leaders alike, and little was done without his prior approval.[10]

On May 2, the king appeared at the Scots' camp near Newcastle-upon-Tyne. He was immediately escorted by Leslie's troopers into the city

---

[9] Lambeth MSS. #943 contains this vow, probably written in the king's own hand.
[10] The deference shown Sheldon by such persons as Samuel Fell, the Oxford vice-chancellor, and other college heads when they were concerting strategy, and by Bishop Duppa and Robert Sanderson while they were treating with parliament on the Isle of Wight, can only be explained by the increased stature which he now possessed. Sheldon had become the man who had to be satisfied in Church affairs.

where he was virtually held a prisoner from May 13, 1646 to January 28, 1647 when the Scots' army returned home.

During this period every effort was made to convert the king to Presbyterianism and to get him to take the League and Covenant. Over several months the eminent Scots' divine, Alexander Henderson, conducted a written colloquy with the Stuart monarch in a vain effort to convince him that presbyters were divinely sanctioned while episcopacy was in no sense a necessary part of God's plan.[11] In face of all the arguments which the Scottish divines could muster, Charles held staunchly to his faith, answered argument for argument, and pled his coronation oath as a sufficient reason why he could not authorize such a change in church arrangements.[12]

Although he succesfully thwarted all Presbyterian conversion attempts, practical politics seemed to decree that some measure of the hated system must be allowed. But to what extent? And for how long? Charles was not sure, but by late September he was apparently ready to make some concessions. On the last day of the month he wrote to William Juxon, bishop of London, seeking advice. Could he, he wanted to know, permit the establishment of Presbyterianism for a limited time despite his coronation oath? He urged Juxon to consult with Brian Duppa, bishop of Salisbury, and Dr. Sheldon, and send him their opinions "with all convenient speed." [13] What answer they gave, we do not know. But it must have been a clear negative, for the Scots could not move Charles on the religious issue. Hence when they returned home three months later, they turned the king over to his parliamentary enemies at Westminster.

On February 16, 1647, Charles was ordered transferred to Holmby Castle in Northamptonshire. Arriving there the next day, he immediately wrote parliament asking that several of his chaplains, including "Dr. Sheldon, Clerk of the Closet," be permitted to attend him. Again on

---

[11] DNB, Henderson's Biography. Henderson died in late summer, supposedly brokenhearted at his failure to convert the king to Presbyterianism.

[12] The king's arguments, which we are told were effective at Newcastle, see *ibid.*, may have been rehearsed with Charles by Sheldon and his friends in the weeks before the Stuart monarch left Oxford. He was talking with Sheldon and the other chaplains almost every day in that period and all arguments would certainly have been thoroughly canvassed. In addition, these same points were debated with Henderson at the Uxbridge treaty negotiations where Henderson had been their principal opponent. They would therefore have been thoroughly familiar with the thrust of his argument and would have "prepped" the king accordingly.

[13] Sir Giles Isham (ed.), *The Correspondence of Bishop Duppa and Sir Justinian Isham, 1650-1660* (Northamptonshire Record Society, Vol. XVII; London, 1956), p. xxiii. Also *CSP, Clarendon*, I, 335.

March 7 he asked for Sheldon, along with some others, but both requests were denied on the grounds that none of the royal chaplains had taken the Covenant.[14] The army, in the persons of Cornet Joyce and some Ironsides troopers, forcibly took possession of the king on Friday, June 4. Shortly after, Charles asked once more for his chaplains, but this time addressed his request to Cromwell and Fairfax. More tolerant than the politicians, they readily gave their approval. Thus on June 21, Sheldon and Hammond arrived at Hatfield House where the king was now being detained.

When some parliamentary commissioners arrived there also, they were scandalized to find, as they reported, Sheldon, Hammond, and another chaplain, Herbert Crofts, using "divers superstitious gestures" as they held services for the king according to the Book of Common Prayer.[15] When their report came before parliament, the House of Commons immediately ordered Sheldon and Hammond removed as persons "unfit to serve the king." The army leaders chose to ignore the order. The Speaker of the House then wrote directly to Fairfax upbraiding him for permitting Anglican chaplains to attend the king. In a conciliatory response, Fairfax assured the House that Sheldon and Hammond were men "who would not do ill offices to prejudice the peace of the kingdom." Anyway, he pointed out, their attendance upon the royal presence had been permitted only "upon his Majesty's continued importunity for it."[16] The House of Commons was loath to accept Fairfax's assurances. Both Sheldon and Hammond were the acknowledged leaders of the Oxford resistance movement which was at that moment attempting to block parliament's control of the university,[17] and to permit such intransigent loyalists to advise the king seemed impolitic to say the least. For this reason on July 1 the leaders of the House of Commons laid a complaint before the lords charging the two chaplains with disrespect for the Directory, and both were ordered to report to the bar of the upper house to answer for their conduct. However, once more the generals refused to enforce parliament's mandate.[18] The

---

[14] Fell, p. xxxix.
[15] J. Cosin. *The Correspondence of John Cosin.* (The Publications of the Surtees Society. Vol. iii, 1868; London, 1869), Part I, 232. Under no conditions would the commissioners stay to take part in this "popish" service. Instead they departed for a church in town. Here they were equally nonplussed to find an Ironsides officer in his buff coat and sword preaching against the Presbyterian government in London as "anti-Christian."
[16] Fell, p. xxxix.
[17] See below, pp. 23ff.
[18] Fell, p. xxxix.

two chaplains thus found it possible to ignore the summons, and both remained with the king for the remainder of the year.

The fact that the army freely permitted Sheldon and Hammond, along with the other chaplains – Sanderson and Morley were also with the king during much of this period – to attend their beleaguered monarch was a source of great satisfaction to the royalists.[19] It seemed to augur well for the future. Hyde, writing from the island of Jersey to John Earle, was overjoyed to hear of it. He was sure that "they who had an impious design on the king's conscience would not have suffered Dr. Sheldon and Dr. Hammond to have ministered to him." [20] Because of the army leaders' generous behavior, he felt certain that events were now going to take a favorable turn for the king, and later in the month he wrote Sheldon congratulating him on the excellent prospects now evident "for a redemption of the kingdom." [21]

Yet the fair prospects failed to materialize. Just as he had alienated the Scots' leaders earlier, the king now followed the same disastrous course in his dealings with Cromwell and Fairfax. Like quicksilver, Charles possessed an elusive quality which could not be pinned down nor successfully captured and enclosed. Just when one was certain that the king had firmly committed himself to an agreement, he would shortly find to his dismay that in reality the English monarch had slipped aside and the whole issue was once more up in the air. One might well ask how much of this elusiveness was a product of the king's basic nature and character and how much was it a planned stratagem, advised by Sheldon, Hammond, Morley and his other ministers?

The royal chaplains, led by Sheldon, were with the king daily for the last half of the year 1647. Sheldon, in his position as Clerk of the Closet, not only advised Charles, but during much of the period he was something of a chief minister, aiding, establishing policy, and carrying on much of the royal correspondence.[22] Neal, the historian of the Puritans, ascribes much of Charles' misfortune as well as his later violent death to "those divines whom he took into his counsel during the war" and who would not permit him to make concessions with respect to the Church.[23] To some extent, at least, it would seem that this accusation is just. Sheldon and Hammond were fighters. They would cling stub-

---

[19] Clarendon, *History of the Rebellion*, IV, 228, states that Morley and Sanderson joined Sheldon and the king almost immediately.
[20] *CSP, Clarendon*, I, 384, Hyde to Earle, July 15, 1647.
[21] *Ibid.*, I, 384, Hyde to Sheldon, July 26, 1647.
[22] See *CSP, Clarendon*, I, 380-400, where Sheldon is writing regularly to Hyde sending him the king's instructions.
[23] D. Neal, *History of the Puritans*, (London, 1837), II, 545.

bornly to the Church and its forms as long as there was any hope that Anglicanism or any part of it could be salvaged from the general wreckage of the Civil War. And when all hope was finally gone, they would continue to use the Book of Common Prayer in their private services even though they ran great personal risks by doing so.

It would appear that Sheldon completely misjudged the strength of the anti-royalist sentiment among the army leaders. He seemed to believe with the earl of Manchester that if parliament should "beat the king ninety and nine times, yet he is king still, and so will his posterity be after him." Nothing the army or parliament could do would change that. Ultimately they would have to seek an accomodation with the king, just because he was the king.[24]

Feeling this way, Sheldon throughout this period was urging Charles to hold out against the Presbyterian parliament and the Independent army until some agreement could be reached which would preserve a measure of the episcopal system. This would account for the king's failure with the Scots' army commissioners in 1646. Now in 1647 Sheldon, Hammond, Morley, Sanderson and others of their friends, were in constant attendance upon the king, and it must have been partly at least at their behest that he now proceeded to alienate the army leaders in the same way.

The strength of the royalist feelings about this matter is clearly shown in the late summer of 1648 at the time of the negotiations between the king and parliament conducted on the Isle of Wight. Bishop Duppa and Robert Sanderson were the main ecclesiastical advisors to Charles during the whole of the conference,[25] and both wrote regularly to Sheldon keeping him informed of what occurred there. As the sessions drew to a close, Duppa wrote a lengthy letter summarizing the accomplishments of the Isle of Wight conference. "You may thank your confinement," he wrote bitterly to Sheldon, "that it hath freed you from the saddest employment that ever you were called to." The king, he went on, had just handed in his final answers on church matters wherein he had accepted the Presbyterian system for three years and had confirmed the sitting of the Westminster Assembly, thus making the work of that body official. Two points on which Charles refused to surrender were the abolition of episcopacy and alienation of church lands. On the first,

---

[24] As late as the middle of January, 1649, Sheldon was still quite confident that although the army-dominated Rump parliament might try their monarch, they would never dare do him any personal harm. See a letter from Sheldon to Hammond, January 15, 1648/9, Theologian and Ecclesiastic, VI, 77.

[25] Charles had requested Sheldon and Hammond, but they were in prison at Oxford and parliament refused to release them for the conference.

however, he did agree that the office of bishop should be reduced to its primitive simplicity; while on the second point, he thought that long leases or some other device might be acceptable. The king also, continued Duppa, had yielded complete control of the militia to parliament, "wherein he shows that however it may be thought he hath parted with too much in the one, he reserves in effect nothing at all to himself in the other." Duppa closed his jeremiad with the unhappy prophecy that the timing of the treaty, "like so much else done by the king," would destroy what impact it otherwise might have had. He begged Sheldon and the other church leaders to judge himself and Sanderson charitably. After all they were forced to be upon the place and actually found themselves able to do little to prevent such a distasteful agreement.[26]

From the foregoing, it appears that the Sheldon group – of whom Duppa was one – could not yet in 1648 accept the fact that compromise with the Presbyterians was inevitable. Apparently they were advising the king, even at that late date, to hold out for better terms. It also is apparent, however, that they were critical of their monarch. They disliked his dilatoriness, his timing of the treaty – "like so much else done by the king," as Duppa phrased it – and his instability. Much of the bitterness and frustration expressed in this letter, and those of Sanderson written in the same period,[27] arose from their total uncertainty of what Charles would do next. The king seldom, they found, restricted himself to taking advice from any one person or group. He often promised to do so, but influenced by some glib courtier who happened to gain admittance to his presence, he frequently broke his promises and acted contrary to the best advice his wisest counsellors gave him.[28] It was no doubt recognition of this trait of Charles that led Sheldon in 1646 to secure the king's written vow in regards to the Church and its lands. No matter what action he might take on the spur of the moment regarding religion, he was at least pledged in writing to the ultimate restoration of the Anglican establishment.

Thus although one must conclude that they were incredibly obtuse as to the unhappy end towards which their advice was carrying the king, yet the Anglican chaplains cannot bear the total blame for his death. The fatal flaw in his own character, a flaw which prevented him from boldly

---

[26] Duppa to Sheldon, Oct. 19, 1648. Lambeth MSS. #943.
[27] See especially Sanderson to Sheldon, Sept. 25, 1648, *ibid*.
[28] This trait of Charles is shown particularly in January, 1642. He had just made Hyde responsible for all royal activities in the House of Commons, but influenced by Digby, he shortly after attempted to arrest the five members without ever informing Hyde of his intentions. See DNB, Hyde's biography, for his angry reactions to this incident.

"cutting his losses" and firmly committing himself to some compromise, was not of their making.

Sheldon spent much of October, 1647, back at Oxford bolstering the Anglican leadership in its struggle to ward off parliamentary control of the university's activities.[29] He was again at Hampton Court the first of November; however, it must have been in his absence and without his knowledge that Charles decided upon the ill-planned and ill-advised flight from the army which he succesfully carried out in November.[30] Charles escaped from Hampton Court on November 11 but was recaptured and imprisoned at Carisbrooke Castle under the watchful eye of Col. Hammond, the Puritan nephew of Sheldon's fellow chaplain, just two days later. But it was not until November 27, more than two weeks later, that Sheldon accompanied by two other chaplains – Heywood and Holdsworth – arrived in the Isle of Wight to resume his services to the king.[31] Hammond arrived a few days later. This two-week interlude suggests that the chaplains had to ascertain, first, where in fact the king had gone, and second, whether they wished to hazard their own safety by attempting to follow such an unstable, unpredictable master. But with Sheldon and Hammond an affirmative decision could not be long in coming; they set out to follow the king and thus continue to render to him such service as they could, as long as they could.

However, what must have seemed, to some extent at least, an onerous service now came abruptly to an end. The army's leaders, like the Scots before them, concluded that Charles was totally unreliable and could never be trusted to keep any bargain he might make. Thus his privileged status as a royal guest whose desires and requests were to be treated with deference was brought to an end. All of his chaplains were ordered barred from the Isle of Wight by December 27.[32]

As that date was only a few days off, the king sought permission from his captors to spend one last, undisturbed day alone with one of his chaplains. He chose Sheldon as his confessor and companion, and the two spent the entire day strolling about the grounds at Carisbrooke or

[29] See below p. 25.
[30] There is no evidence to support this point except as is noted in the following sentences. Yet it seems certain that Sheldon knew nothing of the projected flight or else advised against it. His was a practical mind, and he seldom made a move without carefully planning it and knowing exactly what he expected to accomplish. The king's penchant for sudden, rash, ill-planned action could only have been abhorred by someone of his make-up and temperament.
[31] See Egerton MSS. 2618, British Museum, Charles to Fairfax, Nov. 27, 1647, where the king announced the arrival of Sheldon and his friends and requested permission for them to remain with him.
[32] Fell, p. xxxix.

in the royal apartments, so engrossed in prolonged and serious conversation that they were oblivious to everything and everyone around them. It would be invaluable to know what passed between the king and his chaplain on that day. Sheldon later told Samuel Parker that the king entrusted him with many "secret and last counsels, especially commands to be delivered to his son." He dwelt at length upon his own plight and those factors which were responsible for his being brought to such an ignominious imprisonment. He would, he said, remember three things in the future:

First, that he should forgive his rebellious enemies as much as he would, but never trust one of them, unless he were willing to be ruined again.
Secondly, that he should keep his exchequer as full as possible; for subjects would not dare to rebel against any but poor princes.
Thirdly, that as far as it was in his power, he should expiate the sin of sacrilege; and especially that he should be an example to his subjects, by restoring those revenues to the church which the impiety of former times had taken from it.[33]

Yet this was only a bare fraction of the multitude of topics which must have been touched upon during the course of that long winter's day. As evening approached, Charles was so taken by Sheldon's conversation that he insisted upon prolonging their talk until midnight; only then, he reminded his guards, was the day officially over. Col. Hammond generously permitted the king's stratagem to succeed, and thus Sheldon parted from his master for the last time at midnight, December 26, 1647.

The following day, he, Hammond, and the other chaplains, began their journey back to Oxford. There they would continue their struggle with their parliamentary enemies, but with different methods and upon another level.

Shortly after Charles departed from Oxford in May, 1646, Fairfax appeared before the city and proceeded to lay it under siege. By midsummer the city fathers had accepted the terms offered by the army leaders and surrendered their city to parliament. Although they were included in the terms of the treaty, the university's leaders did not plan to submit tamely to parliamentary control. Stubbornly royalist and Anglican in sentiment, the majority of them charted a course of determined resistance to, and deliberate flouting of, every order issued by parliament and every agent sent from London to supervise them. Judging from the brutal punishments meted out earlier to the leaders of their sister uni-

---

[33] Samuel Parker, *History of His Own Times* (London, 1777), p. 51.

versity for a similar course of action,[34] they were certain to endanger their livelihood, their property, and even their lives by pursuing such a policy. Nevertheless, compromise and accomodation were almost unanimously ruled out. Defiant resistance for as long as it was physically possible became their program.

Assembled in full convocation, the university appointed a committee to plan strategy and to deal with the parliamentary visitors which they were sure would shortly be arriving. Since future convocations would no doubt be difficult to arrange, the royalists pledged themselves to follow all instructions issued by their chosen leaders. Members of this strategy committee were the vice-chancellor, Samuel Fell, Sheldon, Hammond, Morley, Sanderson, and a number of others. John Selden apparently aided the group with legal advice.[35] Thus, before parliament's agents ever arrived at Oxford, the university was thoroughly organized, tactics and approaches had been carefully canvassed, and over-all strategy consummately planned by some of the ablest minds the university has ever produced.

The opening gun in the battle was fired by parliament, when, shortly after the surrender, it sent the League and Covenant and the Negative Oath to the university with instructions that they be subscribed to by all "Doctors of the Chair" and all heads of colleges. The university immediately dispatched Hammond to plead with Fairfax – an attempt to divide the army from parliament – that the legislature's order contravened the articles of surrender which the army and the university had only just agreed upon. At the same time the strategy committee drew up a manifesto, which it sent to Westminster and later had published and circulated in the capital, setting forth the reasons why such oaths were in violation of their consciences as well as earlier vows taken to the king.[36] Infuriated by the committee's effrontery in publishing its case, parliament's leaders next sent express orders that no vacancies occurring in the university or in any college were to be filled until they had been consulted. The university ignored this charge and throughout the remainder of 1646, appointments to all vacancies were made as the leadership saw fit.[37]

---

[34] Many of the Cambridge college heads were imprisoned below decks in a coal scow, under horrible conditions, and were even in imminent danger for some time of being sold into slavery in Barbados. See Barwick, p. 37.

[35] See I. Walton, p. 450, and M. Burrows, (ed.), *The Register of the Parliamentary Visitors, of the University of Oxford* (Camden Society Publications, New Series, Vol. 29, 1881), p. lxiii, for the membership.

[36] *Ibid.* Burrows calls this position paper a "skillful" bit of pleading.

[37] Most of these events are given in Burrows', introduction, *ibid.* However, in

In September, parliament sent seven Presbyterian divines to preach the university into submission. They were greeted with scornful laughter, and when they took over the popular St. Mary's for their services, the Anglicans simply moved en masse to St. Mary Magdalene's and left them facing an almost empty church. In addition, there were among the New Model army units stationed in the city some Seekers who voiced strong opposition to the parliamentary preaching mission. They considered it their peculiar task to preach in a frenzy, and they resolved to outdo their Presbyterian brethren in this respect. The result was utter anarchy as services were held almost every day, both in church and out, with frenzied and impassioned oratory and argument going on everywhere. So passed the winter of 1646-7 with Oxford University still firmly under Anglican control.

In the spring of 1647, parliament at last determined to bring the university under its supervision. On May 1 an ordinance was approved by both houses "For the Visitation and Reformation of the University of Oxford and the several Halls and Colleges therein." [38] Twenty-four visitors were appointed who were to compose a regulatory commission. Among other things, they were ordered to see to it that every scholar and college administrator adhered publicly to the League and Covenant and the Negative Oath and that the order of worship prescribed by the Westminster Directory was followed in all religious services. In addition, they were charged with the duty of ferreting out and arresting those college members who had borne arms against parliament. Any scholar who refused to conform was to be banished from the university within twenty-four hours but was to be allowed the emoluments of his office for a subsequent six months. A standing parliamentary committee of twenty-six lords and fifty-two members of the House of Commons was established to hear any appeals that might arise from the commission's actions.

The visitors arrived in Oxford on June 1. They made their headquarters at Merton, the most strongly Puritan of the colleges,[39] and immediately set to work. Their first act was to summon all heads of colleges to meet with them at Merton on June 4 at eleven o'clock. The university leaders learned that the visitors were to attend a preaching service at St. Mary's prior to the meeting, so they planned their strategy ac-

some places Burrows' account is sketchy and one must go to the Wood MSS. f. 35, the Bodleian Library, where many of the documents produced by the strategy committee are available.

[38] E. H. Plumptre, *Life of Thomas Ken* (London, 1890), I, 40, describes this act in some detail.

[39] See Burrows, *Worthies of All Souls,* p. 130.

cordingly. Knowing that most Presbyterian divines were given to longwinded sermons and that they seldom dismissed their services on time, they resolved to meet at Merton but to wait only until precisely eleven o'clock. If the visitors had not arrived by then, the college leaders would leave in a body exactly on the hour. As foreseen, the parliamentary commissioners were late in returning to Merton and met the university officials as they were leaving the hall. Fell, the vice-chancellor, politely pointed out that it was after eleven, doffed his cap, and he, Sheldon, and the other college heads swept imperiously past, leaving the visitors gaping after them. Thus, the first round went to the university.[40]

On that same day, June 4, the army seized Charles and took him from Holmby Castle. Upon hearing of that action, the university immediately challenged the commission's authority, and unsure of their position, the visitors returned to London for a fresh citation. This left the visitation paralyzed for another three months. In the interim Sheldon and Hammond, accompanied by some of the other chaplains, left the university to join the king in his imprisonment. However, the strategy was well-planned, and Samuel Fell and some others remained to see it carried into effect.

By the last of September, satisfied once more concerning the legality of their appointment, the Presbyterian commissioners returned to Oxford and again set to work. They now dispatched citations to all college heads ordering them to appear with their "Statutes, Registers, Journals, Books of Accompt, etc." to answer the commission's charges. No one appeared. Again they wrote, in stronger terms. But again no one appeared. Fell received eight different citations between the first and the eighth of October, and he ignored all of them. So did the other college heads. All were following the advice given on a memorandum circulated by the strategy committee. It stated:

1. Uniformly to resolve instead of submitting with all civility to the parliament to plead statutes, privileges, oaths, in each case. The university not to submit to any but *Regular* Visitations.
2. Reasons for this advice. By not submitting or nonappearance some advantages to be gained, as Time in which debate of the issues. Lesser danger than from appearance, for if they have power to evict or to punish, appearance subjects to all accusations; non-appearance to imprisonment [only] or that one accusation of standing upon Statutes, Privileges, or Oaths.[41]

With its opposition thus tightly organized, the parliamentary com-

---

[40] Burrows, *Register of Parliamentary Visitors*, p. lxiii.
[41] Wood MSS. f. 35.

missioners found themselves completely isolated from the university. They sat at Merton feverishly writing citations to which no one paid the slightest heed, while university life went on as though they did not exist. In desperation, on the eighth, they asked parliament to summon Fell to London to answer to the special committee for his conduct. Upon arrival in the capital, the vice-chancellor was seized and imprisoned. It was hoped that this action would deprive the university of its directing intelligence and the remaining college officials would then become more tractable. However, the resistance continued unabated.[42]

University strategy now changed. Some of the leaders were permitted to appear before the visitors, but only for the purpose of questioning the legality of their commission. The reasoning behind this shift, and the directions from the strategy committee were as follows:

> To appear *coram non judice* is not a submission to or an acknowledgment of jurisdiction without an empartance. Neither is it an empartance to require a sight or copy of his commission. But to receive a charge or to desire any time to answer any charge... is an empartance in law and is an acknowledgment of jurisdiction...
> You may therefore appear. But he that doth appear is to:
> 1. Desire a sight of his Commission or hear it read.
> 2. If they refuse – persist in the requirement.
> 3. If shown or read – desire a copy of it and time to consider it.
> 4. If they refuse or give it – he is to say he is sworn to recognize the King only as Visitor, whereas they are pretended Visitors.[43]

The first scholar to attempt the new strategy was Henry Wightwick. He was shown a copy of the visitors' commission and saw the king's Great Seal attached to it. He then requested permission to travel to the king to ascertain whether he really did approve of their visit, which he very much doubted. For his "smart" answer, Wightwick was ordered banished from the university, but he ignored the order and continued with his work.[44]

Thus the battle continued throughout the fall. Lacking authorization to use force, the visitors continued isolated from the university and powerless to make any impression upon the organized recalcitrance of its leaders. Late in November the frustrated Presbyterians prevailed

---

[42] Sheldon returned to Oxford and remained there during most of October. This indicates that with Fell in prison, and himself and Hammond at Hampton Court waiting upon the king, a leadership problem had been created by the visitors' action in regard to Fell. See Wood MSS. f. 35, where Sheldon is cited to appear before the visitors in mid-October.
[43] *Ibid.*
[44] *Ibid.*

upon parliament to summon a number of the more obstreperous of their enemies to London to stand trial, along with Fell, for their insolent behavior.

This move on the part of the visitors did indeed emasculate the university's leadership. Sanderson, as Regius Professor of Divinity, was among those cited to London; John Selden and George Morley were in the capital during the trial to assist in the defense of the university leaders; and of course Fell himself as among those who were to be tried. With Sheldon and Hammond off with the king on the Isle of Wight, the strategy committee was decimated, and the university very nearly, in late November and December, surrendered to its enemies. Thomas Barlow, fellow of Queen's College and Bodleian librarian, and a Dr. Potter, whom Fell had appointed pro-vice-chancellor, were left to head the resistance struggle alone.[45] A cautious individual, Potter for a while refused to act in any official capacity, and the university was without a head. Barlow and others finally convinced him that he must assume the leadership, but he was wavering, and how long he would stick, they weren't sure.

In this crisis Barlow turned in desperation to the warden of All Souls. He urged Sheldon to write to Potter "to fix him in his determination." He seemed certain that Sheldon's orders would be effective, and without Potter, he pointed out, "no legal publique act" could be accomplished by the university. Also he wished to know, since the strategy committee no longer existed, whether it would not be wiser to call a convocation and "get the approval of the whole university for what heretofore they have done by delegation." They needed assistance desperately, and Barlow ended his letter with: "We desire to receive your commands and advice." [46]

Sheldon received Barlow's letter about the first of December. He responded immediately urging Barlow and Potter to use every effort to keep the scholars united and the resistance movement in full force. However, the army officers provided the answer to the university's leadership problem. When they ordered the royal chaplains out of the Isle of Wight and away from the king, they solved some of their own problems but compounded those of parliament. For by the first of the year Sheldon and Hammond were back at Oxford where they were able

---

[45] Which Potter this is, it is difficult to say. There were four Potters at Oxford in the thirties. Edward Potter, the Head of Queen's College, who had accompanied Sheldon and Steward to Uxbridge, died in 1646, so it would not have been he.

[46] Wood MSS. f. 35, Barlow to Sheldon, no date, but late in 1647.

to infuse new courage and confidence into their Anglican colleagues. The struggle was once again enthusiastically resumed.

In late winter numbers of pamphlets began to appear in London ridiculing the parliamentary visitation. One of these, authored by Barlow, bore the title, "Pegasus, or the Flying Horse from Oxford, Bringing the Proceedings of the Visitors and Other Bedlamites." [47] Others of the same stripe soon followed. If parliament and its visitors were not to become a laughing stock, some drastic action had to be taken.

Thoroughly aroused, parliament now dispatched the Oxford chancellor, the Puritan earl of Pembroke and Montgomery, to take charge of the visitation and exert the government's authority. For all of his choleric anger,[48] Pembroke too found himself at a loss before the organized and disciplined recalcitrance he encountered among the university officials. He thereupon returned to London, explained the situation to parliament, and on March 23 that body voted to place a troop of soldiers at the disposal of the board of visitors.[49] Pembroke returned to Oxford at the head of these forces on April 13 and shortly after began systematically evicting all persons of known royalist sympathies "down to the very cooks and butlers." [50]

When the earl, accompanied by William Prynne, some of the other visitors, and a dozen of his "janizarries," arrived at the warden's quarters, Sheldon met him at the door, and in his usual soft-spoken way, asked to see his commission. Pembroke produced it. After studying the document for a moment, Sheldon pointed out to the Presbyterians that it was dated March 8 and authorized them to evict those heads who had been voted out by parliamentary action prior to that date. His own expulsion had not been voted until March 30. Therefore, he argued, he did not come within the scope of their commission and legally they could not evict him. Nonplussed, the visitors returned to the quadrangle to discuss the matter; Sheldon stepped back into his quarters and bolted the door. After an hour's discussion, Prynne resolved the difficulty by arguing that although Sheldon was not within the letter, he certainly was within the equity of their commission, and anyway "Parliament must not be fooled with." Encouraged by this bit of casuistry, Pembroke sent

---

[47] Barlow's Biography, DNB. Sheldon probably was behind these broadsides. He was well aware of the value of creating public opinion and gave it more and more attention throughout his career.

[48] When Fell appeared before the parliamentary committee in London, Pembroke denounced him as "an incendiary of the whole kingdom," wanted to see him "whipped through the streets and hanged." Wood MSS. f. 35, Fell to Sheldon, Nov. 13, 1647.

[49] Theologian and Ecclesiastic, VI, 163.

[50] Plumptre, I, 140.

his soldiers to break down the door and take Sheldon prisoner.[51] The same hour Hammond was seized at Christ Church, and the courageous Mrs. Fell, who had defiantly barricaded herself in the vice-chancellor's quarters, had her door battered in and was bodily carried into the quadrangle. Hundreds of students and fellows gathered to watch as their champions were led away to jail. By nightfall all colleges were in Presbyterian hands; the Oxford resistance movement was at an end.

We are told that all of the foregoing events were managed by Sheldon "in concert with John Selden." [52] However, one must include in the Oxford leadership Samuel Fell – until his arrest – and Henry Hammond who was of such significance in the eyes of the visitors that only he was chosen to join Sheldon in his imprisonment. All the other rebel leaders were ordered banished from the university within the prescribed twenty-four hours.

One might accuse Sheldon and Hammond of fighting a hopeless, rear-guard action here which could only have one outcome – complete and total defeat. Yet Sheldon was preeminently a practical man, and ordinarily he would have shunned any irrational action, however romantic it might appear in retrospect. Nor would he have been attracted to such a course of action simply for its nuisance value in annoying parliament. To make it worthwhile, the resistance program would have had to have more significance than that, and it did.

When the university inaugurated its resistance campaign – late 1646 – the king was still negotiating with both parliament and the army, and either attempt might yet have been successful. At that moment too no one could have known what would be the outcome of the struggle between the predominantly Independent army and the predominantly Presbyterian parliament. The Independents were concerned, said Barlow in one of his letters to Sheldon written at the time of the college leaders' trial, that Oxford, like Cambridge, might be molded into a Presbyterian institution. They feared that if that happened the whole country might in time be influenced to that position, and that would mean the end of their own form of worship. Because of this, Barlow wrote, "we find the Independents generally favorable to us... and indeed 'tis much against their interests to permit this visitation to go on." [53] It was this division among his enemies that Sheldon hoped to exploit, and indeed it was to gain time to see this split widen that motivated his whole plan. Stall,

---

[51] This interesting by-play is recorded by Walker, *Sufferings of the Clergy* (London, 1714), II, 98.
[52] Burrows, *Register of Parliamentary Visitors*, p. lxviii.
[53] Wood MSS. f. 35, Barlow to Sheldon, Dec. 11, 1647.

delay, postpone – these were at the core of the Oxford leaders' program, and the delaying tactic was eminently successful. Oxford surrendered in July, 1646, but it was not until nearly two years later that parliament secured control of the university. That in itself was no mean feat. Furthermore, the whole plan came close to succeeding. The vote in the trial of the college leaders conducted in London was thirteen to ten.[54] This close division in itself indicates that the attempt made by Sheldon and his friends to retain independence for the university was no hopeless, last-ditch effort.

[54] *Ibid.*

CHAPTER III

SHELDON DURING THE INTERREGNUM

Sheldon's place of imprisonment was "James Chesterman's House over against Cross Inn." [1] Hammond was lodged in another residence close by. Both were constantly guarded by New Model soldiers. However their imprisonment was alleviated by permission to have visitors – a permission which was freely granted – and very soon such a stream of scholars and students began to seek them out to ask their advice about university and church affaires that their jailers grew nervous. The extent of their influence, the depth of their opinions, the strength of their leadership – all of these gave the new Presbyterian university officials pause. Was it desirable to keep such influential royalists imprisoned so close to Oxford? They decided not, and on May 30, a month and a half after their arrest, the "Committee of Lords and Commons for the Reformation of the University of Oxon" met at Westminster and moved to correct what was becoming a difficult situation. "Taking into consideration that his confinement there [at Oxford] may be of dangerous consequences, in regard of the great respect of persons to him," they ordered that Dr. Sheldon, "be conveyed to Wallingford Castle, there to be kept in safe custody by the governor of the said castle" until the committee decided what further to do with him.[2] Subsequently, Hammond was included in the order.

Then there occurred one of those strangely perverse situations, the frequency of which makes seventeenth-century England such a delightful subject of study. The governor of the castle, a Col. Evelyn, was acquainted with both Hammond and Sheldon, and although he strongly opposed their religious and political principles, he admired the men, and he flatly refused to accept them as prisoners. As guests and friends, he said he would gladly entertain them; but as prisoners in his castle,

[1] Burrows, *Worthies*, p. 184.
[2] Wood Mss. f. 35. Order dated May 30, 1648.

he simply would not receive them.³ Balked by this independent stand, the committee uneasily permitted the two royalist leaders to remain in their prison quarters at Oxford throughout the summer and into the fall.

By September the Oxford Visitors were determined that the two royalist leaders should not be allowed to remain longer in the vicinity of the university. Permitting them their freedom seemed preferable to that. Therefore on September 20, the Committee for the Reformation of Oxon ordered both Sheldon and Hammond to certify where they wished to reside.⁴ Hammond elected to live with Sir Philip Warwick at Clapham in Bedfordshire. Sheldon, however, had business to conduct on behalf of his nephews and some friends in exile, and "because," as he wrote, "I know not any place where, nor friend with whom, I may for the present be associated or settled," requested that he might be free to reside in any place not prohibited by parliament. He pledged himself to keep "Mr. Richard Newdigate of Gray's Inn" informed of his whereabouts and promised to appear at any time the committee should desire.⁵ A month later, October 24, 1648, by order of parliament, the royalist leader was free to pursue his business anywhere in the realm, "except within five miles of the city of Oxford, or in the Isle of Wight." ⁶ The committee thus insured that Sheldon's influence would not in the future be exercised upon either the king or the university.

However, the warden was no sooner free than he again ran afoul of the authorities and shortly found himself once more a prisoner at Chesterman's house. In preparation for his departure he had gone to All Souls and collected some horses from the stable there. Someone saw him leading them away, and reported it to the new warden, John Palmer. In high dudgeon, Palmer immediately secured an order from the Visitors sending some officers from the garrison to repossess the horses, "which belongeth to the said college," and return them to the All Souls' bursar. The same order placed Sheldon once more under arrest.⁷ It took the ex-warden another month to convince the Presbyterians that the animals were actually his personal property and not that of the college; thus it was not until December 18 that he was free once more to begin his preparations to leave the city.

Prior to his departure, Sheldon wrote a lengthy letter to Hammond

---

³ Fell, *Life of Hammond*, p. xliv.
⁴ Burrows, *Parliamentary Visitors*, p. 187.
⁵ Wood Mss. f. 35.
⁶ *Ibid.*
⁷ *Ibid.* Burrows in his *Worthies of All Souls*, p. 197, has Sheldon taking *houses* which belong to the college. He is a bit at a loss to explain how houses could be seized by soldiers and returned to the college bursar.

who was now residing in Bedfordshire and whom he had not seen for the nine months of their imprisonment. He had heard that Hammond was ill – the first of his attacks of "the stone" – and he wished to hear that his friend was well again "before I take myself to my country retirement which will be at a great distance from London." In discussing the king's plight – he was undergoing trial in London – the ex-warden attempted to encourage Hammond. "I do not think," he wrote, "that we have been in the wrong notwithstanding the ill-success of our friend; therefore these adverse times trouble me the less, as being more patient of other men's faults than my own." He felt relatively certain that the Rump Parliament would never dare put the king to death. But, he admitted, one could not be sure, since in his opinion those men were "more to be feared for their ignorance than their wisdom." [8]

Sheldon was still at Oxford when news of the king's execution arrived. To all the royalists this was the most shattering blow of the entire conflict. It represented the total destruction of all they held dear, of all that gave meaning to their lives. They were evicted from their college positions, their parish livings were appropriated by others, their beloved Church was outlawed. Now the principle of monarchy itself was dealt a crushing blow. Hammond could only write bitterly, "God hath spit in our face." [9]

Sheldon himself was prostrated by the news. It was weeks before he recovered his customary tranquility and calm, and years later, when discussing the matter with his chaplain, he still could not help but display some emotion.[10] As he himself said, nothing ever really touched him in this period, "but only the misfortune of the king." [11] Perhaps it was a sense of guilt, a guilt that arose because he held himself in some degree responsible for the king's tragic end, but whatever the reason, only this one event in his whole life is reported as having cracked what was a monumentally cool composure.

The impact upon all Anglicans was traumatic. If the rebels would go to such lengths as to behead their monarch, then who of lower rank was safe? Any one of them might be selected as the next to be martyred for the cause. As a consequence, an exaggerated fear permeated all levels of the Anglican hierarchy for the next year or two, and all overt activity on behalf of the Church ceased. The question of personal safety took precedence over all others. Many Anglican clergymen fled to the con-

[8] *Theologian and Ecclesiastic*, VI, 77.
[9] *Ibid.*, VI, 4.
[10] Parker, p. 52.
[11] *Ibid.*

tinent where they sought employment in various capacities but often ended by accepting charity in the form of grants and loans extended to them by friends and relatives in England. However, most determined to remain there, in poverty or otherwise, until "that cursed ayre at home" was safe to breathe once more.[12] Those who stayed in England sought some position – usually as a chaplain or tutor to a landed family – where they could live inconspicuously far from the capital. Even Hammond and Sheldon, those two truculent fighters who up to this point had boldly captained the royalist resistance to both parliament and the army, now joined the ranks of those seeking refuge from the storm. During the early 1650's the Anglican cause in England was at its nadir.

Hammond found a secure asylum when, in violation of the terms of his parole, he left Clapham in order to render spiritual assistance and comfort to the family of Sir John Pakington. Early in 1650 at the urgent request of Sir John's perennially ill wife, he took up his residence at Westwood, the Pakington estate in Worcestershire. He was to remain there as chaplain, friend, and member of the family until his death in 1660. Apparently content as long as he stayed far from London and Oxford, the Cromwellian government made no move to return him to the Warwick residence at Clapham.[13]

Sheldon found his "calm in the midst of a tempest" at Bridgford in Nottinghamshire where he obtained employment as chaplain to the Okoevers, a minor landed family of the county. Here he lived comfortably, "well-pleased with the rivers and fields [he was an ardent fisherman] and honoured by the neighbors," until old Mrs. Okoever, the matriarch of the clan, died in 1653.[14] He then transferred his residence to the home of an Okoever daughter who had risen above her station by marrying the wealthy Sir Robert Shirley. Until the Stuart restoration, Sheldon made his home with the Shirleys, standing godfather to the Shirley sons and performing duties as spiritual guide and trusted advisor to the whole family.[15]

Once safely ensconced in their separate places of refuge, the two clerics turned to survey the wreckage of the Church. The outlook could only have been a discouraging one. The outward organization had all

---

[12] A phrase used in a letter from Edward Hyde to his wife in 1651. HMCR, Bath II, 88.
[13] Hammond's biography, DNB.
[14] J. Thoroton, *A History of Nottinghamshire* (London, 1839), p. 151.
[15] Sheldon looked upon the Okoever and Shirley families as his own. Their births and deaths are recorded in his personal bible, he performed many services for both families after the Restoration, and he was godfather to Sir Robert Shirley's grandchildren who were born in the 1660's. See Ms. Bib. Eng., 1648, d. 3, Bodleian library.

but disappeared. Of the leaders, some were in prison, some had fled the country, and most of those who remained were so demoralized that they were content to sit quietly, doing nothing. Church lands were seized, whole congregations became Presbyterian or Independent overnight, and the universities – those erstwhile strongholds of Anglicanism – were now in the hands of the enemy. It has been estimated that two-thirds of the clergy made peace with the government and renounced their allegiance to the Book of Common Prayer and all Anglican forms of worship.

Abroad the morale of the expatriate Anglicans was equally low. One correspondent wrote mournfully to Sheldon, "We hope, but that is all." [16] Catholic-leaning Anglicans were bombarded with appeals like the following:

> You have lived a long while in heresy, which hath brought God's anger and indignation upon you: Your kingdom of England is ruined: Your church is lost: Your bishops and priests are put out of their places and never likely to be restored: Your nine and thirty articles are at an end – nobody regards them.... The head of your church aches and is ready to perish: The members are scattered and torn in pieces.[17]

One could scarcely argue with that description of the Church of England and many of its adherents succumbed and defected to Rome. Nor could one hope for aid and comfort from the Protestant churches on the continent. The Church of England held most of them to be in error and would have no intercourse with them. Even if, by some stroke of fate, the king were to be restored to his throne and power, the Church would very probably still be lost, since any restoration seemed ultimately to depend upon assistance from either Presbyterian or Independent. In a restoration engineered by either there would certainly be no place for the prelatical Anglicans. Perhaps the greatest danger of all was the impossibility of consecrating new bishops. When the remaining ones passed away, would not the Church of England cease to exist? Assuredly the danger was great.

Amidst all the gloom, however, a few assets were visible. There was a hard core of clergymen who remained loyal to the Church and its forms. While it was true that many of these were dispossessed of their livings and were even, in some cases, in want for the necessities of life, yet a few had been overlooked and still retained benefices and income.[18]

---

[16] *Theologian and Ecclesiastic*, XII, 166.

[17] *Ibid.*, XI, 89. Cosin's only son was a Catholic convert at this time; Cosin disinherited him and would have no more to do with him.

[18] Sheldon himself retained the rich benefice of Ickford until 1653 with all of its income and even held services there regularly in the early 1650's. *Ibid.*, XIII, 328.

In addition, among the defectors there were some clerics whose hearts and minds were still Anglican and who only grudgingly left off the prescribed forms in order to retain an income and provide bread for their families. Indeed some of these latter, although outwardly abandoning the Book of Common Prayer, successfully retained the essence of its liturgy in forms of their own contriving. Finally, there were many laymen who remained doggedly loyal to king and Church. They liked the old forms and the old religion, and many of them still had property, money, and other resources at their disposal. The only thing lacking in order to make use of these elements was leadership. This Sheldon and Hammond began to supply as early as 1650. They provided a rallying point about which loyal Anglicans could gather and to which they could look for direction.

Their first problem was to locate the scattered Anglican clergy. In the summer and fall of 1650, the two friends made a determined effort to trace all clerics who were likely to be loyal and to prod them into keeping in touch. Their letters of this period are full of discussion regarding the whereabouts of mutual acquaintances, and gradually their correspondence widened as they brought these friends and acquaintances into their sphere of influence. Early in 1650 Robert Payne, one of the dispossessed Oxford leaders, now residing at Abingdon, began writing to keep Sheldon informed of all significant events occurring at the nearby university.[19] About the same time, George Morley began to report regularly upon the activities of the Anglican community at Antwerp. Upon being reprimanded by Sheldon for not having performed this service earlier, he excused himself with, "it was for your sake only I forbore to write, as fearing letters from here might be as prejudicial to you as I heard they have been to others." [20] From Paris reports began to arrive regularly from "Belleau," a Sheldon correspondent who kept the two Anglican leaders posted on their friends who lived there.[21] Richard Steward, Sheldon's old All Souls colleague, now chaplain to Charles II, reported on the activities of the court. Frances Mansell, another All Souls fellow and ex-principal of Jesus College, reported from Wales, along with Jeremy Taylor. From Yorkshire, Sheldon received letters from Henry Ferne, and from Salisbury both he and Hammond heard regu-

---

[19] See a series of letters from Payne to Sheldon, *ibid.*, Vols. VI through X.
[20] *Ibid.*, VII, 124.
[21] For letters from "Belleau" to Sheldon, see *ibid.*, X, 328; X, 329; XII, 166; XII, 167. "Belleau" was probably William Lloyd, later a bishop but in the early 1650's he was living in exile in Paris.

larly from Humphrey Henchman.[22] There were others also.[23] Bishop Duppa was a frequent correspondent of Sheldon's, and Mathew Wren, bishop of Ely, who spent the entire Interregnum period imprisoned in the Tower, was consulted regularly by Hammond about scholarly problems as well as church matters.[24]

From the available evidence, it appears that Hammond and Sheldon were constructing an underground correspondence net. Each working in his own area and beginning with his own friends, extended his correspondence to include as many of the Anglican clergy as could be found who were interested in taking part. Its purpose was to look after the interests of the Church, its clergy, and its loyal members to whatever extent was possible under the circumstances. It was through this organization that the two clergymen picked up the reins of church leadership, abandoned by the bishops, and gave some cohesion to the scattered personnel of the Anglican establishment. Since it was an illegal apparatus, its members in constant fear of government apprehension, and since the government made a practice of opening the mails, Sheldon, Hammond, and their correspondents seldom wrote openly of what they were doing. They made oblique references to most projects, used initials, partial names, nicknames, place names – i.e., "the knight at Rufford," "the conjuror," "a fellow of the Angle," "our sick friend," etc. – when referring to mutual acquaintances, and in some instances lapsed into outright code.[25] The most important matters were transacted through verbal orders only.

All of this, coupled with Sheldon's angry insistence that no "file copies" be retained by anyone [26] – for fear that government agents might through a sudden raid obtain information which would expose the whole net – makes the task of the historian extremely difficult. However,

---

[22] Numbers of letters from these people are reproduced in *Theologian and Ecclesiastic*. Mansell returned to Oxford in 1651, but Taylor was a regular correspondent of Sheldon's in the years after that. There is much evidence of Henchman's correspondence, and his biographer (see DNB) states that he was in touch with Anglican and royalist leaders during this period.

[23] See later this chapter, where Duppa and others are in constant correspondence with Sheldon and Hammond. They even extended their net to include Bishop Wren, imprisoned in the Tower of London.

[24] *Theologian and Ecclesiastic*, IX, 290-298, gives the text of several letters from Wren to Hammond and the reverse.

[25] Sheldon invented a completely new alphabet which he proposed that the net use. Hammond wrote one letter in it, found it too cumbersome, and went back to the system of oblique references.

[26] See *ibid.*, VI, 167, where Payne apologized profusely to Sheldon for losing a copy of a letter. He promised never to retain a copy of any message in the future.

a careful reading of the Sheldon-Hammond correspondence for the period reveals the outlines, even though blurred and indistinct, of a considerable organization engaged in an amazing amount of activity on behalf of the Church, the clergy, and English royalists.[27]

The problems involved in keeping a *sub rosa* net of this dimension functioning were manifold. The ordinary mails could be used only for innocuous messages. Therefore dedicated and courageous royalists had to be found to carry any message of significance to the Church or exiled court. To travel around the country secretly visiting known royalists was to invite the attention of a suspicious and ruthless government. To have oneself smuggled back and forth across the channel involved even greater risks. Yet volunteers for such hazardous duty were seldom lacking. For the first year or so, the chief Anglican agent operating within England was Isaac Barrow, later a renowned scholar and bishop, but at that time Hammond's secretary and protégé. However, frightened by the seditious nature of the messages he was called upon to carry, early in 1652 Barrow absolutely refused to serve further. In reporting his refusal to Sheldon, Hammond commented wryly, "I hoped that he might have adventured to continue in his employments until he had been forbidden particularly." [28] Anyway, as Hammond saw it, there was far more danger to Sir Robert Shirley, the recipient of some of Barrow's messages, than to Barrow himself. But Barrow could not be prevailed upon to continue his travels, so Hammond suggested a young student, "one of six at Dr. Heywood's" who volunteered to replace him. Others who assisted in this dangerous work were Dr. Eleazor Duncan who crossed the channel on church business in 1655; Sir Leoline Jenkins whom, we are assured, was a Hammond-Sheldon agent for a part of the period; [29] and Richard Allestree and John Barwick.

A scholar of Christ Church and a close friend of Hammond's (Hammond bequeathed his entire library to him when he died), Allestree apparently was the main agent employed to carry messages between the Church leaders in England and the court on the continent. He made the cross-channel trip on several occasions – all of them successful until

---

[27] Much of the two divines' extant correspondence has been published in *Theologian and Ecclesiastic*. Unfortunately, what has come down to us covers only the first five years, 1649-1654. of the Interregnum period. All these letters are taken from Harleian Mss., 6942, The British Museum, and were edited by W. N. Clarke in the mid-nineteenth century. This is the best single source on the Church during the Interregnum period.

[28] *Ibid.*, XII, 168.

[29] W. G. Simon, *The Restoration Episcopate* (New York, 1965), p. 101.

he was apprehended and imprisoned by the government in 1660.[30] However, his colleague, John Barwick supplied the organization and was the focal point for all messages going and coming from the continent. After being released from prison, where he had been kept under close guard for two years for receiving suspicious messages from abroad, Barwick was in constant contact with the court from 1652 onwards. Clarendon provided him with the necessary keys and cyphers, and he and the Lord Chancellor regularly exchanged encoded messages concerning church affairs all through the Interregnum period.[31] Sheldon and Hammond were in touch with Barwick continually, and it was through him that they dispatched much of their business with the court,[32] as well as with other Church leaders in England.

---

[30] See Allestree's biography, DNB, and Barwick, appendix, where Allestree is at the court and is dispatched into England with messages for the Anglican leaders.

[31] *Ibid.*, appendix, contains a long series of letters from Edward Hyde to Barwick and vice-versa.

[32] There is a lengthy letter to John Barwick, undated and unsigned, which is reproduced in Barwick, pp. 537-47. It was written in answer to a query from Barwick about church discipline, and how, and if, it should be imposed. This letter can now be definitely ascribed to Sheldon and dated from internal evidence: 1) The author is having difficulty with his eyes — they are constantly filling with rheum, making it difficult for him to read or write. Between 1651 and 1653, on several occasions, Sheldon suffered from this same disability, but particularly in the spring of 1653, when this matter of church discipline came to a head. See *Theologian and Ecclesiastic*, VI, 170 and X, 329, for letters from both Morley and Hammond commiserating with Sheldon about his eyes. 2) This letter is written in Sheldon's inimitable style. He writes in a straightforward, almost modern fashion — especially when he is strongly moved — as though the ideas are mounting steps, one imposed upon the other. This imparts to his writing a peculiar strength. Nor can one mistake this style when he meets it again.

Also in the series of letters between Barwick and Clarendon, reproduced in *Life of Barwick*, appendix, Sheldon is mentioned in almost every exchange. However, in every case, the editor of the *Life of Barwick* mis-identifies him, via footnotes, as William Juxon. The primary reason for this mistake lies in the frequent use of the initials "B. L." (Bishop of London) for Sheldon. This led the editor of the work to settle on Juxon as the best identification he could make of "B. L.". However, "B. L." can now be identified as Sheldon for the following reasons:

1) Clarendon and Barwick were discussing the new bishops to be made, and the list of nominees for the vacant sees had just been sent to Barwick when the series of letters opens. Sheldon's name was at the top of the list, and he was scheduled to be made the bishop of London when Juxon became archbishop. This is the position he received immediately after the Restoration, and of course this is the reason Barwick and Clarendon call him "B. L.".

2) Clarendon is extremely worried about B. L., "our sick friend," as he calls him. Sheldon almost died in 1659 from a plague that broke out in England in 1658-59. It took him over a year to recover.

3) Clarendon anxiously inquires about him in every letter and laments the fact when he is needed so at that moment to supervise the Church and help get the bishops made, he is not available. Sheldon was the leader who, all through

Once they had constructed their apparatus, and the agents had been found to transmit intelligence and keep the net functioning with some degree of efficiency, how were the two friends able to use it to aid the Church? What did they actually accomplish?

As they extended their correspondence to take in more and more of their former friends and colleagues, they found many clergymen and scholars living in near destitution. They discovered some, both at home and abroad, who lacked even the basic necessities of food and clothing. To supply the needs of these desperate clerics, the two friends established a "Charitable Uses Fund." Into it they themselves paid large amounts, and for it, all through the decade of the fifties, they constantly hectored their friends and acquaintances with pleas for contributions.[33] In addition arrangements were made with friendly congregations throughout the country to take up regular offerings for the fund – John Evelyn reports in 1658 that a collection was taken for this purpose during a church service he attended in London[34] – and the amounts gathered over the decade must have amounted to a significant total. Both Samuel Parker, Sheldon's chaplain in the 1660's, and Anthony Wood, who was personally acquainted with the archbishop, report that Sheldon dispatched such large amounts to the court of Charles II that the king considered him his

---

the Interregnum was pushing for the creation of new bishops. (See later this chapter.) Juxon was very lukewarm in the matter.

4) In talking of "our sick friend," Clarendon expresses the hope in one letter (p. 398) that "the time is [now] drawing on that we may [again] enjoy one another" – meaning that we may again enjoy one another's company. Clarendon was never a close friend of Juxon's. He was for years on the most intimate terms with Sheldon who was noted for his great wit and humor.

5) Clarendon assures Barwick, as the Restoration draws on, that the king has promised only one church preferment to anyone, and that one is the deanship of Worcester, which he has agreed to give to Morley. And, he said, you can check with "our sick friend" who will assure you that Morley is in every way qualified for it. He knows him well. Sheldon and Morley were life-long friends; Juxon and Morley were never close.

For all these reasons, Sheldon can now be positively connected with Barwick. He was working closely with him and was transmitting information on the Church and upon loyalist projects to the court through Barwick and Allestree.

[33] The "Charitable Uses Fund" is mentioned by name only once in the whole Sheldon-Hammond correspondence (see *Theologian and Ecclesiastic*, XII, 170), but there are innumerable references to money-raising projects. Periodic contributors to the fund, besides Hammond and Sheldon, were Sir John Pakington, Sir Robert Shirley, Sir Orlando Bridgman, Sir Philip Warwick, Lady Coventry, Lady Savile, Lord Scudamore, and "Mr. Chichley." There were others also who assisted from time to time. See comments by W. H. Clarke, *ibid.*, XII, 173; also the following Hammond-Sheldon letters: *ibid.*, VII, 54; VII, 127; XII, 373; as well as almost any letter chosen at random in the series for some discussion of money projects.

[34] E. S. de Beer (ed.), *The Diary of John Evelyn* (London, 1959), p. 389.

chief financial and business agent in England; [35] while Hammond's biographer declares that in this period that scholar was "the most zealous promotor of almsgiving that lived in England since the change of religion." [36] Throughout the decade of the Interregnum, the two Anglican clerics wrote their letters, made their pleas, and struggled constantly to replenish their coffers. Thus throughout the period the two friends had in their hands "the disposal of large charities." [37]

And they had need of vast amounts. Sheldon and Hammond are on record as having, at various times in the Interregnum, supported: John Cosin at Paris; [38] "Monsieur," his preaching assistant there; [39] "Belleau," another Anglican cleric preaching at St. Germaine; [40] Richard Steward, Charles II's chaplain; [41] John Earle, Steward's replacement at Charles' court; [42] George Morley at Antwerp; [43] Jeremy Taylor; [44] the children of John Prideaux, deceased bishop of Worcester; [45] the children of Thomas Howell, deceased bishop of Bristol; [46] and Charles Steward, the son of Charles' favorite chaplain, after the latter died in 1651.[47] All of these and most certainly – since only a fraction of the Hammond-Sheldon correspondence remains in existence – many others also received assistance from the "Charitable Uses Fund."

By mutual agreement the fund was limited to the support of clergymen and their families, although the plight of some laymen was often as grievous and presented a constant temptation, particularly to the soft-

[35] Parker, p. 53, and Anthony Wood, *Athenae Oxoniensis* (London, 1820), IV, 853.
[36] See comment by John Fell, quoted in Hammond's life, DNB.
[37] Quotation from Hammond's life, *ibid*. The fund was still functioning effectively up to the Restoration. Hyde makes reference to it in November, 1659, in a letter to Barwick. See Barwick, p. 466.
[38] *Ibid.*, XIII, 329.
[39] *Ibid.*, XIII, 330.
[40] *Ibid.*, X, 328.
[41] *Ibid.*, VI, 300.
[42] *Ibid.*, XII, 376. Hammond in this letter, written Dec. 28, 1652, points out the great danger to the Church if no chaplain was provided for the king, without "bringing charge to him." John Earle subsequently became the chief Anglican chaplain at the royal court, and he was supported from the "Charitable Uses Fund."
[43] *Ibid.*, XIII, 246.
[44] *Ibid.*, XV, 179.
[45] *Ibid.*, VII, 55.
[46] *Ibid.*, VII, 51.
[47] On Charles Steward see *ibid.*, XII, 372; XII, 171, where Hammond discusses using "Grey of Wellingbourough," a lawyer, to attempt to arrange a composition on behalf of Steward's young son. Once that was arranged with the government, the young boy would then inherit some of his father's property and have money of his own. Until that time, however, Sheldon and Hammond looked after him and supported him.

hearted Sheldon, to extend the charity to include all royalists who needed help, clergy or not. On one occasion, Morley wrote describing in the most heart-rending terms the condition of an old lady living at Antwerp in absolute penury. He closed with a plea for Sheldon's help. "If I were in England," he wrote, "I know I could collect something for such charitable cases; pray, think on't." [48] Unable to resist such requests, Sheldon suggested to Hammond that they enlarge their charity to include certain destitute laymen. Hammond would not hear of it. Their money, he pointed out, was limited. If they aided one layman, would they not open the door to a flood of requests from others just as needy? "If you [can] secure from that consequence, I shall agree to what you propose," he wrote.[49] Sheldon could find no satisfactory way of drawing such a line, so the arbitrary restriction of their bounty to clergymen was continued.

However, there were some exceptions. From his own pocket, Sheldon sent a considerable amount of money to Hyde's family at Antwerp while Hyde was away at Madrid during 1650-51.[50] He also is on record as lending money to Sir William Ailsbury, Hyde's brother-in-law,[51] and to "old Mrs. Ailsbury," Hyde's mother-in-law, he sent regular amounts during the early 1650's.[52] He also paid her outstanding debts when she died in 1653. And of course there was the king himself. He *had* to be maintained.

At times during the decade of the 1650's, Charles and his court were living in such poverty that they were unable to pay their grocer and were in imminent danger of going hungry. John Barwick and Thomas Holder were transmitting funds from England to the court during 1648 to 1650. When Holder was arrested and imprisoned for his royalist activity in 1649, Barwick continued sending funds Holder had collected and others which he himself collected.[53] When in his turn Barwick was also sent to prison in 1650, methods were still available by which money was transmitted to the king.[54] Upon his release in 1652, the unregenerate Barwick again became the channel through which funds reached the royal court. Much of this money, perhaps a majority of it, came to Charles via the Sheldon-Hammond correspondence net and ultimately from their friends who solicited for it. When it came down to it, neither

[48] *Theologian and Ecclesiastic*, XIII, 244.
[49] *Ibid.*, XII, 170.
[50] *Ibid.*, VII, 59, 119, 123.
[51] *Ibid.*, VII, 61.
[52] *Ibid.*, XIII, 240, 241, 244.
[53] Barwick, *Life of Barwick*, p. 95.
[54] See *ibid.*, p. 128, where Lady Savile transmitted £ 1000 to Charles II in 1651.

could resist the importunate pleadings of these impoverished erstwhile associates, and besides the great amounts they collected from others, both came close to beggaring themselves in their efforts to supply the needs of the court, clergy, and other acquaintances at home and abroad.[55]

But maintaining poverty-stricken clerics and friends was only one of the activities the two Anglican leaders were engaged upon during this period. Their correspondence shows them deeply involved in a great deal of other business on behalf of the Church. They found and assigned tutors to many landed families;[56] they encouraged their unemployed colleagues to open schools, and when many did so, Sheldon and Hammond found them scholars and encouraged them in their work.[57] Thus many of the gentry's children were educated and nurtured in the Anglican faith at the same time. They assigned chaplains, both to loyal Anglican families at home and to many who were living abroad, including the king himself.[58] They found pastors for the expatriate Anglican congregations which met regularly during the Interregnum at such places as Antwerp, Caen, Rouen, Paris, St. Germaine, The Hague, and of course wherever the court happened to be located,[59] and in most cases, as indicated above, they helped support the divines who ministered to those groups.

---

[55] On several occasions Morley apologized for his own indebtedness, since he had heard that Sheldon himself was in need because of his financial aid to friends. "I am sorry," he wrote once, "that one of your large munificence should be straightened in the means of exercising your virtue... but your friends are not to expect more that you are able to give, straightening of yourself to do for them." *Theologian and Ecclesiastic*, XIII, 240.

[56] On the problems related to finding tutors, see *ibid.*, XII, 176, 372, 374, 376; XIII, 329 – all letters from Hammond to Sheldon – and letters from Morley to Sheldon, dealing with the same subject, XII, 373; XIII, 241.

[57] It seems as though almost every significant Anglican clergyman in the post-Restoration period taught school at some time during the Interregnum. Those mentioned in the Hammond-Sheldon correspondence include, Hickes, Heywood, Gunning, Barrow, Sterne and an outstanding teacher named Thomas Triplett who was a member of the Falkland Circle in the 30's. Others were Geoffrey Palmer, later Charles II's attorney-general, and a friend of Sheldon's, always referred to by Robert Payne as "the Conjuror." For references to various members of this group, see *ibid.*, XII, 173; VII, 48; VI, 223; VI, 172; XII, 170; and VI, 218; and H. R. Williamson, *Jeremy Taylor* (London, 1951), p. 42. There were others also.

[58] Richard Steward was assigned by Sheldon to stay at the court as Charles' chaplain, *Theologian and Ecclesiastic*, VI, 300, and upon his death, Earle was assigned to replace him and was maintained by the "Charitable Uses Fund." *Ibid.*, XII, 376.

[59] Sheldon and Hammond were seeking ministers to replace Morley at Antwerp, *ibid.*, XIII, 244; to assist "Monsieur" at Paris, XIII, 330; and someone to help Cosin at Paris, XIII, 329.

They took promising young scholars as their servants and secretaries, educated them as far as they were able, and, in many instances, paid their expenses to the universities; [60] and they encouraged those of their friends who had sufficient means to do likewise. In this manner a number of future Anglican scholars and churchmen received their education during the 1650's.

In addition they encouraged, and in some instances were themselves instrumental, in the organization of various projects to employ the numbers of talented scholars who, on account of their religion, had been turned out of the universities.[61] The most significant of these efforts, but by no means the only one, was Brian Walton's *Polyglot Bible* – an edition of the scriptures printed concurrently in seven languages. On this project scholars of all persuasions were employed in the 1650's, and for it Sheldon, Hammond, and John Selden, among others, were the principal undertakers.[62] And, finally, they were totally and heavily committed to scholarly writing and partisan pamphleteering on behalf of the episcopalian position.

In this latter area Hammond, one of the outstanding scholars of the period, took the lead. He seemed equally facile whether producing a learned *Commentary on the New Testament* – a work that was a stock item in ministerial libraries down to the nineteenth century – or in employing a savage invective to devastate a Presbyterian opponent. Despite a debilitating illness which he mentioned in almost every letter to Sheldon, published works flowed from his study at Westwood at an astounding rate. Yet he could not keep up with the projects which he fashioned, or which were fashioned for him, and he continually begged Sheldon to assume some of the burden or to enlist others in the pamphleteering battles in order to provide him some assistance.[63]

Sheldon undertook to do both. Jeremy Taylor's writings owe much to Sheldon. He supported Taylor with financial aid on several occasions, gave him much encouragement, and it was at his suggestion that Taylor

---

[60] Hammond educated Isaac Barrow and Peter Stanynough, Sheldon paid Richard Waring's way through the university, and Morley had his brother's youngest son with him as a servant and secretary on the continent, "whom by that means," he said, "I shall be able to maintain and breed." *Ibid.*, XIII, 246.

[61] Hammond proposed at one time that he, Sheldon, and Humphrey Henchman, collect £ 600 per annum to maintain twenty persons to be chosen by Bishop Bramhall as a colony of exiled scholars on the continent where they could safely pursue their studies. *Ibid.*, XV, 183. Nothing came of the venture.

[62] See *Life of Brian Walton*, I, 290, for Sheldon's contributions to the Polyglot Bible. The project is discussed on numerous occasions in Sheldon's correspondence also.

[63] *Theologian and Ecclesiastic*, XV, 186; XV, 285, for letters from Hammond in June and July, 1654, where he is seeking assistance in his pamphleteering.

agreed to submit his works to the judgment of Bishop Duppa before he sent them to the printer.[64] It was due to Sheldon's initiative that Peter Gunning was enabled to spend his time writing in defense of the church.[65] Humphrey Henchman was also brought into the lists by Sheldon, as was the unknown author of *The Whole Duty of Man* whom, at Sheldon's instigation, Timothy Garthwaite, the London printer, induced "to come to the press again." [66] Sheldon was less successful with his friend, Robert Sanderson. When John Selden published his work *De Synedriis* in late 1650, Hammond sent a copy to Sheldon, noting that "he has spent eight parts of the whole in writing against the practice of excommunication." And, Hammond added, "we are a sort of very temperate men if it be not replied to." [67] Sheldon attempted to persuade Sanderson, who was very capable of making the answer, to enter the debate. But, although he exerted his best efforts and Sanderson was one of his oldest and dearest friends, Sheldon failed to enlist him in the battle. To the contrary he found to his amazement and sorrow that Sanderson was flirting with the enemy; at that very moment he was writing in defense of those Anglican ministers who had taken the Engagement.[68]

Perhaps because of this failure, Sheldon attempted to fill the gap himself. Between 1650 and 1652, he produced several works which he intended to send to the press. One was centered around the problems of the Apocalypse, and the remainder were tracts upholding episcopacy.[69] In no instance, however, did he send his treatises to the critical Hammond for an evaluation. Rather he dispatched the Apocalyptic manuscript to Thomas Triplett and the tracts to Sanderson in order to fortify himself with their approval before sending them to the publisher. Had they wholeheartedly endorsed his works, he then no doubt would have sent them to Hammond. But his friends were critical – although both urged him to continue his efforts – and Hammond only heard of Sheldon's writings at second hand.[70] Administrative and personal letters

---

[64] Reginald Heber, *Works of Jeremy Taylor*, p. xlix. Also *Theologian and Ecclesiastic*, XV, 179.

[65] *CSP, Clarendon*, III, 385. Sheldon, Hammond, and Bishop Wren were trustees for this fund on behalf of their friend Gunning. The fund was established by Sir Robert Shirley.

[66] Isham, *Isham-Duppa Correspondence*, p. 175.

[67] *Theologian and Ecclesiastic*, VII, 127.

[68] See later this chapter.

[69] For reference to one of these works, see *Theologian and Ecclesiastic*, VI, 50, where Hammond discusses it; the others are mentioned by Sanderson in a letter to Sheldon in 1652. W. Jacobson (ed.), *The Works of Robert Sanderson* (Oxford, 1854), VI, 376.

[70] *Theologian and Ecclesiastic*, VI, 50.

were to be Sheldon's only significant literary productions for the period of the Interregnum.

Because Hammond was thus so furiously, and so publicly, engaged in upholding the Anglican position, and because Sheldon published nothing at all in these years, the mistaken opinion has become current that Hammond was the moving spirit, the master-mind, who led the Anglicans in England during the 1650's.[71] Yet even the most casual reading of their letters for the period reveals Sheldon as the dominant partner in their relationship. While it was true that Sheldon, the man of business, with his more prosaic, practical mind, showed great respect for the scholarly brilliance of his colleague – the exaggerated respect which the businessman always seems to accord the successful author – still in all matters of a practical nature, Hammond bowed to Sheldon's judgment. This dependence of Hammond can be seen in numbers of instances in their exchanges, but it is revealed most clearly in their discussions of Falkland affairs.

Prior to his death, Lucius Cary had named Sheldon, Hammond, and Morley as guardians for his young son. As a result a good percentage of the Sheldon-Hammond correspondence of the early 1650's deals with problems relating to the young Lord Falkland – his education, his marriage, his place of abode, his relations with the Cary family, his tour of the continent, and most important, the supervision of the Falkland properties. Being close to Great Tew, it became Hammond's duty to review periodically the estate accounts and to deal with the executors who were assigned to manage the Falkland holdings. On one occasion, when the managers failed to send him the accounts at the proper times, Hammond wrote helplessly to Sheldon, "What shall I do?" [72] On another he could not answer Sheldon's questions concerning some details of a Falkland transaction even though he had just gone over the estate accounts. At Sheldon's insistence, he sent for the account books again, saying wearily, "I will with Jeffrey Palmer look more closely at them.... I heartily wish you could undertake this, who have so far more weight and dexterity in such affairs." [73] Later when John Maplet, the young lord's tutor who was traveling with him on the continent, became so

---

[71] This mistake was made by Dr. John Owen, Puritan vice-chancellor of Oxford, when he wrote to Hammond in 1654 wanting to talk with him about composing the differences between the two religious bodies. See *ibid.*, XV, 186. For a modern assertion of this idea, see Hammond's biography, DNB. His biographer makes Hammond responsible, single-handedly, for maintaining the Anglican church during the Cromwellian interregnum.

[72] *Theologian and Ecclesiastic*, XII, 170.

[73] *Ibid.*, VII, 54.

disgusted with the boy that he wished to send him home to England and be done with him, Hammond again begged Sheldon, "Tell me by your next what I shall do." [74]

In his own writings, although he seldom discussed scholarly problems with his friend, Hammond was explicitly guided by Sheldon's advice when it came to the practical impact of his publications. An example of this occurred in 1650 when Hammond was preparing a treatise, *Dissertationes Quatuor,* which was a scathing attack upon the views of Salmasius and Blondell, two Presbyterian scholars active at that time writing from the continent. Upon hearing that Sheldon questioned the wisdom of publishing such a work, Hammond abruptly halted his preparations and sent Sanderson to Sheldon to discuss the project. He hoped from the description Sanderson gave of the proposed writings "you," he wrote to Sheldon, "may give me your positive opinion on the fitness of printing them." He pointed out that the bishops of both Sarum and Ely had urged him to speed them to the press. "But your opinion," he admitted, "(after some preparations made with [the printer] Royston) hath given me reason to stop that speed." [75]

Sheldon advised against the publication for two reasons. First, he objected to Hammond's treatment of Salmasius who had only recently published an able defense of the monarchical principle – a work commissioned by Charles II. An attack upon the Presbyterian now, of such bitterness as that which Hammond proposed to mount, might well redound to the Church's disadvantage by alienating its prospective head. Secondly, Sheldon thought it politically imprudent to attack Presbyterianism at the very moment the king was opening negotiations with the Scots in an effort to obtain their military assistance. Until they knew the outcome of the proposed Scots' alliance, Sheldon suggested that Hammond withhold his work from the press. Hammond followed his friend's instructions to the letter. The work was not published until after the battle of Worcester; and when finally it did come from the press, Hammond assured Sheldon that it contained "nothing of Salmasius but magnificent." Instead he had aimed his criticisms primarily at Blondell, although he had, he admitted, criticized some opinions of Walo – a pseudonym under which Salmasius sometimes wrote.[76] Thus, in administrative and political matters, Hammond almost always bowed to the more penetrating judgment of his colleague.[77]

---

[74] *Ibid.,* VII, 384.
[75] *Ibid.,* VII, 61.
[76] *Ibid.,* VII, 147.
[77] See *ibid.,* XII, 171, where Hammond wrote to Sheldon about whom they

But all of the industry employed by the two clerics – whether devoted to providing for the material needs of loyal Anglicans, or to caring for the dispersed congregations, or to defending Anglican theology – would prove useless if the Church of England, as a unique religious entity, disappeared from the face of the earth. The possibility of that occurring by the 1660's appeared excellent. The danger was two-fold: The Church might disappear as a result of loyal Anglican clergymen refusing to use and enforce the use of the Book of Common Prayer in their services; or the Church might well expire with the last of its bishops.

The problem of Church discipline, the necessity of preserving "a being for the church," as Duppa phrased it,[78] was a thorny, complex matter which was never satisfactorily resolved during the Interregnum. It has been estimated that two-thirds of the Anglican clerics made their peace with the government, accepted its oaths, and gave up the use of the Common Prayer completely. Even among those who professed loyalty to the old forms and who were judged by their contemporaries to be committed Anglicans, there was a wide variety of thought on this issue. As Sheldon phrased it in a lengthy letter to John Barwick in 1653: [79]

> He that hath either his eyes or ears open, must needs know the confusion to be great, and the state of it [the Church] most lamentable; and that not only in regard to the wild schismaticks, but even of those who would be owned and would pass for the better and sounder part. To instance in one particular, to which at present I shall... confine myself. Amongst those that either are or would be thought loyal subjects of the king, and obedient sons of the church, there is great diversity of opinion and practice about prayer, and the public worship of God; some believing themselves excused by the times, if they wholly omit it; some contriving the substance of it into a prayer of their own making; supposing they have done their duty well if they pray nothing against the old form; others retain part, some more, some less according to their several judgments; and some again holding themselves obliged to use all, according to their former engagements, and not so much as to communicate with any that use it not supposing them schismatical, they are consequently deprived of the benefits or other ministry and excluded from any public employment themselves to their

could find to aid Steward's son in his dealings with the government. At that time he said, "I suppose you understand the bottom of it (which I profess not at all to do), and if you apprehend my fears vain in respect of these men, as before you did in respect of Mr. St. [sic] etc., do it in a word, and I subscribe and will punctually follow your directions."

[78] *Ibid.*, XV, 465.

[79] *Barwick*, appendix, pp. 537-47. This letter can definitely be ascribed to Sheldon for the reasons I have given in footnote 32, this chapter. It bears the date, "Jan. 10." I have placed it in 1653 because it was late 1652 before Barwick was released from his solitary imprisonment, and the first meeting was held on this problem in early summer, 1653. The letter is clearly written before any meetings have been held and after Barwick was released. Therefore it has to be January, 1653.

own great prejudice.... Thus it is already; and 'tis like time will produce more divisions, both in this particular and many others; and in the confusion the church be wholly lost if timely remedies be not taken.[80]

It was a faction led by Wren and Hammond who would not "so much as communicate" with those who refused to use the Book of Common Prayer in its entirety. On the other hand, Sanderson, with his Calvinist leanings, wrote papers advocating the taking of the Engagement if necessary in order to retain a living and the wherewithal to support one's family.[81] Sheldon was between his two friends. He refused to attend any service where the Prayer Book was not carefully employed, but he refused also to condemn those who on occasion "contrived the substance of it into a prayer of their own making."[82]

But as shown in the above letter, Sheldon was upset at the lack of uniformity in Anglican practice, and he was fearful of the effects upon the Church if such a variety of forms of worship were permitted to continue for an indefinite period. He was not opposed to compromise. He simply wanted some agreement on the degree to which accomodation was to be permitted. In other words, if there was to be a retreat in this matter, in his opinion it ought to be properly shepherded so that all clergy were granted the same degree of latitude – whatever that should be.

In discussing with Barwick how such a regimented retreat could best be accomplished, Sheldon was adamant upon one point. It should *not* be attempted, he thought, by disputation and debate in a conference. That way he was sure "would be endless and fruitless." Rather he thought it should be done

by the bishops themselves, could they agree in opinion how far this remission ought to extend; and did they but state the whole matter as a case of conscience, what might or might not be done; and either command or recommend it to the practice of the clergy, they would certainly be obeyed if not by all, yet by the most and best of them.[83]

But when it came down to it, Sheldon was not optimistic about the above method. To get the bishops to agree, let alone act, would, he foresaw, be a very difficult matter. Thus he turned to a second method – that of

---

[80] *Ibid.*, pp. 539-540.
[81] When Hammond heard of Sanderson's writings, he wrote to Sheldon in a rage: "Our dean's brother-in-law hath from Dr. Sanderson an answer to all reasons against taking the Engagement, and the conclusion is that... he may take it; tell me what you know of this." *Theologian and Ecclesiastic*, XV, 465.
[82] See letter to John Barwick, *Barwick*, p. 538, where he condemns a paper on this matter produced by Wren, as "very rigid," and later the same page where he states his own position.
[83] *Ibid.*, p. 542.

getting the secular authority (the king) to intervene and by "commission, leave, or at least some intimation" to a board of three bishops, permit them to order the necessary changes in worship. This way, he thought, if done secretly would not be dangerous to anyone and would be more apt to bring some action.[84]

Despairing of ever getting the timid bishops to act in a body, and unable to get the necessary "commission" or "intimation" from the king, Brian Duppa, on his own initiative, chose Sheldon's least attractive alternative and called a conference to discuss church discipline in the early summer of 1653. He invited all interested Anglican leaders to attend.[85] Sheldon's health was so poor that spring that he was unable to journey up to Richmond for the meeting, but it was probably just as well. As he had predicted, no decisions were reached. However, those who did attend agreed to try again in late September, and Duppa was determined that this time they must reach some decision in this vital matter. "To this end," he wrote to Sheldon, "your presence and advice is very necessary." [86] Once more, however, Sheldon was unable to attend, and once more the divisions of opinion were so great that no agreement could be reached.

During the winter a group of clergymen, led by Jeremy Taylor, petitioned Bishop Warner, requesting that the use of the Book of Common Prayer be temporarily discontinued and that some other compromises be made.[87] Hearing of this, Duppa determined to try yet again to get an agreement from the Church leaders. This time both he and Hammond exerted their utmost persuasiveness to insure that Sheldon would take part in the meeting. Discussing the clergy's petition and what it might mean for Anglicanism in the future, Hammond wrote to Sheldon, "I cannot but wish that you were there to interpose your judgment and authority." [88]

Yielding to the pleas of his two friends, Sheldon did attend the conference held in the early summer of 1654. But, as he had foreseen, nothing could be accomplished in this critical area by debate and discussion. The issues were too tightly drawn, the feelings between the compromisers and the "bitter-enders" were too intense, and agreement proved impossible. According to Thomas Barlow, it was only the timely interruptions and arguments of Robert Sanderson that kept this third confer-

[84] *Ibid.*, p. 543.
[85] *Theologian and Ecclesiastic*, XV, 465.
[86] *Ibid.*
[87] *Ibid.*, XV, 184.
[88] *Ibid.*

ence from declaring those who swerved in any degree from the prescribed forms in the Book of Common Prayer excommunicate.[89]

Nor were any further attempts made to discipline the Anglican clergy during the Interregnum. The king, no doubt, was loath to dictate to any minister what his practice should be in such dangerous times; the bishops could not agree among themselves on these vital issues – the Richmond conference proved the uselessness of that method of resolving the problem; and even if an agreement were forthcoming by any method, would not some clergy, who now considered themselves loyal churchmen, desert to the enemy rather than forfeit their livelihoods by conforming to the new orthodoxy? Such would certainly seem to be the case, and the Church, already weakened, would only become more so by losing the material and moral support of the defectors. Thus Sheldon opposed any further attempts to discipline the clergy, and diversity in Anglican practice continued to the Restoration.[90]

While important, the matter of discipline was relatively insignificant compared to the dangers facing the Church due to the impossibility of consecrating new bishops. The Church of England would expire when its last bishop passed away, and all of the remaining ones were of an advanced age. Somehow the episcopal bench had to be replenished. But the problem was – how could it be accomplished? Furthermore in this matter, unlike the problem of discipline, it was impossible to by-pass the old and fearful prelates. It took bishops to consecrate bishops.

The normal method of creating new bishops called for the king to send the *congé d'élire* – his permission to hold the election – along with his nominee for the see, to the dean and chapter of the vacant diocese. The dean would then call a meeting of the chapter in the chapter house at which the canons would vote for the man indicated. Notice of their action would then be communicated to the monarch who, in turn, would signify his assent and order three bishops to proceed with the consecration. As pointed out by John Barwick, in a letter to Edward Hyde, the problems preventing this procedure being followed were great.

For the dean and chapter to petition for such a license would be difficult, as to elect if they had it, many of the deans being dead, some chapters extinguished,

[89] Jacobson, *Sanderson's Works*, V, 37.
[90] See Williamson, *Jeremy Taylor*, pp. 101-107, where Taylor is engaged in 1657 and 1658 producing new liturgies and forms, based for the most part on older practices – particularly that of the Greek church – which a cleric might substitute for the Book of Common Prayer. He was trying to supply his brethren with forms, the use of which would not make them heterodox in the eyes of their fellows and which would, in addition, not make them liable to arrest if their services were discovered by the authorities.

and all of them so disturbed as they cannot meet in the chapter house, where such acts are regularly to be performed.[91]

Several alternative methods were proposed. An Irish prelate suggested that since by custom the royal appointment alone sufficed to create a bishop in the Irish church – no election being required there – the king might make whomever he pleased an Irish bishop and them subsequently translate him to an English see. Others thought that, since suffragan bishops could be created solely by a royal warrant, during the interim the same procedure might be deemed sufficiently legal for the making of bishops themselves.[92] Both of these methods were appealing, since they by-passed the consecration ceremony, and thus obviated the necessity of stirring the laggard bishops to action. However, for that very reason, either of these plans could be decried by the Church's enemies; whatever the method, it had to be in accord with accepted tradition. John Cosin, a brilliant church scholar, offered an acceptable solution to the dilemma. Since, as he noted, Queen Elizabeth had created bishops by simply collating the nominee to the see and then ordering four bishops to consecrate him, the same procedure could easily be followed by Charles II from his place of exile on the continent.[93] Support for this plan gained ground rapidly among the scholars and lawyers, and Sheldon, Hammond, and most of the important Church leaders eventually gave it their approval. The problem then was to build a fire under the king and his advisors abroad as well as the bishops at home in order to bring them to act. Interesting either group proved difficult.

Within a few months of Charles I's death, Sheldon was assessing this danger to the church and attempting to provide a solution. In October, 1649, he wrote to Hammond suggesting a method by which he thought bishops could be consecrated.[94] He urged Hammond to use his utmost influence with any of the bishops he knew to stir them to some action on this critical problem. Hammond approved of Sheldon's plan, urged him to perfect it, and then propose it to the bishops, although he was emphatic in the opinion that the young king must be brought into the

[91] *CSP, Clarendon,* III, 503.
[92] R. Bosher, *The Making of the Restoration Settlement, 1649-1660* (London, rev. ed., 1957), p. 91, discusses these suggestions. This work is a brilliant recent study of the Anglican maneuvering which led to the restoration of the Church.
[93] *CSP, Clarendon,* III, 50.
[94] One author – W. H. Clarke, *Theologian and Ecclesiastic,* VI, 30 – denies that this letter dealt with the bishop-making problem on the grounds that no attempts were ever made this early to solve this problem. However, Sheldon was extremely farsighted about practical problems such as this, and as the text of Hammond's letter indicates, Sheldon's letter quoted here referred to nothing else.

matter first. "The beginning," he said, "must be from abroad." [95] But at this time Sheldon's efforts were to no avail. The execution of Charles I was too recent; the bishops were in a funk, and no one would move.

Prideaux of Worcester died in 1650, and Sheldon again grew worried about the future of the Church. In October of 1651 Hammond wrote to Bishop Wren in the Tower,

> I am this week put in mind by G. Sh. to be a remembrancer to some of those who are concerned to think of doing somewhat to preserve a church amongst us lest it perish with their order which is now reduced to a small number.[96]

Wren had no idea who "G. Sh." was, and he had to write back to Hammond to make the identification.[97] He then reported to Sheldon, via Hammond, that he was well aware of the problem but had no contact with any of the other bishops and therefore saw no way in which he could aid the venture himself.[98] Sheldon's agitation of this problem in 1651 did, however, produce some reaction among the bishops. A meeting was proposed to discuss the matter, and Brownrigg of Exeter even came to Highgate to attend.[99] But the bishops' fears overwhelmed them, and as far as is known no conference was held.

Sheldon continued his agitation of this matter throughout 1652 and 1653. He wrote to all the bishops and urged those of his friends who knew any of the prelates to add their influence to his. But the response was always the same – excuses, delays, and refusals. Wren refused to commit anything pertaining to such a dangerous project to paper – he wanted a "living conveyance" – while most of the others argued that the best course to pursue at the moment was to wait and see what the government was going to do. Perhaps a more propitious occasion would present itself later.[100]

It is possible that the major reason nothing was done earlier in this matter was Hyde's opposition to any premature action which might be

---

[95] *Ibid.*, VI, 30.
[96] *Ibid.*, IX, 294.
[97] *Ibid.*
[98] *Ibid.*, XII, 92.
[99] *Ibid.*, XII, 161. Apparently this was the only time Brownrigg gave any assistance with this problem during the Interregnum. He was Calvinist by inclination and, making his peace with the Cromwellian government, he managed to retain his position and income. See *Barwick*, p. 213, where Hyde is severely critical of Brownrigg and Skinner, bishop of Oxford, for their lack of interest in the consecration problem.
[100] See *Theologian and Ecclesiastic*, XII, 168; XII, 170; and *Sanderson's Works*, VI, 390, for references to Sheldon's efforts in the bishop-making process in 1652-53.

labeled as illegal by the Church's enemies.[101] By 1655 Sheldon had aroused his friend to the critical nature of this problem, and in that year Dr. Eleazor Duncan was dispatched from the continent to prod the bishops into taking some concrete action. He brought with him a list of persons approved by the king to be elevated to the episcopal bench, along with Cosin's proposal, noted above, which eliminated the problem of the chapter elections. Immediately upon arrival, Duncan consulted with five bishops, Sheldon, Hammond, and a "prime common lawyer," concerning the legality of Cosin's scheme. All pronounced it a perfectly legal method of making bishops. He also reported to Hyde that of the five bishops, Lichfield (Frewen) and Chichester (King) were ready to go overseas to consecrate new bishops if that was the king's desire, while Sarum (Duppa), Armagh (Ussher), and Exeter (Brownrigg) were perfectly willing to hold the consecration services in England. All agreed that the collaboration of only three bishops would make the consecration ceremony a valid one.[102] It looked as though the problem would at last be resolved.

Yet once again the bishops failed to act. Some were frightened by government surveillance, some were sick, and it proved impossible to bring three bishops and the king's nominees together long enough to accomplish the consecrations.

In 1658 Hyde became Lord Chancellor, and he was now fully aroused to the danger of the Church's expiring. In the next year and a half – almost to the moment of the Restoration in 1660 – he exerted every effort to get some bishops consecrated. He sent letter after letter to the bishops, urging them to action.[103] He encouraged, he ordered, he threatened, he cajoled, he begged, he lectured, he shamed the bishops. But is was all to no avail. He could not persuade them to perform the consecrations. Even the loyal Duppa, resentful of Hyde's badgering tactics, wrote angrily to Sheldon that Hyde had no real understanding of the difficulties which the bishops faced in England. Had he been nearer to home, Duppa was sure that instead of expressing amazement "that so little care is taken of our great business ... he might pity some of us and there should be no place for wonder left." [104]

In this matter Hyde wanted everything to be done by the bishops in England. He promised them faithfully that the king would approve

---

[101] See Bosher, p. 90, for this curiously complacent attitude on the part of Hyde.
[102] *CSP, Clarendon,* III, 50.
[103] For this long series of letters in 1659 and 1660, see *Barwick,* appendix.
[104] *Isham-Duppa Correspondence,* p. xxv.

whatever action was taken just so some bishops were consecrated and the Church remained alive. However, the bishops refused to take the initiative until they received orders from the king. Even Wren, the most aggressive of them all, used this excuse. He would not exert himself in any way in the project until he got express orders from the king along with a complete list of nominees. When that list arrived in 1659, there was anger and outrage that some names were left off, and jealousy on the part of the older prelates that some of the new men were to have the more lucrative sees. The bishops in the province of York were all dead, and until they could make the new ones in the proper order, beginning with York itself, they refused to consider making any of the others. And since no one would take Sodor and Man, the most poverty-stricken of all the sees, the elderly bishops used that as an excuse to refuse to consecrate anyone in York at all.[105] With all of this wrangling, jealousy, and dilatoriness, Hyde was beside himself, and it was not to be wondered that he heartily wished Sheldon's presence on the scene in order to provide the great "affair of importance" with some aggressive leadership.

But Sheldon had fallen ill in late 1658 – of the same sickness which carried off Cromwell, – and although some "Jesuit's powder" brought from China finally saved his life, his recovery was slow, and he was not available to conduct any business until the spring of 1660. In June of 1659 Hyde particularly lamented the warden's incapacity.

> I am very sorry [he wrote to Barwick] that our sick friend doth not recover as fast as we wish and as is necessary for the publick [good]. It is heartily wished that as soon as his health will give him leave, he would return to you and consult upon the great affair, which considering the delays have been hitherto used, is not like to move as it ought to do, without another kind of prosecution.[106]

Hyde re-affirmed his regret about Sheldon's illness in almost every letter he sent to Barwick. In the early spring of 1660, despairing of getting any action from Wren and with Sheldon still incapacitated, the Lord Chancellor dispatched Morley to England to spur the project on.[107]

In 1659 the bishops agreed finally that the consecrations would take place near London. However, an abortive royalist uprising occurred in that year, and as an aftermath about the time the prelates were to gather, government agents broke into Duppa's house and searched all of his

---

[105] For all of these excuses and problems, see *Barwick,* appendix, letters between Hyde and Barwick, pp. 398-524.

[106] *Ibid.,* p. 407. As I have pointed out earlier, the editor of *Barwick's Life* mistakenly identified "our sick friend" as Juxon in every reference. Hyde was actually referring to Sheldon for the reasons I have given in footnote No. 32.

[107] *Ibid.,* p. 515.

papers. This so unnerved the other bishops that they called the project off. Hearing of this fearful cancellation, Hammond, who along with the sickly Sheldon was waiting vainly for the bishops' summons, wrote to his friend:

> I hear nothing lately from Mr. Barwick, but I believe you must enlarge your prayer, and extend it not only to danger, but fears, though never so causeless ... or else the granting it will be no effect to our church business.... I pray do not you give over attempting to awaken these concerned, whilst there is any hope of success.[108]

But prayers had no effect upon the fearful bishops. In order to postpone the moment of action, they now quibbled about the oral list of nominees sent to them from the king. They argued that this was not a satisfactory indication of their monarch's will for such an important matter and insisted upon seeing a written list, signed by the king himself, before stirring themselves further.[109] Early in 1660 Richard Allestree once more crossed the channel in order to secure the necessary papers and pacify the elderly bishops upon that point.

As the Restoration approached, and as the government and people of England became more uncertain of what the future held, it seemed possible at last that the consecrations could finally take place. Hyde fully expected that the episcopal rank would be bestowed upon some of his nominees early in 1660. However, ill-luck, cowardice, and wilfulness on the part of the old leaders once more conspired to block the consecration ceremonies. Upon his return to England in February of 1660, Allestree was seized at Dover and placed under arrest; at the same time some of Hyde's dispatches dealing with the project were purloined at Dunkirk by Puritan agents and carried to the government in England; and, finally, to the great consternation of the royalist leaders, Barwick learned that John Wallis, the Oxford cryptanalyst, had broken their cypher, and all their plans were, and for some time had been, revealed to the English government.[110] These circumstances effectively cancelled all further thoughts of episcopal consecrations until after the Restoration.

Despite their failures during the 1650's and their fears for the Church's future, Sheldon and Hammond watched developments in England during 1658-59 with growing hope. The king's return would surely at long last

[108] Harl. Mss. 6942, Hammond to Sheldon, Aug. 20, 1659.
[109] *Barwick*, p. 464.
[110] *Ibid.*, p. 491. Matthew Wren, the son of Bishop When, was a friend of Wallis. From the mathematician he obtained copies of letters which some of the conspirators had sent to the court. He sent the copies back to their royalist originators and asked them if they had actually written those messages. The copies were letter perfect of course and finally convinced Hyde, who heretofore had refused to believe it, that the government was privy to all of his plans.

offer them the opportunity to revive and rebuild the Anglican organization, and they were determined to pursue every possibility open to them. Unfortunately, the indefatigable Hammond was not to see that glorious day. Beset by the passage of a train of gall stones of a steadily expanding diameter, his effectiveness declined markedly in the later years of the Interregnum, and he died an excruciating death on April 17, 1660, the very day parliament voted to invite the king home. It must have been with a great sense of loss that Sheldon turned to the task of planning the Church's restoration.

Although the Sheldon-Hammond correspondence for the period of the Interregnum is far from complete, enough is known of their activities to allay, at least to some extent, the criticism which has been leveled continuously at the Anglican leadership in this period. Some have maintained that the Anglican catacombs were a myth invented to cover the very unheroic performance by almost all Anglican clergy in this period.[111] Others have castigated the bishops for their cowardice and neglect of the Church in her hour of trouble.[112] Some have concluded that the Anglican clergy took almost no part in any of the royalist conspiracies – they had no stomach for such dangerous projects.[113] And still others have asserted that there was no Anglican leadership to speak of in England at all in this period, that what leadership did exist was provided by the expatriate clerics – Morley, Earle, Cosin, and their friends abroad.[114]

Dealing with these assertions in reverse order, it can now be stated categorically that leadership of the Anglicans during the Interregnum came from the island itself, not from the expatriates abroad. Cosin, Morley, Earle, and the other exiled leaders were maintained for the most part by the Sheldon-Hammond Charitable Uses Fund, and they received their instructions from the two leaders in England. Leadership came to Sheldon and Hammond by default. The bishops would not or could not provide the direction which the demoralized Anglicans desperately needed. Having been Charles I's most intimate advisors and the directors of the Oxford resistance movement, the two friends already were churchmen of national importance before 1650. As the Interregnum wore on, they were the only clerics with the courage and ingenuity to step into and fill the vacuum which the bishops created when they abdicated

[111] H. R. Trevor-Roper, "The Restoration of the Church, 1660," *History Today*, II, (1952), pp. 540 on.
[112] Bosher, p. 26.
[113] D. Underdown, *Royalist Conspiracies in England, 1649-1660* (New Haven, 1960), p. 182.
[114] Trevor-Roper, p. 540.

their authority. Thus the two royal chaplains provided a rallying point for all the loyal Anglican clergy. Of course the Charitable Uses Fund greatly strengthened their position, both at home and abroad. They were the only Anglican leaders with financial resources which could be tapped on behalf of the Church, and as it always does, money brought authority. Any Anglican needing aid must perforce apply to Sheldon and Hammond, and instructions and orders, they found, invariably came with the financial grant. So responsibility for the Anglican establishment devolved upon the two Oxford scholars. For years before the restoration Sheldon and Hammond were in effect *de facto* bishops who directed Anglican activities, and they were accepted as such by almost everyone, including the king and his closest advisors. The two lists of nominees for episcopal office which have come down to us – Duncan's in 1655, and another composed from memory by Allestree some years after the Restoration – merely confirm this view. Sheldon's name headed both lists; Hammond's was second in each case.[115] Sheldon was to go to London from where he could exercise supervision of the Church until the elderly Juxon died, and Hammond was slated for Worcester, one of the richest of the English sees.

One did not get such plums for nothing. Although Anglican priests may not have been as forward in their support of conspiracy as some wished, still Sheldon and Hammond were involved. John Pakington, as his biographer states,[116] was a leader in almost every uprising of the decade – he compounded for his estates on at least three different occasions, at great financial loss to himself – and Sir Robert Shirley died in the Tower for his part in a royalist uprising. Could not these two have been advised and inspired by their chaplains? Shirley, we know, was in the process of making peace with the Cromwellian government in 1651, but was dissuaded from that course and returned to the royalist camp by Sheldon.[117] In addition we have the record of one Sheldon agent who was so frightened by the seditious nature of the messages he was

---

[115] See W. H. Hutton, *A History of the English Church* (New York, 1903), VI, 166, and a memorandum from Allestree, reproduced in Bosher, p. 94.
[116] See DNB.
[117] *Theologian and Ecclesiastic*, XV, 183, where Hammond discusses Shirley's approaching defection. When Sheldon won the latter back to the Anglican position, in order to proclaim his renewed faith in the Church, Shirley built, under Sheldon's direction, the only Anglican church to be constructed in England in the period of the Interregnum. The wall of the church at Staunton Harold still bears Sheldon's tribute to his patron – "In the year 1653, when all things sacred were throughout the nation destroyed or profaned, this church was built to the glory of God by Sir Robert Shirley, whose singular praise it was to have done the best things in the worst times, and hoped for them in the most calamitous." Sheldon used almost the same words to describe himself a year or two earlier.

required to carry that he absolutely refused to serve further, and we know too that at least some of the messages which frightened him were destined for Shirley through Sheldon's hands. Finally, we know that Sheldon and Hammond operated a correspondence net which covered most of England and even reached to the continent. When these facts are coupled with Bishop Parker's flat assertion that Sheldon "was concerned with almost every prudent design against the tyrannical usurpers" in this period,[118] it would seem that some Anglican clerics were doing more in this area than they have ever received credit for. The Anglican story for this period really suffers from two severely crippling disabilities: Sheldon's order that no copies of any documents be retained by anyone – making the Anglican record extremely scanty – and the fact that most historians have based their assessment of the period on the activities of the bishops.

As far as the occupants of the episcopal bench were concerned, one must realize that all were superannuated, and all were so constantly under government surveillance that they found it exceedingly difficult in those times even to assemble to discuss their problems. Bishop Duppa, whose courage has never been questioned, bore witness to this official harassment. He thought the difficulties which hindered the bishops acting were almost insuperable.

Although the story of the Anglican catacombs may be a myth, yet the reality is not nearly so discrediting as has been asserted. Proven and determined leaders were acting on behalf of the Church, and they did direct all aspects of its severely circumscribed, but still very considerable, activity. Against great odds, this *pro tem* leadership was able to keep the Church alive and to preserve to it some spiritual identity, and vigorous and able Anglican leaders did appear when the Restoration became a reality. During the Interregnum Sheldon and Hammond performed yeoman service for the Anglican cause, and members of the Church of England everywhere owe them a debt of gratitude.

See *Theologian and Ecclesiastic*, VI, 77, where he proposes to "Make use of ill-times to make me better and that will make me merrier."
[118] Parker, p. 53.

CHAPTER IV

THE RESTORATION

As the Restoration graduated from the status of remote possibility to near certainty in the spring of 1660, many Anglican clergymen at home could not restrain themselves. Finally, after all their suffering and all their troubles, it seemed certain that the king was again to come into his own. Many took to their pulpits to offer thanksgiving to God for his salvation and also, with newfound courage, to excoriate their Puritan enemies. Publicly and exultantly they predicted dire retributions upon their foes once the king was returned. One even had the effrontery to publish a sermon containing such sentiments and dedicate it to General Monk! [1]

This was too much for Hyde who, with the king, was awaiting developments at Breda. On April 16 – the day before the Convention Parliament voted the king's return – he wrote a stiff letter to Barwick, pointing out that negotiations were far too delicate for that kind of thing. In the king's name, he ordered Barwick, Morley, and the bishops of Ely and Sarum to take prompt steps to silence those foolish clerics before their precipitate actions brought untold "inconvenience and mischief" upon the Church and the king.[2]

One hears no more of such rash talk; therefore, it can be assumed that Hyde's orders were obeyed. Yet this was only the first, and perhaps the least, of the problems confronting the Anglican leaders. With the Convention's invitation, the king was clearly about to leave the wilderness. But could the Church accompany him? Did the return of monarchy mean the return of the Anglican establishment? Certainly not in the minds of those Presbyterians and Independents in the Convention Parliament who had voted Charles' return. But did they represent majority opinion in England? How much support for the Church of England

[1] *Barwick*, p. 515.
[2] *Ibid.*

might there actually be in that homeland which some of them had not seen for ten or more years? No one knew. But the religious issues were critical, and they had to be handled cautiously, circumspectly, carefully. Hyde recognized that. He was determined to restore the Church if at all possible, although he saw that this intention would have to be masked for the time being. Until the king was safely on his throne and until the religious temper of England could be properly assessed nearer at hand, Anglicans and Anglican sentiments must be kept carefully concealed from public view.

For this reason Hyde wrote, through Barwick, to Morley and Sheldon in England, assuring them that regardless of what the Presbyterians were saying, "there would be a better bargain made for the Church than is yet imagined." However, at that moment – late April, 1660 – all that he wanted them to do was to enter into conversations with some of the Puritans, sound them out, and see if some could not be won over to an acceptance of episcopacy. Hyde thought that it might help to promote a spirit of moderation in some of them "to assure them of good preferments in the church." [3] Morley, always more sympathetic than Sheldon to the Calvinist position, began to arrange such conversations.[4]

This same cautious approach characterized Hyde's handling of several other problems. For instance, it dictated the Breda Declaration, with its very reasonable and soothing statements about religion. In that document Charles declared "a liberty to tender consciences," and promised "that no man shall be disquieted, or called in question, for differences of opinion in matters of religion which do not disturb the peace of the kingdom." Furthermore, he expressed his willingness to abide by the judgment of parliament and to accept whatever laws that body chose to enact in order to guarantee such liberty.[5] This no doubt reassured many a fearful Presbyterian.

But the Anglican dissimulation had to go further. With the Restoration appearing imminent, the leading Anglican divines met in London to discuss what attitude they should take and what part they might play in the celebration of the king's return. Most of the remaining nine bishops were present, as were Sheldon, Morley, and some of the other leading

[3] *Ibid.*, p. 524.
[4] Morley ultimately won Gauden over to episcopacy by offering him church preferment.
[5] Clarendon, *History of the Rebellion*, XVI, 193. Charles was no doubt sincere in his statement about religion in the Breda Declaration; to Hyde it was merely the politic thing to say at that moment. It certainly reassured many a Presbyterian and did much to reconcile them to the Stuart restoration. They quoted it frequently in their debates with the Anglicans.

Anglican clergy. Unable to decide among themselves, they addressed a letter to the king, asking his advice. They thanked him for some recent expressions of friendliness for their church, pledged their loyalty, and asked several questions: Should they be present at the time of the king's landing in England? Should they attend in their episcopal habit? If so, at what time and place? And how many? Were they to arrange the traditional service of thanksgiving at St. Paul's? They desired an indication of the court's thinking on these important matters.[6]

The Anglican leaders must have been disheartened at the answers which they received. For when the king stepped ashore at Dover, at one o'clock on the afternoon of May 25, not one bishop or other Anglican minister in habit was present in the welcoming delegation, nor were any visible in the crowd of 50,000 who gathered to welcome their monarch home. The official religious delegation was composed of a group of Presbyterian divines who stepped forward and presented Charles with a new bible.[7] But none of the old bishops or other Anglican leaders was present. Nor were they in evidence four days later when Charles was joyously welcomed to the capital. Apparently cassocks, miters, and surplices were no longer a part of the English church – only Geneva gowns.

Furthermore, no thanksgiving service was held at St. Paul's. The excuse offered was that it was not fit for services – the New Model's horses, which had been stabled in the cathedral, had seen to that. But in fact no service of thanksgiving was held at all until a full thirty days after the king's arrival in London. Then, on June 28, Sheldon celebrated "the happy return of his Majesty" with a solemn service at Whitehall. In his sermon he held up David's deliverance and his thanksgiving as a proper pattern for the English king and his people. "A sad bargain it is," Sheldon orated, "to save wealth, honour, crowns, and scepters, life itself, anything we have, at the loss of our God, at the expense of our souls . . .; an horrid sin it is instead of thanking God to sacrifice to Bacchus, to express *publicum gaudium per publicum dedecus*."[8] This last may have been a threat aimed at many of the Anglicans whose celebration of the king's return often led them into excesses and drunkenness. However, it also could have been a first circumspect criticism of Charles II. Reportedly, the "merry monarch" spent his first night in London in the arms of the beautiful Barbara Palmer, Lady Castlemaine, and this

---

[6] Carte Mss., Bodleian Library.

[7] Charles thanked them and remarked solemnly that "this was the object which he valued above all else on earth."

[8] Gilbert Sheldon, *David's Deliverance and Thanksgiving* (London, 1660).

was but the prelude to many, many more nights passed in that same pleasant fashion.[9] However, there was nothing in Sheldon's presentation with which the Presbyterians could find serious fault – except that the service was Anglican in form.

Shortly after the king's arrival, in order to conciliate the Presbyterian group even further, a round dozen of their ministers received appointments as royal chaplains. Among them were Richard Baxter, Edward Reynolds, Edmund Calamy, Thomas Manton, and William Bates – all popular London preachers.[10] Up to this point – June, 1660 – the Presbyterians must have felt fairly content with the way the restoration was proceeding. However, two things had occurred which, had they become general knowledge, must have given them pause.

In their visit to The Hague to wait upon the king, the Presbyterian ministers had been distressed to find royal chaplains, dressed in surplices, holding services according to the Book of Common Prayer. When they upbraided Charles for these "popish practices," they met a stone wall of resistance. Charles quickly let them know that he would not be dictated to in the matter of his personal religion. Upset by his intransigence upon this point, they departed with some misgivings.[11]

The other incident occurred on the evening of May 26 when Charles broke his trip to the capital with an overnight halt at Canterbury. After dark a solitary figure was admitted to the king's lodgings. The visitor was Sheldon. Hyde had long planned the meeting between churchman and king. Early in 1659, he had written Sheldon, "When you meet, as meet you will, I think you will be satisfied with the king, and nobody is like to do so much good upon him as you are, for sure he reverences nobody more." [12] One can only surmise what passed between Sheldon and the young king at that surreptitious night conference. Robert Baillie, writing two years later from Scotland, asserted that Charles had been willing up to that point to accept Presbyterianism in its entirety as the English religious system. It was not, he thought, "till the Saturday at night, in the cabinet council at Canterbury" that the king was convinced otherwise.[13] This surely is a guess on the part of Baillie; it does not square with Charles' behavior over the next several months. More likely, both Sheldon and Hyde described the restitution of the Church as the *sine qua non* toward which they intended to work. However all three

---

[9] A. Bryant, *Charles II* (London, 1931), p. 141.
[10] M. Sylvester (ed.), *Reliquiae Baxterianae* (London, 1696), p. 229.
[11] R. Bosher, *The Making of the Restoration Settlement* (London, 1957), p. 129.
[12] Add. Mss. 4162, Hyde to Sheldon, Jan. 21, 1658/9.
[13] Robert Baillie, *The Journals of Robert Baillie* (London, 1842), II, 459.

men were realistic politicians, and all must have realized that many difficulties lay ahead and that their future religious program would depend more than anything else upon the temper of the country.

This was Sheldon's first meeting with the king and much depended upon it. Of course he came well recommended. His service to Charles I, his staunch resistance at Oxford, his work during the Interregnum, and the large sums of money he had transmitted, plus Hyde's great confidence in him – all these could only have predisposed Charles in his favor. In addition, when he wished, Sheldon could be gay, witty, and affable, qualities which Charles himself possessed and which ranked high in his estimation.[14] From all the evidence, their initial meeting proved a great success. Although fundamentally of very different temperaments, cleric and king found that in some areas they had much in common, and Sheldon was courtier enough to exploit those areas to the utmost. He shortly had ready access to the throne, and Charles found in him an exceptionally congenial counselor.

Thus over the next several months it became apparent to all observers that Sheldon's influence with the king was daily increasing. It was Sheldon who baptized the young duke of Cambridge into the Anglican faith. It was he also who read the burial service for the duke of Gloucester when the latter died of smallpox in 1660. When Juxon found himself too weak to perform the coronation ceremonies in 1661, Sheldon stepped into his place and took over the more onerous parts of the service. In the fall of 1661, he was reported as being at the theatre with the king to see a play satirizing two of London's best-known Presbyterian preachers. And in May, 1662, it was Sheldon who officiated at the marriage ceremonies which made Catherine of Braganza Charles' wife. Pepys, who was in an excellent position to know of these things, noted that by the fall of 1662 Sheldon had become "one of the most powerful men in England" by reason of his influence over the king.[15] In the spring of 1663, he reported again that "the bishop of London [Sheldon's title after October, 1660] keeps as great with the king as ever." Pepys was sure at that point that Sheldon, "being a man of great business, and yet of pleasure, and drolling too," would shortly be made Lord Treasurer upon the removal of the ailing earl of Southampton.[16]

---

[14] Sheldon's company was eagerly welcomed and even sought after. He must have been an extremely interesting person to be around. Later when he was archbishop, young noblemen thronged Lambeth Palace to eat with him and to enjoy his conversation. See Parker, p. 36.

[15] Pepys, I, 322.

[16] *Ibid.*, I, 419. This of course did not come about, but it shows something of what Sheldon's influence was reported to be.

With his growing ascendancy over Charles in religious and even secular matters, and with his long, intimate friendship with Clarendon, the fortunes of the ex-warden of All Souls took a turn for the better. He had boldly occupied the master's quarters at Savoy hospital when the incumbent died in 1658 – thus finally obtaining a preferment awarded to him seventeen years earlier by Charles I. Ickford came into his possession again with the Restoration, and Newington, where his rights were challenged, was secured for him by Clarendon's intervention.[17] The king himself wrote to the dean of Gloucester Cathedral, where Sheldon still claimed a prebendship, to preserve Sheldon's share of the money from the new leases which fell due at the Restoration.[18] Sheldon also became dean of the Chapel Royal – another income – with the duty of providing court preachers. It may have been for this reason that, as Baxter points out, only four of the new Presbyterian chaplains were ever called upon to preach before the king, and those four but once each.[19]

Thus the first hurdle was surmounted. The king was home and established on his throne once more. Although he was surrounded by high churchmen and Anglican clerics, still there were Presbyterians at his court, seemingly on intimate terms, and it was certain that they would do their utmost to protect their fellow religionists throughout the land. There was good reason to believe also that Charles' affinity for Anglican forms was only a personal matter and would not influence the religious settlement which soon would be effected for the country. Presbyterianism, or at least some acceptable compromise between presbyter and bishop, seemed now a certainty, and the Presbyterian leaders in the summer of 1660 set themselves the task of securing official and legal sanction for their system. Sheldon and Hyde also shifted their tactics. Their purpose now became one of blocking any permanent religious settlement until it could be made on terms which were satisfactory to them. Also they proposed to resurrect episcopal church government wherever and to whatever extent possible.

This latter task was made somewhat easier for them because they were beginning to get some grass roots support. Some of the old bishops almost immediately began, probably with Hyde's and Sheldon's tacit approval, to enforce the use of the Book of Common Prayer. Some also began to eject all Puritan ministers who would not conform or who had no proper claim to their benefices and to replace them with the old Anglican priest, where he was still alive, and with loyal younger men

---

[17] *CSP, Clarendon,* V, 360.
[18] *Cal. of State Papers, Domestic,* 1660-61, p. 283.
[19] *Reliquiae Baxterianae,* p. 229.

when he wasn't. In some instances this change-over to Church of England practices was the result of dispossessed Anglicans returning in full fury to reclaim their own. We are told that at Halifax on a June Sunday in 1660, "while Eli Bentley was preaching in the parish church, the old vicar, Dr. March, marched up the aisle, displaced Bentley, and went through the service according to the Prayer Book." [20] There were no doubt many other individual actions of this kind – although probably few so dramatic. In some cases and in some areas, through the collaboration of loyal justices of the peace, legal persecution of dissent began almost immediately. Before the end of June, 1660, it was reported that the jails of Wales were full of dissenters – many of them pleading the king's Breda declaration.[21] Also, almost as soon as the king arrived, Sheldon inaugurated a campaign in the press to generate popular support for episcopacy, while at the same time and through the same medium, the League and Covenant, as Baillie phrased it, "was torn to pieces." [22]

But the Puritans were not without weapons in this area either. Besides their own able pamphleteers who answered the royalists charge for charge, they used the more insidious weapons of scorn, execration, and vicious gossip. All bishops and Anglican priests found that they were continually subjected to contumely and spiteful, malicious abuse wherever they went. They were accused of being greedy and dissolute placeseekers, interested in nothing so much as squeezing the last farthing from their lease-holders. If any elderly clergymen found it necessary to use a cane, "he was pointed out as one who through drunkenness was not able to control himself." If a cleric had poor eyesight, making it necessary for him to peer carefully up the street to determine where he should go, there was always someone nearby who would remark, "That parson has already devoured five fat livings; see with what prying eyes he is seeking after a sixth." When a few days before his death John

---

[20] Repeated in F. Bate, *The Declaration of Indulgence, 1672* (London, 1908), p. 8.

[21] A. G. Mathews, *Walker Revised* (Oxford, 1948), p. 165.

[22] Baillie, II, 443. Morley put a pamphlet into the press supporting episcopacy, and probably Sheldon did too. See Morley, *A Modest Advertisement Concerning the Protestant Controversy About Church Government*, (London, 1661), and G. S., *The Dignity of Kingship Asserted* (London, 1660). In an introduction to this latter pamphlet, William R. Parker, an Indiana University scholar, makes "G. S." George Starkey, although he admits that except for the fawning dedication, it sounds like Sheldon himself. I rather think that "G. S." was George Stradling, one of Sheldon's chaplains. It could well have been written by Sheldon himself except for the introduction. Most of Sheldon's chaplains – Myles Smith, Robert Tompkins, Samuel Parker, Mr. Pell, and George Stradling – recommended themselves to the Church leader by publishing pamphlets on behalf of the Church in this period.

Barwick was bent over on the street coughing up blood, some bystanders laughingly accused him of vomiting up good, red wine to relieve his overcharged stomach.[23]

But great numbers of Anglicans were regaining their church holdings. In addition, persecution and prosecution of Puritans very quickly evidenced itself – even though sporadic in time and restricted in geographical extent.[24] Even if this latter development were mostly the result of overzealousness and vengefulness on the part of some local authorities, still to the Presbyterians these were evil portents, and they determined to bend their best efforts to secure for themselves, if not a place in the national church, at least a certain and secure toleration.

Through the efforts of the earl of Manchester, Charles' Lord Chamberlain, some of these Puritan leaders inaugurated a series of talks with the new governing officials looking to a settlement of the religious issues. Held at Sion House before the king, this conference ran through the early summer of 1660.[25] No Anglican clergy were present, although their faithful ally Hyde reported to Sheldon all that occurred there. Unhappily, Hyde noted that Charles took more than a cursory interest in these religious discussions. On one occasion, having discoursed at length on the peacefulness and loyalty of the Presbyterians and of their basic differences with the Episcopalians, Richard Baxter pointed out that only the monarch himself could bring an agreement between the two parties; and he urged the king to exercise his power in order to secure an acceptable compromise. Charles agreed wholeheartedly, and, he continued, the final settlement "must not be by bringing one party over to the other, but by abating somewhat on both sides and meeting in the midway." Furthermore he assured the Presbyterians that if such a compromise agreement were not reached, the fault would lie with themselves and not with him. The king ended his discourse by stating firmly that "he was resolved to see it brought to pass" in that manner, and he promised that he would personally look after the business himself.[26] Charles' sincerity and determination were so apparent that a flood of relief ran through the group of Puritans who heard him. Old Simeon Ash burst into tears of joy. All felt certain that their faith was now secure.

However, the inherent weakness in the Presbyterian camp evidenced

---

[23] Barwick, p. 338. All of these accusations are reported bitterly by Barwick's brother and biographer, Peter Barwick.

[24] Mathews, pp. xii, xiii, estimates that over 700 Puritan ministers were ejected in 1660 alone.

[25] Baxter records these meetings in *Reliquiae Baxterianae*, pp. 230-232.

[26] *Ibid.*

itself almost immediately. There was no leader who would take the responsibility for speaking for the whole party. When Charles asked them to set down on paper their views on church government, yielding as much as they possibly could, they refused. They said they had no commission to act on behalf of all Presbyterians and requested a delay so that they could take the matter up with their congregations around the country. The king objected that such a procedure would take too long and attract far too much publicity. He countered with the suggestion that they could at least speak for all the London ministers. Again they refused, saying that they could act only for themselves alone – those who were physically present at the moment. Charles was visibly disappointed, but he reluctantly agreed that their proposals should represent nothing more than the views of the handful of leaders who were present.[27]

The summer sessions at Sion House failed to produce anything concrete in the way of a religious settlement. Sheldon and Hyde were no doubt quick to seize the opening which Baxter and his colleagues offered. They could easily point out to the king that the Presbyterian delegation represented no one – not even all the London Presbyterians – and that to continue negotiations with such an insignificant group was of relatively little value.

From a personal predilection Charles certainly favored a compromise settlement. If he had any sincere religious sympathies, they lay with the Roman Church. Besides he owed a great deal to those English Catholics who had rendered him such valuable succour after the battle of Worcester. On the other hand, his experience with the Scots preachers in 1650-51 had developed within him an acute distaste for their religion and their somber way of life, thus the prospect of seeing Presbyterianism enthroned as England's official religion could only have appalled him. He certainly did not intend ever again to submit to their domineering surveillance of his private life or listen to their hectoring diatribes from the pulpit. Yet he was no doubt sincere also in wishing to see them tolerated at the least. Such toleration might be extended to include Catholics, as well as the other Independent sects; in any event, Charles Stuart opposed religious persecution on principle.[28] Of course there was also the political factor. Charles was home to stay. If the majority of the country were Presbyterian in sentiment, which at that time seemed

---

[27] *Ibid.,* p. 232.
[28] See A. Bryant, *King Charles II* (London, 1931), p. 155, for an assessment of Charles' religious outlook.

probable, then Presbyterianism it should be. He would not oppose it. Just so he himself were free to worship as he pleased.

For all of these reasons the Anglicans came to view the king as a serious threat to their plans. In addition all through the summer of 1660 Charles opposed any overly-hasty action to consecrate new bishops. He wanted to be sure of himself before he committed the government to that step. To some extent no doubt Hyde and even Sheldon were also of this view. But their disagreement with the king was over how long they should wait. In Sheldon's opinion episcopal consecrations should be held at the earliest possible moment.[29]

As the summer passed, the outlook for the Anglicans became more and more bleak. The Convention Parliament, which up to his time had reacted favorably to proposals for postponing the religious settlement, or for leaving it in the hands of a synod to be appointed by the king, now began demanding some action in this area.[30] Furthermore, as the younger members – most of whom were Cavalier in sentiment – began to straggle away home, the advantage shifted toward the Puritan side.[31] They of course desired a settlement on the basis of the Covenant. After all, they said, Presbyterianism had been England's religion for many years now, and people were generally devoted to it. Whereas if the Book of Common Prayer – "which few had even heard" – were re-introduced, many would be offended, and the peaceable composition of the kingdom might become impossible.[32] They pressed these plausible arguments upon their colleagues in parliament, upon every one at court, and upon the king. The London ministers hung the Covenant in their churches and called everyone's attention to the clause which called upon them "to defend the king's person, to take up arms if need be on his behalf." [33] They were loyal monarchists, and it was due to their intervention, they insisted, that the king had been invited back. While not wholly acceding to their arguments, Charles was impressed by them, and he postponed even further the elections for new bishops.

At this juncture of affairs – August, 1660 – Duppa became worried about the Church's future, and he sat down and wrote a letter to Sheldon.

---

[29] See a letter from Duppa to Sheldon, August 11, 1660, where Duppa can't understand why episcopal consecrations have not been held. Tanner Mss. 49.
[30] Clarendon, *Continuation of His Life* (Oxford, 1759), p. 9.
[31] L. F. Brown, "Religious Factors in the Convention Parliament," *English History Review*, VOL. XXII, (1907), p. 52.
[32] Clarendon, *Continuation of His Life*, p. 9.
[33] *Ibid.*, p. 8.

You are the only person about his Majesty [he wrote] that I have confidence in, and I persuade myself as none hath his ear more, so none is likely to prevail upon his heart more, and there was never more need of it; for all the professed enemies of our church look upon this as the critical time to use their dernier resort to shake his Majesty's constancy.[34]

Years before Duppa had been Charles' tutor, and he was aware of the great respect which the king professed for his father's memory. He now suggested to Sheldon that this was the moment to recover "those buried papers" and show them to the king. They "can't but have," he said, "a powerful influence upon so dutiful a soul as his." [35]

Duppa knew the king well. Sheldon immediately sent orders – probably to All Souls – to dig up Charles I's vow where he had carefully buried it fifteen years before. Ten days after Duppa's letter was written, he had the vow once again in his possession, and he hurried off to Whitehall to show it to the king.[36] What took place between clergyman and king is not known, but shortly after Sheldon's interview, the government made three moves which aided mightily in tipping the balance once more in favor of the Anglicans. Parliament was speedily adjourned; the consecration of new bishops was begun during the recess; and, to disarm the Puritans and to recapture the initiative for the government, negotiations with the leading Presbyterian ministers were re-opened.[37] A side-effect of all this was that in ecclesiastical matters Sheldon's voice was the dominant one for the next several years.

That first summer back in England was a busy one. There were a world of matters to be cared for, all of which demanded immediate attention. Clarendon himself could not do everything, and when a petition came to him from one Abraham Allen who wished to be returned to the rectory at Westmane, Hampshire, he referred it to "Dr. Sheldon, Dr. Earle, and Dr. Morley, or any two of them," asked them to certify

---

[34] Tanner Mss. 49, Duppa to Sheldon, Aug. 11, 1660.
[35] *Ibid.*
[36] Sheldon certified the validity of the royal vow in his own handwriting on August 21, 1660. It is surprising that he had not shown it to Charles before, but apparently it had completely slipped his mind. See Lambeth Mss. #943.
[37] For the most part, I follow Robert Bosher's brilliant study for the general cause and effect of the moves which led to the Anglican restoration. In some cases I have changed the emphasis. For instance, he does not mention the use of Charles I's vow in any context. I think it was of prime significance. Within two weeks after Sheldon showed his father's promise to Charles, Juxon was ordered elevated to Canterbury (Sept.3); Sept. 10 saw Duppa translated to Winchester; and on Sept. 28, Sheldon was recommended for London. The others soon followed.

the petitioner's merits to the king, "and his Majesty will certify his further pleasure." ³⁸ Thus were practically all of the routine Church matters decided throughout those months.

In addition, when Barwick visited London during the early summer, he found Sheldon busy with the problem of appointing new deans and filling up all the vacancies in the cathedral chapters. Barwick himself became dean of Durham, Sancroft of York, and Morley was appointed to Worcester.³⁹ All the remaining vacant deaneries were soon filled, and every cathedral shortly had its full quota of canons. Sheldon was preparing for the episcopal elections from the moment the king arrived in London.

With this groundwork already completed, and once they had secured the king's assent, it was a simple matter to conduct the elections and begin the consecrations. Juxon was elevated to Canterbury in September – for his services to Charles I on the scaffold – and later in the same month Duppa was translated to Winchester. Sheldon was the king's first nominee for a vacant see – London, on September 28 – and one month after the nomination he was consecrated bishop along with Humphrey Henchman, elected to Salisbury, and George Griffith, who received St. Asaph. These were the first consecrations in sixteen years, and it must have been with great relief and joy that Sheldon, who had been working assiduously for twelve years to bring them about, finally saw them come to pass. Other consecrations quickly followed in the next two months, and by the feast of Epiphany, January 6, 1661, the bench again had its full complement of prelates. Sheldon insisted that these events be crowned, as they always had been in the old days, with a magnificent, sumptuous feast, paid for by the new bishop. We are told on the good authority of John Evelyn, who was invited to John Earle's consecration a year later, that Earle's banquet cost that prelate a full £ 600.⁴⁰ We can be sure that Sheldon, who knew how to carry off such things with style, did not pay less.

At the king's insistence, bishoprics had been offered to some of the leading Presbyterians also. Richard Baxter, Edward Reynolds, and John Gauden, among others, had been approached. Reynolds and Gauden accepted – Gauden received Exeter and Reynolds Norwich – but Baxter,

---

³⁸ *Cal. of States Papers, Domestic*, 1660-61, p. 93. See *ibid.*, pp. 113 and 436 for other examples of petitions assigned to Sheldon and his friends.
³⁹ Barwick, p. 287.
⁴⁰ Evelyn's *Diary*, p. 448. The equivalent in modern American money is about $ 50,000.

Calamy and the others turned the proffered promotions down.[41] In his own case Baxter was in a quandary about the offer for some weeks. He asked for time to consider it, and all the Presbyterians agreed in advance that they would act together in the matter. However, one day, when he was alone with Hyde, the Lord Chancellor suddenly turned on him and demanded an answer. Would he take the bishopric or not? Much to the relief of Hyde and Sheldon, this maneuver worked. Baxter refused the appointment. He felt he could do nothing else, since he had as yet come to no agreement with the other Presbyterians as to what their action would be.[42]

Aside from Gauden and Reynolds, Sheldon's voice was the most influential in choosing the men who were to be raised to the episcopal bench. Hyde implicitly trusted his judgment – although the two often held discussions about church affairs – while the king, once the political factors had been determined, left almost all Church appointments completely in Sheldon's hands.[43] Already by the fall of 1660, Sheldon was primate of England in all but name.

When the king prorogued parliament, he alluded to its failure to achieve any religious agreement. "Since you have not settled it," he said, "I shall try my hand at a settlement." [44] True to his word, he activated the third part of the Anglican strategy by calling a conference to meet at Hyde's quarters at Worcester House. During October, he, Hyde, and a group of ministers representing both Anglican and Presbyterian viewpoints spent many hours trying to work out an agreement that was acceptable to both groups. The Anglicans were represented by Sheldon, Morley, and six bishops, while the Presbyterian contingent of nine ministers was headed by Baxter, Calamy, Manton, and Wallis. The king and Clarendon acted as moderators. After several days of discussions,

---

[41] Reynolds apparently was a sincere low churchman who thought he was doing the correct thing by accepting a bishopric. Gauden was assisting the Anglican party at this time and received Exeter as pay for betraying his colleagues. Sheldon had no use for the latter – Morley won him over to the Anglican cause – and strongly opposed his elevation. See *Barwick*, p. 368 and *CSP, Clarendon*, V, Part I, 68 and 81, for letters from Gauden to Hyde regarding his elevation. Also G. Burnet, *History of His Own Times* (Oxford, 1897), I, 324. Burnet attests Sheldon's dislike of Gauden.

[42] *Reliquiae Baxterianae*, p. 283.

[43] Isaak Walton in *The Complete Angler* and *Lives* (London, 1678), pp. 158-9, states: "Dr. Sheldon ... was by his majesty made a chief trustee to commend to him fit men to supply the vacant bishoprics." Bishop Nicholson was fully aware of Sheldon's power also. In 1661 he wrote to him: "In all gratitude I do acknowledge that next to his majesty ... your endeavors from an obscure man have advanced me to a place of honor and dignity." Reported by Bosher, p. 183.

[44] Clarendon, *Continuation of His Life*, p. 74.

it became evident that the two sides could not agree.[45] Yet some temporary arrangement seemed essential. Therefore, Clarendon set to work to produce a declaration on religion which he proposed to have the king issue. On October 22, he read a proposed draft to both sides and asked that both accept it. As set down by Clarendon, its main provisions were:

> That none should be presented to bishoprics but men of learning, virtue, and piety; that suffragan bishops should be appointed to the larger dioceses; that the censures of the Church should not be inflicted without the advice and assistance of presbyters, who should aid Bishops, Chancellors, and Archdeacons in their respective offices; that Confirmation should be rightly and solemnly performed; that no bishop exercise any arbitrary power; that the liturgy should be revised, but that until the revision was effected, the unexceptionable portion only of it should be used; that no existing ceremonies in the church should be at once formally abolished, but to gratify the private consciences of those who were grieved with some of them, they should be dispensed with for the present. The sign of the cross in baptism, bowing at the name of Jesus, the use of the surplice, and the oath of canonical obedience, were things ... left to individual opinion and choice.[46]

Clarendon's proposal was based for the most part on a scheme of comprehension drawn up by Archbishop Ussher in 1641 which he was fairly certain would be acceptable to the Presbyterians. Had the final church settlement been on this model, it would have been a clear victory for the Puritans. It was pretty much what most of them had been advocating all along. Much of the bishops' power and authority would have been curtailed, and many elements of the Presbyterian system would have been incorporated into the Anglican establishment. With this agreement, nearly all the Presbyterian ministers would have remained within the established Church, future dissent would have been of insignificant proportions, and the religious issue, which was to divide the country for decades, might have been permanently laid to rest. Recognizing all of this, the Presbyterian ministers unanimously approved Clarendon's draft.

But this royal declaration was only a maneuver of Sheldon and Hyde. It was necessary to allay Presbyterian fears for the moment, so they retreated and accepted a compromise position. As Sheldon carefully pointed out, the royal declaration was an interim measure, effective only until a church synod could be called to arrange permanently and officially all matters dealing with the liturgy and the Prayer Book. With this proviso, the bishops too gave their approval to the declaration.

[45] *Ibid.*
[46] Reproduced in J. Stoughton, *History of Religion in England* (London, 1908), III, 116-117.

Once that matter was settled, Clarendon drew forth another paper and informed the group that the king had been petitioned to grant toleration, at least for the moment, to Independents and Anabaptists. The Lord Chancellor desired therefore to read a clause, which the king wished inserted in the declaration, which would have that effect. There was a pause of silence while all parties considered this new development.

This was an even more devious maneuver than the Worcester House Conference itself. Its purpose was to cut away Independent support from the Presbyterians in the Convention Parliament, and it would work this way: All present knew that the king had strong sympathies for Roman Catholics, and that he would no doubt attempt to extend any such grant of toleration to include them. Neither of the religious parties represented at Worcester House were prepared at that time to permit toleration for the independent Protestant sects, let alone Catholics – nor was the country itself. Therefore, if the Presbyterians did not veto this clause, then Sheldon, speaking for the Anglicans, must. However, by this time both he and Clarendon were well acquainted with Richard Baxter. They knew that he had a strong propensity for rash, impetuous speech. Nor were they mistaken in that judgment. Vainly, Wallis tried to restrain Baxter, so that the Anglicans would have to bear the onus for refusing the proposed grant of toleration. But, impatiently, Baxter shook Wallis off. He spoke out boldly, outlining a number of reasons why, in his opinion, the inclusion of such a clause would be a terrible mistake. Clarendon listened politely, agreed with him, and the matter was dropped. It was not referred to again at Worcester House, but Baxter's ill-considered speech would shortly prove costly to the Presbyterians.[47]

One other incident at Worcester House gave the Anglicans some leverage which they gleefully proceeded to exploit. A clause had been proposed by the Anglicans urging all ministers and people everywhere to use the Book of Common Prayer in their church services. Several Presbyterians opposed its inclusion, especially Calamy. He asked that it be omitted, although he assured the king that he and the other ministers would use the Prayer Book themselves and in addition would urge others to do so. However, if there were no mention made of it, he argued, then in no sense would it appear that they were merely obeying the king's injunction in this matter, and their influence over their congregations on this issue would be even greater as a result. Thus they would gradually bring their parishioners to accept the Prayer Book and its forms.

[47] For an account of this incident see *ibid.*, III, 114. It is interesting that in his account of this conference, Clarendon makes no mention of this matter.

Calamy's argument was accepted, and the clause was omitted. Shortly afterward, however, Hyde intercepted letters from some of the Presbyterians – and one of them was from Calamy – advising and entreating their fellow ministers to hold fast to the Directory and not to admit the Book of Common Prayer into their services under any condition. There was no question, they said, but we "shall still prevail further with the king than he has yet consented to in his declaration." [48] Hyde showed the letters to Charles and used them effectively to destroy Calamy's influence with the king. "From these instances," indignantly wrote the Lord Chancellor, "all men may conclude that nothing but a severe execution of the law can ever prevail upon that classis of men to conform to government." [49] Sheldon most certainly seconded him in these opinions.

What neither Sheldon nor Hyde could ever see was that they were heaping scorn and abuse upon the Presbyterians for engaging in the very same tactics they themselves regularly employed. Subterfuges, devious maneuvering, trickery, reading others' mail – all of these were *de rigueur* when employed by the Anglicans but scornfully condemned when used by their opponents. Neither side dealt honestly, in a straightforward manner, with the other. Exaggerated partisan spirit permeated all religious groups throughout the whole period. This, as much as anything, made a compromise religious settlement impossible at the Restoration.

On October 25 the king issued his declaration much as it had been hammered out at Worcester House. The Presbyterians were delighted. It seemed as though they surely were to be safe from persecution and would be free to worship as they chose. Just to make sure, however, when the Convention Parliament reconvened in November, they moved that the king's October Declaration be enacted into law. Thus the religious question would be disposed of once and for all.

This was the most critical moment in the Restoration period for the Anglicans. Had the Convention Parliament passed this bill, it would have been nearly impossible to reverse its action later, and Anglicanism as Sheldon, Hyde, and their friends knew it could never have been resurrected. And had they been politically more astute, the Presbyterians could have seen the matter settled as they desired. According to the authority on the Convention Parliament, the Anglicans – or the "sober, prudent men" as Hyde always called them – had a bare plurality. Presbyterian and Independent together – both of them bitterly opposed to

[48] Clarendon, *Continuation,* p. 76.
[49] *Ibid.*

an Anglican restoration – held a majority.[50] The key vote came in December, and the measure was defeated by a mere twenty-six votes.[51] The defeat was made possibly by the Independents, some of whom inexplicably voted with the Anglicans. Their reason: Sheldon and Hyde informed them that Baxter and the Presbyterians had been responsible for the omission of any grant of toleration to them at Worcester House. They now repaid the Presbyterians in good coin; they voted with the Anglicans. So the Sheldon-Hyde maneuver paid off. The religious settlement was still to be concluded.

The first week of January, 1661, saw the Fifth Monarchy Men erupt into violence led by Thomas Venner. The duke of York found it a relatively simple task to bring in a troop of soldiers and suppress the rising and capture the rebels. However, the government and some London citizens panicked. Were they never to be safe from these rabble-rousing, religious fanatics? Sheldon made good use of their fears.

He secured a royal declaration prohibiting all unlawful and seditious meetings.[52] This was aimed primarily at Anabaptists, Quakers, and Fifth Monarchy men – all, he thought, were equally dangerous – and he requested permission to wage a campaign to enforce uniformity upon all congregations. He was sure that a vigorous campaign, directed to this end, would go far towards composing the kingdom.[53] The government agreed, and over the next several months the bishop of London used all the power he could muster to force the Book of Common Prayer upon all the London churches. He proposed to oust any minister who refused to conform, and even the most prestigious Presbyterian preachers were harassed with demands that they be ordained according to episcopal forms.

Sheldon drove furiously towards his goal. When the popular William Taylor of St. Stephen's, Coleman St., refused ordination, he ejected him from his pulpit. He proceeded against Bates and Manton. The latter accepted Anglican orders and agreed to use the Prayer Book, although he only did so under protest and pleaded the king's October Declaration. Bates compromised and used part of the Prayer Book service, but he admitted "he didn't know if that would satisfy or not." Jacombe refused

[50] Brown, p. 55.
[51] *Ibid.*
[52] See D. Wilkins, *Concilia Magnae Britanniae et Hiberniae* (London, 1737), IV, 564.
[53] Sheldon could not have begun his ruthless attacks upon the Puritans in February and March without government approval. The line of reasoning he used is only surmised here, but it is based on knowledge of his opinion and outlook and is justified by his subsequent actions against the Puritans.

any semblance of Anglican forms and prepared to defend himself in a court of law if necessary. Sheldon warned him bluntly that if he did not conform and read the Common Prayer, he would be replaced by someone who would. When parishioners of St. Mildred's Poultry petitioned the bishop for permission to keep their minister, a Mr. Wills who was not in episcopal orders, Sheldon angrily replied that "he was unfit for his place if he knew not best who were fit for them." [54] Thus he applied pressure ruthlessly to high and low alike, and although some stubbornly resisted his efforts, a number of Puritan ministers did accept Anglican orders and conformed their services to the Book of Common Prayer. Even Baxter thought it wise to visit Sheldon personally and obtain his license before preaching in the London diocese.[55]

But the bishop overdid it. The City was seething with anger at Sheldon's callous disregard of its religious sensibilities. In the parliamentary elections held in March these resentments flared up into a huge demonstration at the Guildhall. Amid cries of "no bishop, no bishop," the elections were completed, and all of the members chosen were of pronounced Presbyterian views.

This gave the Anglican leaders pause. Were they frightening the country into the arms of the Puritans by their precipitate attempts at discipline? It appeared so, and therefore a halt was ordered, and concessions were offered which were intended to soothe Puritan feelings.[56] Probably as a result of all this, a commission was issued by the king on March 25, ordering a synod, composed of twelve bishops and twelve Presbyterian divines, to meet for a period of four months and compose the religious differences which divided the country. Each side was authorized nine additional scholars who were to act as assistants. Accepted Frewen, the bishop of York, was named as chairman for the gathering. According to the commission, they were to advise and consult together about the Book of Common Prayer – to compare it to the "most ancient liturgies which have been used in the church," to look at

[54] Most of these incidents are reported in *Cal. of State Papers, Domestic,* 1660-61, pp. 537 through 552.
[55] Baxter reports: "The archbishop [Baxter is writing later] received me with very great expressions of respect; and offered me his licence, and would let his secretary take no money of me. But he offered me the book to subscribe in. I told him that he knew that the King's Declaration exempted us from subscription. He bid me write what I would. I told him that what I resolved to do... I would do of [free] choice, though I might forbear. And so (in Latin) I subscribed my promise not to preach against the doctrine of the church... in his diocese while I used his licence." *Reliquiae Baxterianae,* p. 369.
[56] Again, in general, I am following Robert Bosher's excellent study of the various moves which led to the Restoration.

several Presbyterian directories, to examine the objections raised against the "rules and forms of prayer," and to make "such reasonable corrections and amendments as should be agreed upon to be needful or expedient for the giving satisfaction to tender consciences." [57] The king himself no doubt had a hand in writing these instructions, and the commission's directions probably represented what he sincerely desired. But to Sheldon and Hyde this was only one more retreat, dictated by the tactics of the moment, and designed to bemuse and to confuse their opponents. Sheldon set himself the task of obstructing and nullifying the conference.

At the first meeting on April 15, held at Sheldon's lodgings at the Savoy, Frewen resigned the chairmanship to the bishop of London as one who "knew more of the king's mind in it." Sheldon then proceeded to lay down three ground rules under which the conference would operate. He pointed out that since he and the other bishops were essentially satisfied with the Prayer Book and the Church's ceremonies as they presently existed, they would have nothing to offer during the conference. They would, however, entertain whatever changes the Presbyterians chose to suggest. But, he continued, the Presbyterians must first prove that the changes they requested were indeed necessary before they would be accepted and incorporated into Anglican practice. Secondly, he announced that all proposed changes should be submitted at one time, so that the bishops might know in advance how far they were expected to go in compromise before any single change was discussed. And, thirdly, he proposed that all exchanges between the two groups be conducted in writing.[58]

Some of the Presbyterians protested this high-handed procedure. They pointed out that such rules would prohibit any free and open debate of the issues – a debate which they held to be vitally necessary – and to their way of thinking they also contravened the spirit of the royal commission. With these differences, it seemed as though the conference must break up in disagreement at its very first sitting. However, Baxter once more came to the aid of the Anglicans and persuaded his colleagues to accept Sheldon's proposals.[59] With their concurrence, the bishop of

[57] The complete commission is reproduced in W. H. Hutton, *A History of the English Church* (New York, 1903), p. 185.
[58] *Reliquiae Baxterianae,* p. 305.
[59] Baxter's reasons for this surprising agreement were as follows: 1) They were expected to submit new forms and this would give them the opportunity to do so in writing; 2) they could, he felt, reach agreement even with this stilted arrangement; 3) verbal disputes among themselves would be easier to resolve in private; 4) they could subsequently publish their case, in the event of failure.

London recessed the meetings until May 4 in order to give the Presbyterians time to draw up their list of objections.

During the interim Calamy, Bates, and the other Presbyterian leaders devoted themselves to cataloguing the errors in the liturgy, while Baxter, working alone, composed a whole new Book of Common Prayer – a book that unfortunately bore little resemblance to the accepted version. As Bishop Burnet commented:

> Sheldon saw well what the effect would be of putting them to make all their demands at once. The number of them raised a mighty outcry against them, as people that could never be satisfied. But nothing gave so great advantage against them as their offering a new liturgy. In this they were divided among themselves.[60]

The conference reconvened on May 4. Sheldon was not present – he attended only the first and last sessions and took no part in the debates – but Morley, his good right hand, was manager for the episcopal side. The Presbyterians handed in their exceptions to the liturgy. Shortly after the bishops handed back to them papers stating why the exceptions were unacceptable. The Presbyterians again handed in carefully considered rebuttals to the bishops' answers, only to find once again that their reasons were all coolly disallowed. Baxter doubted whether the Presbyterian papers were even read, except possibly by the persons selected to answer them. After several days of such fruitless exchange, the Presbyterians finally urged the bishops to go over their suggestions in a friendly way and tell them how much of the Prayer Book they would be willing to abate. All the principals on the Presbyterian side, including Bishop Reynolds, urged the bishops to take a more conciliatory approach. "But they resolutely insisted upon it," said Baxter, "that they had nothing to do till we had proved that there was any necessity of alteration, which we had not yet done." [61] Even though the Presbyterian leaders quoted to their opponents from the very words of the king's October declaration and from the royal commission calling the conference, the bishops remained adamant. They would not change their procedure.

Thus the wrangling continued for several weeks, with no single alteration which the Presbyterians suggested ever admitted by the Anglicans as being valid. With the termination date of the conference rapidly approaching, the Presbyterians requested that the debate be made a verbal one, and ten days before they were to adjourn, the bishops finally agreed to that procedure. But open debate proved even worse. Morley and

---

and make it known throughout England and the continent. It would be difficult to publish verbal discussions with the bishops. *Reliquiae Baxterianae*, p. 306.
[60] Burnet, p. 319.
[61] *Reliquiae Baxterianae*, p. 335.

Cosin freely interrupted the Presbyterian speakers and cruelly baited them whenever they chose. Baxter complained that they often laughed at what he had to say, as though it were foolish or stupid. In addition, they complained frequently that he spoke too long and too continuously; they could not remember what he said. One of them accused him of being a traitor because he inadvertently used the word *nation* instead of *kingdom* – "he wouldn't own a king." [62] No coherent discussion or debate was permitted, and the conference ended on a note of farce.

Sheldon was present when both groups reported to the king that no agreement was possible. The palpably surprised and confused monarch abruptly asked, "Then who shall be judge?" Baxter responded quickly with a glib definition of judgment, and the Savoy Conference was at an end.

This Savoy meeting was the last time the Presbyterians would sit down with the bishops on anything like an equal footing. It was also the last opportunity which the Puritans would have to influence the Church settlement in any direct fashion, and it was Sheldon, with his unyielding attitude and his rigid rules of procedure, who effectively torpedoed the whole effort before it even began. He set the tone and the strategy for the meetings. At his direction the bishops came to the conference not in the spirit of reason and compromise, but as judges to whom the Presbyterians were forced to petition for a hearing for their views. At Baxter's insistence, the Presbyterians acquiesced in the conditions imposed, and the conference was doomed from the start. From Sheldon's standpoint it could not have worked out better. He did not intend to permit any Presbyterian to have a hand in arranging the Church of England's liturgy.

The main reason why Sheldon and the bishops could offer the Presbyterians such short shrift at Savoy Hospital was the new parliament which convened in late spring, 1661. On May 8, just shortly after the Savoy Conference opened, it had its first sitting, and as one of its first acts, the new House of Commons ordered every member to take communion in the Church of England form. The Cavalier Parliament had come into existence, and its appearance signified a profound shift in political alignments and strengths. Sheldon, who for a year had been fighting a desperate rear-guard action to prevent the Church's enemies from arranging a Presbyterian religious settlement, now had a secure base from which to operate. At one stroke the Presbyterians had been reduced

---

[62] *Ibid.*, p. 340. One must beware of being influenced too much by Baxter who has given us the most complete account of this conference. Yet there is too much sincere indignation and hurt pride evident in his writing to doubt but that he was describing exactly what they were doing to him.

to the status of a sect. They could now be summarily dismissed from the Savoy Conference, and in the future they could expect only what the king could salvage for them in attempting to carry out his promises. Sheldon and the bishops were now in a position where, with the help of the new parliament, they could re-establish the old Church forms as they chose. If the restoration of the king were a divine miracle, to Sheldon and his colleagues the Cavalier Parliament was a clear continuation of that miraculous intervention. Hyde and Sheldon now proceeded to summon convocation.

Traditionally the clerical assembly had always convened at the same time as parliament. Uncertain of the religious tenor of the country, however, Hyde had chosen in this instance to delay its meeting.[63] Once it was ascertained that Anglican sentiment did indeed predominate in the House of Commons, the orders immediately went forth and the lower clergy proceeded to choose their proctors. Here again, however, Sheldon was careful to use every wile and pressure at his command to insure that convocation would be composed of a substantial majority of Anglicans. While the elections were not rigged – as Baxter claimed – "yet such care was taken in the choice and returns of the members of the convocation, that everything went among them as was directed by Sheldon and Morley." [64] The only contretemps suffered in the selection of proctors was in the city of London. Its Puritan sentiment was clearly evidenced by the choice of Baxter and Calamy, among others, to represent the London clergy. But even this setback was cancelled by Sheldon. Always one to know his legal rights, he recalled an old custom whereby the bishop of London was permitted to veto two of the city's delegates to the lower clerical house. He therefore excused Calamy and Baxter from attending, and thus when it convened, the convocation proved solidly Anglican.[65] In the absence of Archbishop Juxon, Sheldon presided over the opening ceremonies. "In excellent Latin, he addressed the lower house, desiring them to go together and choose their prolocutor, whom they should present the Thursday following in King Henry VII's chapel." [66] Now Sheldon and his friends were ready to reform the Anglican liturgy.

---

[63] There is a story that Laud's old secretary, Peter Heylin, was responsible for the summoning of Convocation in 1661. He wrote a letter to Hyde suggesting it. See W. H. Hook, *Lives of the Archbishops of Canterbury* (London, 1875), XI, 430. However, it is unlikely that Sheldon would have needed such prodding. My explanation seems more valid.

[64] Burnet, p. 325.

[65] *Reliquiae Baxterianae*, p. 333.

[66] Mercurius Publicus, (1661), No. 20, p. 305, cited by Bosher.

Since the House of Commons was eager to pass an Act of Uniformity – they actually passed one during the summer to which they attached the old Book of Common Prayer – Sheldon recognized that speed would be vital in the matter of Prayer Book revision. However, nothing could be done in the summer session, since the Savoy Conference, arranged at the order of the king, was sitting for that very task. Until it was concluded, convocation had to content itself with passing various ordinances which would help to bring a proper order and respect once more into English worship services.[67] To speed the business of revision, when it finally did get under way, Sheldon proposed that the province of York send its bishops, along with proxies from its lower house, to London. In this way, since both provinces had to approve the revision, both would be sitting at Westminster as one, and much time would be saved. His suggestion was adopted, and when parliament and convocation were reconvened in November, both provinces were represented.

Revision began in earnest on November 22 and was completed by December 20 – just a month being required for the actual work involved. Such speedy action would of course have been impossible without a great deal of preparation and forethought. That this was given is shown by a comment which Sheldon made to the clerk of the convocation. On the eve of the session the latter suggested hopefully that the convocation would, "so reform the liturgy as that no sober man might make exception." Taking this as a Presbyterian criticism, Sheldon answered shortly, that "what should be was already concluded or resolved." [68] The bishops had been working on their own revision for some months.

Several groups had been assigned to the task. Bishops Wren and Cosin, firm supporters of Laud in the old days, penciled their changes into a copy of the 1619 Prayer Book, a book which was later found in the library of Durham Cathedral and is known consequently as the "Durham Book." They based their proposals on the Scottish liturgy, published in 1637 by Laud, on some suggestions which Wren had produced in 1660, and on a paper of suggested changes, composed by Cosin for Laud in the 1630's. The Durham Book thus represented the Laudian view. It tended toward a more ceremonial, liturgical form of service than

[67] One of these ordinances provided that: 1) All churches and chapels were in the future to be guarded from promiscuous and common usage, 2) The Book of Common Prayer only was to be the order of service, 3) All persons were to come on time and not leave until the service was over, 4) All persons were to uncover their heads during church services, 5) There was to be no walking, talking, or any other misdeameanor during services, 6) All persons were to perform due reverence at the mention of the name of Jesus. David Wilkins, *Concilia Magnae*, IV, 577.
[68] Bosher, p. 246.

that contained in the old Prayer Book. The Durham Book, however, was rejected by the bishops, and Sheldon's voice no doubt was dominant in securing this decision.

The 1662 version of the Prayer Book was written by Sanderson, assisted by Wren, Cosin, and five other bishops, with Sancroft, dean of St. Paul's, to correct the printing.[69] There were some 600 changes made, most of them of a minor nature, although nearly all the concessions which the bishops had made to the Puritans at Savoy were included. One author counts twenty-seven of these Puritan changes. In no sense of course was that group satisfied with the end product. But neither were the Laudians. As Bishop Sanderson wrote in the preface, "It hath been the wisdom of the Church of England . . . to keep the mean between the two Extremes," and that is what Sheldon and his colleagues attempted to do – to retain the liturgy much as it had been in the past. Sheldon and his friends were essentially conservative in outlook, and they showed it nowhere more than here.

It was February 4, 1662, before a copy of the new liturgy could be read and approved in council and passed on to parliament. Both the House of Lords and the Commons had been impatiently calling for it for some weeks.[70] On May 19 the bill for uniformity, with the new Prayer Book attached, was again passed by parliament and sent to the king. It required "every parson, vicar, or other minister whatsoever, who now has and enjoys any ecclesiastical benefice or promotion within this realm of England" to declare his "unfeigned assent and consent to all and everything prescribed in . . . the Book of Common Prayer." The deadline for taking the oath was – an unfortunate choice – St. Bartholomew's Day, August 24, 1662. After that date no minister or priest who had refused the declaration would be able to serve any congregation in England.[71] The king had requested that he be granted the dispensing power so that certain deserving and loyal dissenters might be excused from taking the oath. Parliament decisively refused to add a proviso to that effect.[72]

The Act of Uniformity was the most important topic of discussion during the summer of 1662. Could conformity to Anglican ritual really be imposed on the English population at this late date? Might there

[69] H. M. Gwatkin, *Church and State in England to the Death of Queen Anne* (London, 1917), p. 352.

[70] See *Journals of the House of Lords*, XI, 383, for Sheldon's answer to the Lords when they requested a copy of the new Prayer Book.

[71] Henry Gee and Wm. Hardy (eds.), *Documents Illustrative of Church History* (London, 1914), p. 604.

[72] *Journals of the House of Lords*, XI, 409-10.

not be another rebellion against a new Stuart king, who had, after all, only been back in England for two years? A few days before the 24th, there was a debate in council over the wisdom of attempting to put the act into effect. The earl of Manchester, a Presbyterian sympathizer, vehemently opposed the act. He felt the times were much too dangerous for the government to attempt to enforce it. Sheldon was equally passionate in support of the measure. Englishmen, he thought, were accustomed to obey laws, so while they stood on that ground they were safe. Furthermore, he was sure that none of the dangers which seemed to threaten would actually occur. He promised that all vacant pulpits in London would be filled, and that the new ministers would be much more satisfactory in the eyes of the city's parishioners than those who were ejected. Finally, he argued that very few of the Presbyterians would actually be deprived of their livings. He was sure that, when pressed to it, most of them would conform. Convinced by these arguments the council decided to put the law into effect as planned.[73]

Among the people of London too the consensus was that it would be impossible to enforce the act in a city so predominantly Puritan in sentiment as the capital. Fortified by this belief, a large group of Presbyterian ministers covenanted together to refuse the oath – sure that because of their very numbers there would be such an outcry raised by citizens deprived of their church services that the government would be forced to relent. However, they reckoned without Sheldon's exact knowledge of what was going on in the London churches. Through spies in most of the Puritan congregations, he carefully informed himself of those ministers who were most likely to refuse the oath. Thus when August 24 arrived, he had in the city an equal number of well-qualified, orthodox divines "who, the sign given did, as it were, come out of ambush and take possession of the [empty] pulpits."[74] Therefore even though in London alone some eighty ministers left their churches, services in all parishes were conducted as usual, and no public outcry was raised. As the surprised Pepys admitted, because of the bishop of London "we are here supplied with very good men."[75] In addition Sheldon advertised throughout the city a special ordination service to be held in St. Paul's on August 21 for those who desired to conform and keep their livings, that "none might plead impossibility or want of notice." On the day appointed he ordained numbers of persons as deacons and priests, many

---

[73] Burnet, p. 341, gives an account of this debate.
[74] Parker, p. 33.
[75] Pepys, I, 324.

of whom "had before been under the hands of the Presbytery only." [76] Because of these skillfull maneuvers, St. Bartholomew's Day passed with very little disturbance in London or anywhere else. On that day, it has been estimated, some 936 Puritan ministers left their pulpits rather than conform.[77]

The matter did not end there, however. Among the Puritans there had been a general expectation that the king, as he had promised, would grant a royal indulgence which would relieve them from the necessity of complying with the Act of Uniformity. When August 24 came and went and no such promulgation was forthcoming, there was great anger and persistent talk of revolt by the disaffected elements throughout the country. Rumor named September 3 as the day appointed for action. This date was chosen, says Pepys, "by the Fanatiques and Presbyters that did intend to rise... as the most auspicious to them in their endeavors against monarchy, it being twice fatal to the king and the day of Oliver's death." [78]

At court, Clarendon was surrounded by people who predicted dire forebodings of what was to happen on September 3. Major-General Brown, who was close to the Puritans, was daily advising him that if the monarchy was to be saved from another rebellion and civil war, then some action on behalf of the ejected ministers would have to be authorized.[79] Influenced by this daily advice, Clarendon apparently lost his nerve and came to the conclusion – which in any case fitted well with the king's desires – that an indulgence would have to be granted. Acting on this belief, he hurriedly had some of the most eminent Puritan divines petition for the indulgence and had it approved at a council meeting without ever consulting Sheldon. Then on August 28 he summoned the bishop to a council meeting and faced him with a *fait accompli*, fully expecting that his friend would be forced to fall in with the plan. However, he underestimated Sheldon's strength of character.

The bishop faced the king, Clarendon, and the council, and told them that it was too late now to suspend that law, since he had only the Sunday before ejected all of those ministers in his diocese who would not conform. No council ruling, he argued, could justify his acting contrary to a law which had been passed with such a unanimous vote in both houses of parliament after a long and mature deliberation. If the council

---

[76] Mercurius Publicus (1662), No. 33, p. 554.
[77] Mathews, pp. xii and xiii.
[78] Pepys, I, 322.
[79] See Clarendon Mss. C. 70, Vol. 77, the Bodleian library, where, in a letter from Morley to Clarendon, Sept. 3, 1662, Morley refers to these talks with Brown.

attempted such an act now, just to satisfy a few factious people, it could only end by making the parliament look ridiculous and contemptible. He warned that he would be no party to such a move, nor would he obey such a council ruling.[80]

The appeal to parliament, or the threat of it, was effective. There was no doubt but that the legislature would feel itself flouted by any such council action. As one author observes, "a resourceful prelate was dealing with a realistic king who could recognize and accept defeat." [81] The council reversed itself and decided against the grant of indulgence.

Sheldon was the hero of the hour to the Anglicans. As one of them reported:

But the bishops... were all gone to their respective dioceses; so as the Lord Bishop of London was to answer all, and stand alone in the gap – which that incomparable prelate did to that height of prudence and Christian resolution (of both which at present there was absolute necessity).[82]

Sheldon was wrathfully indignant at the court and the Lord Chancellor in particular. Two days after the affair he wrote a bitter letter upbraiding his old friend for taking the lead in what the bishop could only consider a disgraceful episode.[83] Had the indulgence been approved and issued, it would have made Sheldon an object of raillery at the very least. Only a few days before he had been responsible for ejecting a great number of nonconformists from their livings; if the king turned around now and reinstated them, the bishop would have been left in an untenable position. Moreover, the Act of Uniformity, which Sheldon had worked so industriously to bring into existence, would thenceforth have been a dead letter. And where would this have left the established church? The Church which Sheldon remembered, and loved, and was striving so desperately to resurrect, would have forever ceased to exist.

By the end of September, 1662, the crisis was past. The king was safe on his throne. Every Presbyterian effort at church settlement had been blocked, and that group was now an outlawed sect. The Act of Uniformity was operational, and Clarendon had been forced to stand by it. The king too had been thwarted, although by no means for the last time, in his efforts to grant an indulgence. The Church of England, now once more the only legal religious body in England, was in the hands of its devoted servants. All of this had been accomplished over two and one-

---

[80] See W. H. Marah (ed.), *Memoirs of Archbishop Juxon* (London, 1869), p. 80, where this confrontation is described in some detail. Also see Parker, pp. 31-33.
[81] Bosher, p. 263.
[82] Mercurius Publicus, (1662) No. 33, p. 548.
[83] Clarendon Mss. C. 70, Vol. 77, Sheldon to Clarendon, August 30, 1662.

quarter years against great odds. All that remained now was to guard the portals and see to it that the Church of England remained what the episcopalians had made her. As the future would show, that would be no easy task, but Sheldon had fifteen years more of active life to devote to it.

The sudden success which attended Sheldon, Hyde, and the Anglicans in their efforts to re-impose the Book of Common Prayer after its fifteen year hiatus, has always remained somewhat of a mystery. Even the Puritans were puzzled by their ignominious defeat. With victory apparently so easy of accomplishment, with the Presbyterians seemingly in an impregnable position at the king's return, with the king himself sincerely willing to accept their system of church government, why was it that they had failed even to secure some measure of toleration for themselves? They were at a loss to explain it.

The reasons, however, are not in any sense enshrouded in mystery. The apparent strength of the Presbyterian position at the Restoration was itself a contributing factor. It gave the Presbyterian leaders a false sense of security. They were confident, even overly-confident, that they represented such a large portion of the population that they would have to be consulted on the religious settlement. The Anglicans on the other hand had no such confidence. They were "running scared" and were not at all certain that the Church of England could ever be restored. But they were determined to make every effort possible to restore the old forms. In their desperation any means seemed justifiable to gain their ends. They were not in any sense a generous enemy.

In addition Sheldon, Hyde, and the Anglican clergy, returned with a bitter hatred of Puritanism. To them it represented republicanism, rebellion, and chaos. All of them had suffered at its hands; they would give it no quarter. Fortunately for them, although it was not immediately apparent in 1660, the majority of the English body politic had come to the same conclusion. Puritanism, Presbyterianism even, had acquired overtones of social revolution, and the country squires wanted no part of that. Thus the Anglicans were riding the crest of a swelling wave of reaction against the Puritans. The Cavalier Parliament was a result of that feeling and it proved enthusiastically royalist and equally enthusiastically Anglican. Without its assistance, Sheldon and the bishops could never have succeeded in re-establishing the Church.

Fortunately too, the Anglicans had their great ally, Hyde, at the seat of government directing policy. Thus the initiative lay with them, and the strength of the government could be wielded by them to help achieve their purpose. The Presbyterians, on the other hand, were outsiders, never sure of what was going on in the inner governing circle. Worse than this was the fact that their group was divided. There was no single leader who could speak for their church with authority or who could command the obedience of all of its members. As has been noted, this very often led them to work at cross-purposes and gave their enemies a considerable advantage over them. In the Anglican camp the reverse was true. There was unity and obedience. Sheldon spoke with authority and provided leadership which was acknowledged by all.

Finally, that very leadership must receive its due. Sheldon was determined to restore the Church, and he let nothing stand in his way. Through offers of preferment – very nearly bribery – he won over some of the opposition leaders and used them and their information in his schemes. John Gauden, for instance, whom both Sheldon and the king scorned, was nevertheless given the see of Exeter "for his great services" to the Church at the Restoration.[84] James Sharp, a Scots Presbyterian, also defected to the Anglican side and was rewarded by Sheldon with the province of St. Andrew's. Robert Baillie was sure that Sharp had become a turn-coat early in 1660, shortly before the king's return. At that time, he wrote bitterly, "Dr. Sheldon... and Dr. Morley did poison Mr. Sharp, our agent whom we trusted." [85] In addition to such sources of information, Sheldon and Hyde regularly intercepted Presbyterian mail and used the information gleaned from that source to help form their plans.[86] Then, as we have noted, Sheldon had informers and spies everywhere, in almost every Presbyterian congregation. Baxter was sure that he never preached a sermon but what it was audited by one of Sheldon's people, and when in 1661 he was finally silenced by Morley, bishop of Worcester, it was on evidence forwarded to Sheldon by "one of the hearers." [87] Through all of these means, Sheldon informed himself carefully of his foes – their thoughts, their plans, and their actions.

And just as coldly, carefully, calculatingly, the bishop devised his own schemes and drove them to fruition. His was the dogged determination

---

[84] Gauden was won over by Morley. See *CSP, Clarendon*, V, Part I, 68 and 81, for two letters from Gauden to Morley expressing his dissatisfaction with his payment. Some have maintained that Gauden received Exeter because he was the reputed author of the *Eikon Basilike*. Both Hammond and Sheldon had been among the first to see the Eikon – Hammond edited it for publication – and both were thoroughly convinced that Charles I was the author. Sheldon would not have been paying Gauden for this service.

[85] Baillie, II, 459.

[86] We have already noted Hyde's interception of Calamy's letters. For another reference – this time to reading Baxter's mail – see *CSP, Clarendon*, V, 274.

[87] *Reliquiae Baxterianae*, p. 302.

that refused to admit defeat; his the shrewdness, the cunning, which directed Anglican councils, and his was the leadership which held the Anglican party together through this trying period. To him must be apportioned a good share of the blame, or credit, for resurrecting the Church of England in 1662.

CHAPTER V

ARCHBISHOP VS. KING I

Supposedly, the second Charles Stuart returned from exile as an indolent, cynical, self-centered man, slightly debauched, devoted to nothing save his own comfort and the gratification of his sensual appetites. To admit the truth of the last of these charges – the facts seem fairly incontrovertible on this point – does not mean necessarily that the others are equally valid. Charles has suffered much because most of his record has been written by his enemies – enemies who were suspicious of his Romanist sympathies, who could not understand him, and who, consequently, were willing to believe the worst. And in this instance the worst was the picture which Charles projected of himself. Apparently he was content to appear very much the indolent young man, interested only in his own creature comforts, his mistresses, and the idle repartee of a debauched court.

But isolated records show another Charles II, with other, more admirable traits. This other Charles could, in 1650, receive £1000 – transmitted from England by Lady Savile – and even though he was in near desperate financial straits himself, he could immediately re-transmit £200 of it to London to help ease the lot of a faithful servant who was dying in prison there.[1] At the height of an official persecution, he could also secretly summon a Presbyterian leader to him and press upon the surprised man 1000 guineas to be used to ease the sufferings of those dissident religionists whom his government was vigorously prosecuting.[2] This Charles Stuart could leave his pleasure-seeking court to hasten to the bedside of his dying tutor, there to kneel and claim a last blessing from a good, old man.[3] And finally, this Charles Stuart could, and did, believe in religious toleration as a principle, believe in it so much that

[1] Barwick, p. 128.
[2] F. Bate, *Declaration of Indulgence* (London, 1908), p. 90.
[3] Burrows, *Worthies*, p. 224.

he was willing to labor for twelve years to establish it within his kingdom. It was upon this latter point that he clashed with Gilbert Sheldon, bishop of London, and later archbishop of Canterbury.

The king was far from satisfied with the Act of Uniformity which went into effect in the summer of 1662. He thought it unnecessarily severe in that it eliminated from the Church many loyal and honest subjects and instituted a period of suffering and persecution for them. He had tried to construct a more comprehensive Church which would have included most of the Presbyterians within the establishment. The bishops torpedoed that idea at Savoy. He then requested an additional clause in the Act of Uniformity itself which would have granted him the power to dispense with that law for those dissenters of proven loyalty to the throne. Parliament emphatically denied that request. And, as has been discussed, he attempted with Clarendon's help to grant an indulgence on August 28, four days after the Act of Uniformity became law, only to be thwarted again, this time through Sheldon's efforts.

But Charles refused to relinquish his projects for comprehension or toleration. In December he again let it be known that he intended to grant an indulgence to the more deserving of those dissenting ministers who were now without congregations or income. Hearing of his master's declaration, Sheldon exploded. What *could* the king be thinking of? The only answer to that seemed to be: the Roman Catholics in England. Charles apparently wished to grant them toleration. In a blunt, most uncourtier-like letter, the bishop warned his monarch off any such project.

> By your act [he wrote] you labour to set up that most damnable and heretical doctrine of the Church of Rome, whore of Babylon. How hateful will it be to God and grievous unto your subjects, the true professors of the Gospel, that your Majesty, who hath often disputed and learnedly written against those heresies, should shew yourself a patron of those doctrines which your pen hath told the world, and your conscience tells yourself, are superstitious, idolatrous, and detestable.[4]

Besides, Sheldon coldly pointed out, any such toleration could be accomplished only by an act of parliament, "unless your Majesty will let your subjects see that you will take unto yourself a liberty to throw down the laws of the realm at your pleasure." [5]

Sheldon was voicing openly the suspicion which was to be current in

---

[4] Reproduced in Molesworth, *History of the Church of England from 1660* (London, 1882), p. 60.

[5] *Ibid.*, probably oblivious to the irony involved, Sheldon signed himself, "Your obedient servant."

England throughout Charles' reign and which would ultimately defeat his toleration project – the fear of Roman Catholicism and its political power. Protestants of all persuasions were united in an irrational phobia concerning the papacy and, handled astutely, this could be a potent weapon against the king's plans. Even the dissenting sects themselves were willing to forego any of the benefits of toleration if those same benefits were to be extended to Roman Catholics. And Charles was adamant in his determination to include them. On principle he was for toleration, but it must include the Catholics. He owed them much, and his feelings ran deep on this point.

Sheldon's outspoken letter clearly reflects the reversal in alliances since Laud's day. The Church under Laud allied itself with a loyal Anglican monarch against a dangerously heretical parliament. Under Sheldon the Church now sought an alliance with a loyal Anglican parliament against a dangerous monarch. Sheldon preached no passive obedience to the king's divine will as did many high churchmen in this period. To preserve the Church in its Anglican purity, he would block Charles in any way he could devise. If that meant marriage to parliament, then Sheldon would become a politician and work through majorities, votes, and parliamentary maneuverings. In method he was eminently flexible; his goal – preservation of the Church – the bishop would never change.

Perhaps warned by Sheldon's letter, Charles withheld his intended declaration. However, when parliament convened for its spring session, he once more requested that he be granted the authority to excuse some dissenters from conforming to the St. Bartholomew's Day act. He spoke emphatically about his desires on this point.

> I hope you all have so good an opinion of my zeal for the Protestant religion [he said], as I need not tell you, I will not yield to any therein, not to the Bishops themselves, nor my liking the uniformity of it as it is now established; which being the standard of our religion must be kept pure and uncorrupted from all mixtures; and yet if the Dissenters will demean themselves peaceably and modestly under the gov't, I could heartily wish I had such a power of Indulgence to use upon occasions as might not needlessly force them out of the kingdom, or, staying here, give them cause to conspire against the peace of it.[6]

Despite the fact that the king very probably was honestly expressing his thoughts here, the Cavalier Parliament again rejected his request, with both houses emphatically concurring.[7] In the House of Lords Sheldon, Clarendon, and the bishops all spoke against it.

Sheldon's outspoken criticism might well have alienated a monarch

---

[6] Lords Journals, XI, 478.
[7] Bate, p. 39.

of a more touchy disposition than Charles, but it seemed, at the time at least, to have no effect at all upon the Stuart king. It was after this event that Pepys was sure that Sheldon would replace Southampton as treasurer – he was "so great with the king." [8] In addition, all through this period Sheldon disposed of Charles' church patronage as though it were his own. Seldom did the king intervene in any matters pertaining to Church appointments.[9] And finally, when Juxon died in the summer of 1663, there was no discussion, as was customary, as to who would replace him. In accordance with everyone's expectations, Sheldon moved up to Canterbury, and he brought his friend Humphrey Henchman into London behind him. His closeness to the king and his influence in Church affairs during the early years of the Restoration were without parallel in England's recent history. Even Laud had been given no such free hand in bestowing Church patronage under Charles I.

None of this, however, indicated any meeting of the minds between the king and the archbishop on the religious question. The former was determined to create a broad church, comprehensive enough to include most of the Puritans, and then to arrange toleration for those who were excluded; the latter was equally determined to retain a monopoly for the Church of England, and to enforce uniformity of practice upon all Englishmen.

As archbishop, Sheldon found that the king's divergent policy created serious problems for his bishops. In their efforts to bring nonconformists into the Church and to extinguish all conventicles within their sees, they were constantly hampered by rumors and "expectations of liberty." What was worse, the rumors proceeded from "that place from whence we might hope for other things," – the king himself.[10] Too many people knew of the king's sympathies for the dissenters, and apparently he secretly abetted many of them in their determination to remain outside the officially sanctioned communion.[11] With encouragement from such

---

[8] Pepys, I, 624.

[9] See letter to Mrs. Paul, wife of deceased Bishop Paul, where Sheldon told her that if her request to remain temporarily in the living Paul had held had been in the King's gift, then he could have assured her that her wish to remain there for a few months following her husband's death could have been easily granted. But since the benefice was in the Lord Chancellor's gift, he would see what could be done in the matter. Sheldon to Mrs. Paul, June 15, 1665, Add. Mss. 5831.

[10] Phrase from a letter from Ward to Sheldon, Jan. 13, 1663/4, Add. Mss. C. 305.

[11] See a letter from Sparrow to Sheldon, no date, Add. Mss. C. 305, where Sparrow reports on a merchant, John Mayne, who had been promised by the king that he would not suffer for his nonconformist views.

a source, large numbers refused to conform, and few justices could be prevailed upon to proceed against them.

To counter this problem – a constant source of irritation in the first fourteen years of the reign – Sheldon instructed his subordinates that they point out to the recalcitrant justices, and to the nonconformists themselves, "that his Majesty's sense is not otherwise known than by his public laws, by them therefore we are only to be guided in our duty." To take his Majesty's sense from any other source, the archbishop warned, was "neither safe nor good manners." [12] Here Sheldon again appealed to the legal enactments of parliament. From these only are we to divine the government's desires and intentions, he said, not from any hearsay or rumor, no matter where it originates. This was a telling argument, and the bishops employed it on many an occasion to bring the justices to a recognition of their duty. As a result in some areas nonconformity did begin to decline markedly.[13]

However, with the government so obviously divided on the religious issue – Clarendon aided Sheldon and the bishops with all of his official power, while the king and some of his counsellors impeded them wherever and whenever they could – the complete elimination of conventicles was almost impossible. What was needed was more leverage in the form of another law, a law that would deal so severely with the dissenters that they would be liable to serious penalties if they chose to persist in their illegal conduct. With this as the motivation, but with the many rumors of risings and rebellions as the ostensible reasons, Sheldon and Clarendon pushed the Seditious Conventicles Act through parliament in 1664. Anyone taken in illegal worship, where more than five persons were gathered together, could now be fined £ 5 for the first offense, £ 15 for the second, and could be transported to the penal colonies for the third. Even this, however, was not considered enough assistance by Sheldon and his supporters. Conventicles still persisted. Taking advantage of the Dutch War which broke out in 1664, they went a step further. Pointing out to the legislators that many dissenters were in sympathy with the Dutch and were therefore potential fifth columnists, Sheldon and Clarendon drove through the Five-Mile Act. This new bill forbade any nonconformist preacher or teacher from coming within five miles of any parish where he had previously taught or ministered. Sheldon wrote both of these laws.[14] He was furiously determined that conventicles would cease

[12] Harl. Mss. 7377, Sheldon to Compton, Sept. 21, 1674.
[13] See Ward's letters to Sheldon, 1664-5, from Winchester, Add. Mss. C. 305.
[14] See Chapter VII for a discussion of Sheldon's production of legislation. While advocating the passage of the bill in the Lords, Clarendon made much of

and everyone would conform, and he now had laws that would be effective regardless of the king's desires.

The ease with which these bills were passed through parliament convinced Charles that neither dispensation nor toleration were possible for the dissenter as long as so much fear of Roman Catholicism existed throughout the country and as long as Clarendon was managing the House of Commons and encouraging that body's enthusiastic Anglicanism. He took steps to correct both problems. When the judges were sent forth on annual circuit in 1664, he instructed them "to cause the Roman Catholics to be convicted." [15] He wanted *all* convicted who were refusing to attend Anglican services so that 1) it would be clear to everyone that the government was not soft on Catholicism, and 2) when it was seen how few recusants there actually were in England, the outcry against them would be considerably diminished. At the same time he made a concentrated effort to halt all conversions to Rome at the court and to keep Jesuits and other priests from coming into the country from abroad.[16] All of these things maintained the Catholic fear at flood tide and reacted against the loyal English Catholics who wished only to be permitted to live quietly in peace.

The problem of Clarendon had to be handled more circumspectly. By 1663, the king had already begun to turn from the chancellor, mainly because of his and the bishops' stubborn opposition to the royal indulgence bill of that year. He had begun to bring along Sir Henry Bennet and Anthony Ashley Cooper – recently created Baron Ashley – younger men who could act as counterpoises to Clarendon's power. He now insisted that the management of the lower house be entrusted to a committee and that his two new favorites be included in that body's membership. Ashley Cooper and Bennet shortly brought in others of their friends to aid them and were clearly moving to oust Clarendon from management of the government's majority in the lower house.[17]

However, what was not readily apparent was that Clarendon was only partly responsible for the strong Anglican majority in the House of Commons. He and the archbishop together, using both Church and

---

the dangers to the war effort from the malignant parties. He urged both houses "to suppress [your] enemies at home that your enemies abroad may be less exalted." Lords Journals, XI, 689. Also there was, we are told, a great deal of activity by the Dutch among the nonconformists – stirring them to rebel and recruiting some to fight for Holland. See *Secret History* (London, 1723), II, 170.

[15] Clarendon, *Continuation* (London, 1723), p. 189.
[16] *Ibid.*, p. 190.
[17] Bate, p. 39, and *Secret History*, II, 18, where Bennett and Coventry add Clifford and Churchill to Hyde's committee.

government patronage, had been carefully nurturing that group.[18] Consequently, the efforts of the new men were not destined to be very effective in frustrating Anglican control of the lower house. Three years later when the king broke with the Lord Chancellor, one reason he gave was that Clarendon, as he said angrily, "had a faction in the House of Commons that opposed everything that concerned his Majesty's service if it were not expressly recommended to them by him." [19] The king at that time determined to end for all time Clarendon's power in Commons by ending his power in the government. Then perhaps a more moderate opinion might prevail in the lower house and the king's plans for remodeling the Church might have better hope of success.

However, it was not then apparent that Hyde's influence went that deep among the members of the Commons, and so it was with high hopes of success that a new plan to obtain toleration for the dissenters was formulated in 1665. Ashley, Arlington, and Lauderdale had taken a long look at the king's two most pressing problems – religion and finance – and thought they perceived a method by which both could be solved. They proposed that the king sell indulgences to individual Catholics and nonconformists. The time, they thought, was propitious for just such a scheme. War with Holland appeared imminent, and it would only compound the government's troubles to continue to prosecute and thus alienate such a large group of citizens in a period of national crisis. They were certain that most people would recognize the logic of that determination. Then, secondly, parliament had only just passed the Conventicle Act, and the enthusiasm of the members for the Anglican settlement was so apparent during the course of the debate that all nonconformists must now surely recognize that they were to be a perpetual remnant, forever outside the legal church system. Therefore, the king's advisors reasoned, the Puritans would now be willing "to compound for liberty at any reasonable rates." [20]

The scheme never really had a chance in the climate which prevailed in England at that moment, but Charles embraced it ardently. Its supporters had even drawn up a detailed schedule showing what the king should realize from such a sale, and it appeared a princely sum indeed. Good revenue and tranquility in the kingdom would both seemingly result. He ordered his counsellors to draw up a bill embodying their proposals and then had it introduced into the House of Lords.

In council Clarendon, Sheldon, and Southampton (the Lord Treasur-

---

[18] See Chapter VI for a discussion of Sheldon and the House of Commons.
[19] Clarendon, *Continuation*, p. 441.
[20] *Ibid.*, p. 245.

er) opposed the whole business, but the king was determined. He made the measure his own, put his prestige behind it, and ordered all those who were opposed but loyal to absent themselves from the house while the act was under discussion. None of the three Anglican advisors gave their promise to remain away. However, Clarendon was ill with the gout when the debate opened, so Southampton and the bishops provided the main opposition in the first days of debate.

Southampton denounced the measure as one purposely designed to destroy the true Protestant religion and to increase the power of the Papists. To his way of thinking its purpose could only be this. The bishops "fiercely" seconded him. They argued that it would undermine the nation's recently established religious structure, and it could only have an iniquitous effect. Arlington and Ashley spoke in favor. Before the second reading Charles called Sheldon in and sharply reprimanded him and the bishops for their opposition. He threatened that if they continued in their obstructionist course "they would repent it." [21] The archbishop was just as determined as the king; and the episcopal bench was just as "fiercely" opposed at the second reading as at the first.

In the debate that attended the second reading, Ashley Cooper made a brilliant speech in which he argued logically and effectively that in these dangerous times such a measure made sense. It would compose the country and unite it in the moment of crisis. Anyway, he argued, the king's loyalty to the Anglican faith was unquestioned, and should it be granted, he would not make an undue use of such a prerogative. Ashley warmly assured his hearers that the king could be trusted in these matters.

Probably because of the effect of this persuasive speech, Clarendon was induced to quit his sickbed to speak against the grant. In a lengthy speech he argued, perhaps a bit too cleverly, that it was not a question of "whether the king was worthy of the trust, but whether the trust was worthy of the king." [22] He agreed that everyone knew of the king's constancy in matters of religion but, he pointed out, if this bill were passed, the nonconformists would flock to him with their importunities and in doing so would create an embarrassing and difficult situation for him. Urged on by Ashley's taunts, Clarendon went to greater lengths than he had perhaps intended. He recklessly called the bill

ship-money in religion, that nobody could know the end of or where it would rest; that if it were passed, Dr. Goffe [a converted Catholic] or any other apostate

[21] *Ibid.*, p. 247.
[22] *Ibid.*

might be made bishop or [even] archbishop here, all oaths and statutes and provisions being dispensed with.[23]

With Clarendon's assistance the tolerationists were turned back, and the bill for the sale of dispensations was rejected by the Lords. Thus another of the king's efforts to grant toleration was blocked. But the cost was great. Charles grew increasingly cold and reserved in his treatment of Clarendon and Southampton, and both were mimicked, mocked, and derided freely in the royal presence. Worse than this, Sheldon and the bishops were now for the first time subjected to the same treatment. The king himself spoke of them slightingly and never after "treated any of them with that respect as he had done formerly." [24] Encouraged by their monarch, Buckingham and the court jesters now turned the cutting edge of their wit against the Church leaders. Their mannerisms, their voices, their sermons, their religion – all were held up to scorn, contempt, and ridicule.

Aware of what was happening and aware also of the possibility of a complete break occurring between the king and himself, Sheldon labored diligently over the next two years on behalf of his monarch and in support of governmental policy. He was trying to mend his fences and prove his loyalty in order to retain Charles' confidence, and he *was* loyal. The only real difference he had with the Stuart king was over the issue of religious liberty.

The archbishop was especially careful to see that the king's prerogatives in Church affairs were not transgressed by anyone. In 1665 we find him warning Bishop Lucy of St. David's against refusing the king's great seal ordering the award of a benefice which Lucy thought was in his gift and not the king's.[25] Again a few days later he wrote to Alexander Hyde, the new bishop of Salisbury, cautioning him about refusing a benefice to a Mr. Gardiner whom the king wished to reward. "You owe his Majesty a great deal more than so small a return," he said, and he hoped that Hyde would not be so foolhardy as to provoke the king in his "very first act of duty and observance." [26] Or, a short time later, we find him remonstrating with the magistrates of Dover, firmly pointing out to them that the curacy of their church was in the king's disposal and not theirs. However, if they would choose some worthy and conformable person, he promised to intervene with Charles in order to secure his appointment.[27] There were other instances of this

[23] *Ibid.,* p. 248.
[24] *Ibid.,* p. 249.
[25] Add. Mss. C. 305, Sheldon to the bishop of St. David's, Jan. 21, 1665/6.
[26] *Ibid.,* Sheldon to Hyde, Jan. 23, 1665/6.
[27] Add. Mss. C. 308, Sheldon to the magistrates of Dover, May 10, 1666.

same exaggerated carefulness of the king's prerogatives, and one can only conclude that Sheldon was bent on proving his own loyalty and zealousness wherever and whenever he could.[28]

Partly for this reason too, when the plague broke out in London in 1665, the archbishop remained at his Lambeth residence all through the months of greatest danger. He assisted in keeping order and in aiding the poor who were forced to remain in the stricken city, and his example was an inspiration to churchmen throughout the country.[29]

When war broke out with the Dutch, he was equally attentive to his duties. He scoured the Church for naval chaplains, so that no ship would be reduced to sailing without a spiritual counsellor aboard. These were hard fought, bloody engagements, and consequently volunteers for these dangerous positions were difficult to find. But Sheldon used his power and persuasiveness to its utmost, and the Anglican ministers went to sea. In one instance when Prince Rupert had no chaplain for his flagship, Sheldon promised faithfully to supply one, and failing that, the sixty-eight year old archbishop added grimly, "I shall come myself." [30]

When the wounded began flowing ashore, it was Sheldon again who suggested to the council that all hospital places which became vacant should be reserved for crippled seamen. He dispatched orders to all the bishops ordering a census of the hospitals in their sees, so that all available places would be known, and wounded sailors could be sent to fill them. All through 1665 he drove his subordinates to supply that information.[31]

In the case of the royal loans requested by the government in 1667 to enable it to carry the war to a successful conclusion, Sheldon was equally diligent. The occasion was the Medway disaster. Charles' treasury being utterly depleted and peace talks in progress, it was decided to put up the fleet in the face of an aggressive enemy still at sea. The result was

---

[28] One might argue, of course, that since Sheldon himself was arranging much of the king's patronage, he was only using the king's name here to bolster his own claim to bestow these benefices. This could be true, but I think my own explanation is better. A spate of these letters at this time seems to indicate a desperate attempt by Sheldon to retain the king's favor.

[29] See Chapter VIII for a further account of Sheldon's activities during the plague.

[30] Add. Mss. C. 308, Sheldon to Prince Rupert, July 12, 1666.

[31] Add. Mss. C. 308, has the letter from Sheldon to his bishops, no date, requiring the hospital census. It also contains a letter from the king to Sheldon, but in Sheldon's handwriting, ordering the census. This certainly makes it appear that Sheldon suggested the census and wrote the king's letter to himself ordering it – with Charles approval of course. Unlike modern hospitals, 17th century hospitals were endowed institutions, managed by the Church which provided In-Brothers and Out-Brothers with an income or an income plus living quarters.

one of the most disgraceful incidents in English naval annals. In June, 1667, de Ruyter, the Dutch commander, sailed boldly up the Medway, stayed there a week, burned four naval vessels with impunity, and coolly sailed out again towing the Royal Charles, the navy's largest ship-of-war, behind him. In panic the government hastily decided to borrow money from all persons who would lend against the next year's revenue and re-outfit the fleet. Charles turned to Sheldon and the bishops to publicize and propagandize for the loans. In placing the matter in his primate's hands, the king wrote:

And we are rather induced to believe your labour herein will be successful because you are to deal with a sort of persons endued with loyalty and ingenuity who cannot forget what tenderness we have for them, what care to protect and support them, and how much their interest and welfare is involved in ours. But arguments and motives of this nature we leave to your proved management.[32]

Nor was the king mistaken in his man. Sheldon seized upon this opportunity to prove to the king and the country what an aroused, zealous, and loyal Church could accomplish in a moment of crisis. He wrote to every bishop, ordering each of them to meet with their clergy and instruct them personally in the preaching up of the loans. He gave careful instructions for the three sees which at that moment were vacant – St. Asaph's, Lincoln, and Llandaff – and appointed senior clergymen to supervise the loan projects in those areas. He included the ecclesiastical and civil courts in his drive and instructed the judges in all of them to see to it that all "Advocates, Proctors, Registers, and officers unto them belonging" subscribed to the loan. In logical language his letters laid out the reasons and advantages which might effectively motivate the "dignified and richer sort... to make a free and liberal advance." [33] He noted the danger to all from the invasion of the Dutch – they surely would not object to parting with a reasonable portion of their money in order to secure the remainder. The loan, he reminded them, was made on "the best security the kingdom can afford" – the word of parliament; and those "that come in earliest," he continued, "are like to have their money soonest repaid." [34] He frequently made reference to the king's letter "wherein his Majesty recommends to my care the promoting of his and the kingdom's interest in this great time of danger and necessity," [35] and he urged his subordinates to apply themselves to the task with all zeal possible. Most of the bishops responded

---

[32] Lambeth Mss. #943, the king to Sheldon, June 21, 1667.
[33] Mss. SR-138, June 24, 1667, Sheldon to his Own Commissary at Canterbury.
[34] *Ibid.*
[35] See *ibid.*, Sheldon to bishop of Rochester, June 24, 1667.

with alacrity to the urgency evident in their primate's messages, and they and their officers immediately sent in their own subscriptions to the loan, and in all their religious services they discoursed at length upon the government's great need.

The result of all of this was an aroused citizenry. Money began to pour into the treasury from all parts of the country. When only a trivial amount arrived from the diocese of Bristol, Sheldon fired off a wrathful letter to the bishop, Gilbert Ironside, angrily chiding him for what he considered disgracefully low amounts. "I do not wonder," he wrote indignantly, "to see the subscriptions so pitifully mean, seeing the clergy of your diocese had not the encouragement of your lordship's example to lead them on." [36] The archbishop doubted that such small sums would even be admitted into the exchequer, and he closed by informing Ironside coldly that he would make no further reference to "the wretched business." [37]

But Bristol was the exception; the loans went very well indeed.[38] However to everyone's relief, peace was signed on July 31, and the crisis was over.

The assiduity with which Sheldon and the church leaders prosecuted these ventures, as well as the success which attended them, could not have helped but impress the king. However, all were to no avail. Within a few months of the completion of the loan subscriptions relations between the king and his archbishop had been severed completely.

Sheldon and his friends went down with the earl of Clarendon. Charles had gradually grown more and more restive under the tutelage of the old Lord Chancellor. Evidence from Clarendon's own writings convicts him of carping, criticizing, and preaching at the young king. He heartily disapproved of the lax morals which prevailed at court, and by his outspoken criticisms made bitter enemies of the royal mistresses.[39] Moreover, as has been noted, he regularly offended the king by siding with the bishops on the religious problem. The country too was outraged. For the sale of Dunkirk, the plague, the London fire, the Dutch in the

---

[36] Add. Mss. C. 308, Sheldon to the bishop of Bristol, June 18, 1667.
[37] *Ibid.*
[38] See Tanner MS. 45, John Hacket to Sheldon, June, 1667, where Hacket of Lichfield, elated at the success of the loans in his diocese, wrote Sheldon that he had received £317 from the clergy in Staffordshire alone, and he had yet to hear from "two of the fattest."
[39] Particularly the duchess of Cleveland. Hyde intervened when the king forced Cleveland into the queen's entourage as lady-in-waiting. He also attempted to restrict the grant of lands and patents which the king awarded to her so freely. But most important, probably, he would not let his wife call on the duchess. Cleveland never forgot, nor forgave.

Medway – all national disasters – someone must pay.[40] Clarendon was the logical scapegoat.

There is a story that the king's determination to rid himself of his mentor came as a result of the lord chancellor's intervention in the Frances Stuart affair. The king was ardently courting this young lady-in-waiting, and Clarendon, fearful that he might attempt to divorce the queen in order to marry her, apparently encouraged the young duke of Richmond to carry the celebrated beauty off in a run-away marriage. The king was furious at Hyde's meddling and determined to be rid of him for good.[41]

He summoned the archbishop to Whitehall, discussed the matter with him, and attempted to win him over to an acceptance of the dismissal. Sheldon stood quietly, saying nothing. Finally, the king turned to him, "Well?" he demanded.

"I wish sire," the archbishop said quietly, "that you would put away that woman [duchess of Cleveland] you have."

"What? Why have you never mentioned this before?" the surprised king asked.

What Sheldon answered is not known, but apparently the conversation went from bad to worse; voices rose and tempers flared, but Sheldon stubbornly refused to desert his old friend. Lauderdale reported that "the king and Sheldon [went] into such expostulations upon it that from that day forward Sheldon could never recover the king's confidence." [42] The doughty old archbishop carried the break a step farther and publicly expressed his disapproval of the king's gross licentiousness in the strongest language possible. Somewhat later when Charles came forward to the communion table, Sheldon, we are told, turned him away. "He refused to administer the sacrament to the king on this account." [43]

It was the last of August, 1667, before the king had fully made up his mind. On the 26th, he sent the duke of York to the chancellor with the request that he resign. Hyde had just lost his wife, was despondent anyway, and really needed a rest, but he stubbornly attempted to cling to his power. The duchess of York (Hyde's saintly daugther), the duke of Albemarle, and Sheldon, all went to the court to intercede for the

---

[40] For an excellent summary of the reasons for Hyde's fall see Feiling, *History of the Tory Party* (Oxford, 1950), pp. 113-122.
[41] *Secret History*, II, 214, repeats this story.
[42] Pepys, II, 750, note.
[43] Burrows, *Worthies*, p. 222. This story was apparently first related by Swift after the turn of the century. However, it must have circulated as common knowledge prior to that time.

old royal servant, but it was to no avail. Hyde had to go.⁴⁴ On August 30, the lord chancellor trudged sorrowfully to Whitehall to deliver up the Great Seal, his badge of office. As he departed from that great palace for the last time, the duchess of Cleveland, unable to resist the opportunity, appeared at her bedroom window – dressed appropriately in her nightgown – to gloat over her fallen foe.

In the weeks that followed Charles frequently and publicly denounced the lord chancellor. He charged him with being "so imperious, he would endure no contradiction; that he had a faction in the House of Commons who opposed everything that concerned his Majesty's service, if it were not recommended to them by him; and that he had given him [the king] very ill-advice concerning Parliament." ⁴⁵ The emphasis on Clarendon's parliamentary sins was deliberate. Charles wished to arrange a rapprochement between himself and the legislature, and he felt that Clarendon's unpopularity was so great that his dismissal could not help but dispose the legislators in his favor. In addition, with Clarendon gone, the House of Commons should now be much more malleable and could, he thought, finally be brought to accept a change in the kingdom's religious policies.

When parliament met on October 18, 1667, Charles announced Clarendon's dismissal in a firm voice, promised never again to return him to power, and requested additional revenues. The effects of the war were still continuing, he pointed out, and further supply was mandatory. The Lords dispatched a perfunctory thanks for the speech from the throne. Commons took longer and expressed particular pleasure at the chancellor's dismissal. Since they had not mentioned the matter themselves, the members of the upper house refused to concur in that portion of the Commons' message and returned it to the lower house for some changes. Commons refused to change it. The Lords, with all the bishops voting in a block, refused to accept it. Charles wanted that message from Commons, and he wanted the clause concerning Hyde included in it. To him it was the symbol of his new relationship with the House of Commons, and he wanted nothing to mar that relationship at this stage. Therefore he summoned Sheldon once more to Whitehall and ordered him "in his Majesty's name" to command all the bishops to concur in the Commons vote of thanks. If they refused, the king grimly promised

⁴⁴ Clarendon, *Continuation*, p. 436.
⁴⁵ *Secret History,* II, 328. This account pretty much follows Clarendon's *Continuation of His Life,* but the writer shows some differences of interpretation and emphasis.

Sheldon, "he would make them repent it."⁴⁶ Hyde reports that he used many other similar threats. But Sheldon held his colleagues steady in their opposition, and the king finally got his way only because his threats proved more effective against the secular lords. Many of the latter absented themselves, and the Commons vote of thanks was finally, reluctantly, accepted by the upper house.⁴⁷

It was the Lords again in November who, by their firm opposition, blocked Clarendon's impeachment and arrest, and once again the members of the episcopal bench stood staunchly by their ally and friend. Their solid block of votes helped hold the house steady in its rejection of impeachment, and the old royal servant was ordered banished instead. Sheldon was thus able to render his friend a last important service.

But with their champion no longer at the head of the government, could the church leaders successfully continue their opposition to Charles' determined tolerationist policies? Would the House of Commons continue steadfastly to uphold the Church now that patronage and management were vested in the new royal favorites? No one could be sure, but to Sheldon the Church's future must have appeared grim indeed.

After November, 1667, the archbishop's position at court for the next several years was an anomalous one. He attended privy council meetings, but Hyde was now gone, and his friends and supporters, Morley, bishop of Winchester, and Dolben, bishop of Rochester – the latter married to the archbishop's niece – had both been dismissed from the council earlier in the year.⁴⁸ Thus Sheldon's voice was now an isolated one and carried little weight in that body. He came and went freely at court and spoke on occasion with the king about Church business, but their relationship was a strained, formal one, with none of the old friendliness.⁴⁹ Sheldon's influence over Charles and his advisors in matters of religious policy was now absolutely nil. As he wrote to the bishop of Armagh in 1670, "Since the king hath cut himself loose from the advice of those that used to counsell him in matters of that nature [religion] many ex-

---

⁴⁶ Clarendon, *Continuation*, p. 442.
⁴⁷ *Ibid.*
⁴⁸ Simon, *The Restoration Episcopate*, p. 98, sees Sheldon as dismissed from the council at the same time as Morley and Dolben. Apparently the king fully intended to include the archbishop, but, as Pepys says, "was at last advised to forbear it." Pepys, II, 761. The Privy Council Registers show Sheldon attending council meetings regularly throughout this period. See the *Privy Council Registers*, II, 59-62, The Public Record Office.
⁴⁹ There are a number of references in Sheldon's letters for this period to his going to court to speak with the king about Church matters. For instance, see Add. Mss. C. 308, Sheldon to Creighton, Feb. 2, 1668/9.

travagant things have been attempted that way and daily will be so yet." [50] All that the primate could do was to keep a wary eye out for the "extravagant things" and attempt to counter them as best he could.

Of course the king himself was the real enemy, but Sheldon could have taken little encouragement or satisfaction from the group of royal advisors who now surrounded the monarch. Of the five members of the Cabal, Clifford was a Roman Catholic, Arlington has been called a crypto-Catholic, Buckingham and Ashley both had strong links with the dissenters, and Lauderdale was of a Presbyterian background. None was Anglican, and that fact alone was a clear warning to the archbishop that some attack upon the Anglican monopoly was imminent.

---

[50] Harl. Mss. 7377, Sheldon to the bishop of Armagh, no date, but from internal evidence, written about 1670.

CHAPTER VI

ARCHBISHOP VS. KING II

Even prior to Clarendon's downfall, there had been almost continuous talk of a revision of the Act of Uniformity in order that the more moderate Presbyterians might be brought into the Church. With the Chancellor's discharge, the advocates of a more comprehensive policy took heart and began openly to advocate such a revision. Several pamphlets appeared in 1667 and 1668 suggesting various schemes of comprehension, and two bills were prepared – one in the fall of 1667 and the other in the spring of 1668 – which were to be introduced into parliament. Both were roughly of the same dimensions. Ordination in either the Presbyterian or the Anglican form would be deemed satisfactory, kneeling at communion would no longer be mandatory, the wearing of the supplice was to be at the individual cleric's determination, the use of the cross in baptism was no longer to be required and the word "consent" was to be omitted from the oath prescribed by the Act of Uniformity. However, the second of these two bills was the more liberal. In addition to comprehension for the Presbyterians, it offered all Protestant faiths the freedom to worship publicly upon complying with some minor legal requirements.[1] Sheldon's old friend and Staffordshire neighbor, Sir Orlando Bridgman, proposed this latter measure. Sir Mathew Hale and the earl of Manchester were active in support of it, and Col. Birch, Pepys' friend and informant, was certain it would pass since it had the king's enthusiastic approval.[2]

Worse than this, from Sheldon's point of view, was the support the bill received from a small group of bishops and other Anglican leaders. John Wilkins – Cromwell's brother-in-law – had been recently made bishop of Chester, over Sheldon's bitter opposition, and he was the avowed leader of this small group of rebels. A known Latitudinarian

[1] Stoughton discusses these two bills, III, 373.
[2] Bate, p. 58.

and low churchman, Wilkins had an intense dislike for the Act of Uniformity and its accompanying penal codes. In his view those enactments "set up [the Church] as a top on the toe, it will not spin or stand longer than it is whipped by penal laws; I would have it stand [he said] on the broad basis [sic], and then it will stand without whipping."[3] Encouraged by the king, Wilkins and some other Anglicans of his persuasion began holding meetings with Baxter, Manton, Bates, and other Presbyterian leaders, in order to arrive at a legislative enactment which would satisfy both sides.[4]

Although these meetings were held secretly, the archbishop was not to be taken unawares. He knew of the meetings, who was attending them, and had daily reports from some member there of the discussions which took place. He publicly reproved the Anglicans for working at such a project "without their Metropolitan's approval" or without waiting for a properly constituted synod.[5] On one occasion he sent for one of these conspirators, along with Samuel Parker, his own chaplain, and strongly reproved both of them for taking part in "those meetings." Parker was innocent and vehemently denied taking any part in the affair. The bishop denied it also – too strongly. When the prelate was gone, Sheldon turned to his chaplain and smilingly asked his forgiveness for the apparent reproof. He continued:

> Now I have too plainly found out the treachery of this man; I can never wonder enough at his impudence and stupidity since by particular expressions I used he should have known that all of the counsels of that meeting, in which he was always present and bore a principal part, were discovered to me.[6]

Sheldon, says Parker, would have nothing more to do with that bishop from that day on.[7]

Sheldon early began to gird himself for the coming battle. He recognized that public opinion was going to be critical, and he saw to it that all published attacks upon the Anglican monopoly were promptly and ably answered. Robert Tomkyns, who acted as one of the archbishop's chaplains as well as his personal secretary, answered one of these advo-

---

[3] P. A. Wright-Henderson, *The Life and Times of John Wilkins* (London, 1910), p. 115.
[4] D. Wilkins, IV, 587, tells of the king's encouragement to Bishop Wilkins. Stoughton discusses the comprehensionist conferences held at this time, III, 373.
[5] Parker, p. 36.
[6] *Ibid.*, p. 37.
[7] This may have been either Herbert Croft, bishop of Hereford, who later came out in favor of Comprehension, or it could have been Sheldon's old associate, Thomas Barlow, who took part in these talks, and was subsequently made bishop of Lincoln in 1675.

cates of toleration as early as August, 1667.[8] Herbert Thorndyke, the Anglo-Catholic divine, opposed both comprehension and toleration, arguing that Presbyterians could not, "any more than Papists" be considered good subjects.[9] Among the Sheldon papers at the Bodleian library there is a pamphlet written in 1669 by Dr. Swadling, still another chaplain, in which the question is posed, "Whether it be not as lawful for us to pray, Deliver us from Presbytery, from Independency, from Quakery, from Anabaptism, as it was for him [David] to pray, deliver us from the heathen." [10] And Samuel Parker, who had joined Sheldon's staff in 1667, entered the fray with a pamphlet entitled, "A discourse of ecclesiastical policy wherein the authority of the civil magistrates over the consciences of subjects in matters of religion is asserted, the mischief and inconveniences of toleration are represented, and all pretenses pleaded on behalf of liberty of conscience are fully answered." Parker's intolerant views were adequately summarized in his opening sentences. He began:

Let any man that is acquainted with the wisdom and sobriety of true religion tell me how it is possible not to be provoked to scorn and indignation against such proud, ignorant, and supercilious hypocrites. To lash these morose and churlish zealots with smart and twanging satires is so far from being a criminal passion, that 'tis a seal of meekness and charity.[11]

Parker had come to Sheldon's attention for another "smart and twanging satire" which he had published earlier, and there is no doubt but that the archbishop was unleashing him now. These are Sheldon's views expressed through the vitriolic pen of his chaplain.

But decision in this matter was not to be reached in the cockpit of the public press, as important as that was. These iniquitous comprehension schemes could only be blocked in parliament. Recognizing this, Sheldon began to muster his forces in that area also. As early as July of 1667, when it became apparent that Clarendon was skidding from power, Sheldon began to assemble his parliamentary forces. He ordered every bishop able to make the trip to be in London for the very first meeting of the fall session. They were needed, as he said, to attend "the service of the king and the Church." [12] If for any reason any one of them were unable to be present, Sheldon insisted on having that bishop's proxy in

---

[8] Stoughton, III, 371.
[9] *Ibid.*, p. 378.
[10] See Add. Mss. C. 307, where the Swadling pamphlet is preserved.
[11] This pamphlet began a literary encounter with Andrew Marvell, the Puritan poet, which ran for the next four years. At the end of that time Parker is supposed to have admitted that the odds were in Marvell's favor. See Parker, Introduction.
[12] Add. Mss. C. 308, Sheldon to all bishops, July 4, 1667.

his hands well in advance of the opening session. "For," he wrote, "there is like to be a very great occasion to make use of your and all the rest of our votes." [13] With the bishops on hand in strength, the archbishop felt that there was a fighting chance at least to block the toleration bill in the upper house.

However, in the event, the lower chamber proved a far more reliable ally for the Church than the upper.[14] There is excellent evidence that Sheldon was using his influence to the utmost on this body also.[15] Working through friends, he began politicking, adding up his votes, and bringing to bear what pressure he could exert in order to hold the members steady in their allegiance to the Church. Whether the archbishop's influence could counter the government's managers in the lower house, no one at that time could be sure. As the day of the opening session approached, many of the members received letters "respecting fanatics who had come in great numbers to certain churches, turning people out, preaching themselves, and pulling the surplice over the parson's head." [16] While these accusations have been called "utterly false," and they may very well have been, such letters could only have originated with Sheldon and his staff. They were covering every angle in their efforts to block the toleration bill.

All of this furious activity was effective. When the House of Commons met early in the year, its bias in favor of Anglicanism proved to be as strong as ever. It vehemently opposed any new measure in religion and suggested dramatically that anyone proposing such innovations "come as the proposers of new laws did in Athens – with ropes about their necks." [17] In February when the Wilkins-Bridgman bill was introduced, it was scuttled immediately by a decisive majority of 176 to 70. Sheldon and his bishops were in an ecstasy of delight. John Hacket, writing to

---

[13] *Ibid*.

[14] In support of this view see the Journals of the House of Lords for numerous occasions when the lower house sent messages to the upper persistently demanding certain actions by that body to support the Church. See VI, 389, where the Lords would have passed the Quaker Bill, but the Commons insisted on adding punitive amendments against several other sects as well; on XI, 540, the House of Commons objected to a clause in the Bill of Uniformity as reported from the Lords, insisted on adding several amendments making it more rigorous. For other similar instances, see XI, 495; XI, 557; XI, 561; XII, 21.

[15] For an account of how the archbishop was able to do this, see below pp. 135 ff.

[16] Pepys' *Diary*, II, 812. There was a flurry of nonconformist activity in 1668. Buckingham was encouraging them, and they apparently were sure the penal laws were at last to be taken off.

[17] Stoughton relates this incident, III, 378.

Sheldon from his diocesan quarters at Lichfield, saw "the holie providence of God" in it. But more than that, he wrote,

> I discern your Grace's great providence and indefatigable industry to prepare the votes of the Commons against they met for so noble and happie concurrence, to discourage nonconformists and sectaries, who did openly boast what assurance they had in the undertaking of a great duke [Buckingham] to procure them a most factious toleration.[18]

Parker was equally exultant and ascribed the victory to the same source – the archbishop who "had so prepared the good members of that House that the very first day of their meeting, they resolved if it was brought into the House, they would not pass it." [19] Thus this "pernicious design of a Comprehension," as the Sheldonians called it, perished. On March 4, the lower house displayed further zeal on behalf of the established religion. They petitioned the king – voted by another good majority – asking that he issue a proclamation calling for the immediate enforcement of the laws against conventicles. They were determined to see to it that the country conformed its religious practice to the Anglican pattern.[20]

So the king was defeated once more, again by parliament, and again by Sheldon's adroit maneuvering. The elimination of Clarendon from power – which had caused the bishops so many misgivings, and which had given the king and his advisors so much hope – had not markedly affected the strength of either party. The Church was still secure in its monopoly, and Sheldon was still sternly spurring his bishops and the justices on to their grim duty of prosecuting the nonconformists. Nothing apparently had changed.

Despite his ignominious defeat, and it must have been galling to

---

[18] Tanner Ms. 45, Bishop of Lichfield to Sheldon, Feb. 15, 1667/8. The duke mentioned here is undoubtedly Buckingham who was actively encouraging the dissenters at this time. See *Secret History*, II, 372.

[19] Parker, p. 40. Sheldon's activities in relation to the lower house were manifold at this time. Both Parker and Hacket bear witness to his adroit politicking. Both of these of course might be termed biased observers since they were both close to Sheldon and admired him greatly. However, Cosin, who took a more jaundiced view of the archbishop – they had fallen out in 1662 over Cosin's treatment of a friend of the king's, and later again in 1665 over Cosin's leasing of Church lands for several lives, contrary to Sheldon's instructions – implies the same range of activity in a letter written in 1666. He said: "What designs soever there are against the Church, I doubt not your Grace's power, zeal, and prudence will be very able to withstand them." Add. Mss. C. 305, Duresme to Sheldon, March 23, 1665/6.

[20] For the Sheldon party's reaction to his good news, see another letter from Hacket to Sheldon, March 16, 1667/8, Tanner Ms. 45, where the bishop of Lichfield almost chortles over "the constancy of the votes of the House of Commons for the suppressing of conventicles and nonconformists."

Charles, the king stubbornly refused to give up his religious project. He did, however, become more devious in his methods. If the Anglican monopoly could not be broken by a frontal assault, then he would try the indirect approach. He issued the proclamation against conventicles demanded by Commons – he had no choice, he had to have supply – but he also met a group of Presbyterian leaders at Arlington's lodgings. He told them that no matter what his official actions, he resolved to comprehend them; but they must wait until the time was ripe. In the meantime, he urged them to constrain their people to be more circumspect in their preaching and meeting. In the king's opinion they had stirred up a groundswell of opposition throughout the country by their flagrantly illegal open meetings. He particularly took Baxter to task for "drawing too many people to himself." [21] He reiterated his determination in this matter, saying that "he had been too long king of a party, and now he resolved to be king of all of his subjects." [22]

However, Charles would have to abide his time as far as toleration of dissenters was concerned. Parliament was the chief obstacle. That body was determined to enforce conformity to the official worship. Not only did the legislature reject toleration, but the House of Commons proceeded to pass another Conventicles Act in the summer of 1668 with almost the same resounding majority with which it had rejected the toleration bill – 138 to 78. Without this new measure the 1664 Conventicles Act – which had been enacted for only five years – would expire in 1669. Like the 1664 act, Sheldon and his colleagues were responsible for the terms of this new bill too.[23] To their dismay, however, the Conventicles Act was not renewed in 1668. The Skinner vs. Bernardiston controversy caused a bitter division between the two houses, and seizing upon this as an excuse, the king prorogued parliament and sent the members home. They did not come together again until October, 1669.

In the interim the Conventicles Act expired and with it went much of the bishops power to suppress dissent. Even the Five-Mile Act of 1665 was generally held to be unenforceable without the penalties of the earlier law to back it up.[24] Thus once more throughout England nonconformists openly assembled together to worship, and many justices could not be brought to proceed against them. Sheldon and his suffra-

---

[21] Stoughton describes this meeting, III, 384.
[22] Bate, p. 62.
[23] See earlier this chapter where Sheldon was writing legislation; also see Chapter VII for further information on this matter.
[24] Cardwell, *Annals*, I, 276.

gans could only fume and express angry indignation at such a state of affairs.

At this juncture Sheldon took two steps which seemed to him to offer possibilities of assistance for the Church. He knew full well that parliament favored a new conventicles act, and when they met, it was almost certain to be enacted. Therefore he wrote to his bishops ordering them to take a careful census of all the conventicles in their diocese, where they met, and who led them.[25] Since they were now congregating openly, such an enumeration would be easy to compose. Thus when the new Conventicles Act went into effect the census of dissenters would be a convenient tool to use in their suppression.

The other approach employed by the archbishop was to urge upon the king the necessity of a royal proclamation against conventicles and ordering all justices to assist the bishops in their efforts to halt them. The primate upbraided the king for his lack of support for the established church and argued that the growth of dissent was mostly due to the rumors, repeated everywhere, that Charles himself secretly encouraged the nonconformists in their illegal activities. Were it not for that encouragement, Sheldon was sure, and said so to the king, the country could have been brought to conformity by this time. Charles angrily rebutted this accusation. The blame for the large numbers of dissenters in the country he placed upon Sheldon and the bishops. He was sure that if only they and their clergy had attended to their religious duties, they could have won those people to the Church. "But," he sneered, "they [the clergy] thought of nothing but to get good benefices and to keep a good table." [26] Surprisingly, however, Charles agreed to issue the declaration which the archbishop requested, and it was forthwith promulgated from Whitehall on July 16. In it the king placed the government squarely behind the Church. He ordered all laws to be firmly and fully executed against dissenters.[27]

While puzzled by the king's ready compliance with his request, Sheldon nevertheless was quick to take advantage of the royal proclamation. He wrote to Henchman, bishop of London, informing him that

---

[25] For Sheldon's letter to his own commissary on this problem, written in June, 1669, see Wilkins, IV, 588. The archbishop sent identical instructions to the bishops.
[26] Stoughton reports this conversation, III, 384.
[27] Wilkins, III, 384. The reasons for the king's shift in policy can only be surmised, since his whole policy was subject to many devious and sudden twists and turns in this period. He opposed the Conventicles Act, and it may have been that he wished to show that uniformity could be enforced wihout it. Thus when Parliament met, he could argue that such penal laws were no longer needed.

his Majesty lately speaking much against these disorderly meetings and expressing an indignation against all reports of him, as if he either favored or connived at them, was pleased after he had laid some blame upon the bishops, for want of care in this affair, to declare that henceforward they should not want the assistance of the civil magistrates to support them.[28]

Therefore he ordered Henchman to write to all of the bishops, instructing them to report to him at Lambeth Palace the names of any justices who refused to assist in the suppression of conventicles. The archbishop promised to make good use of that information at court. He also urged the prelates to hurry forward the census of nonconformists and their meeting places which he had requested a month earlier.

When parliament met again in late October, 1669, the lower house turned immediately to the Conventicles Bill, but once more they were prorogued, and it was the spring of 1670 before it could be brought to fruition. By February of 1670 Charles was in desperate need of supply. He discussed his financial needs in his opening speech to parliament, and he was emphatically seconded by the lord keeper.[29] When a group of Presbyterians came petitioning the king to refuse the new act, he sadly pointed out to them that they were applying to the wrong party. They must, he said, address themselves to the House of Commons. He frankly acknowledged that he could not afford to disoblige his friends there, otherwise "he had gone without money." [30]

So in the spring Sheldon and the bishops got their bill. In some ways it was even stronger than the earlier one. It provided for fines of £ 100 to be levied against justices who refused to prosecute known conventiclers, and even better in Sheldon's view, one-third of all fines assessed went to the informer who reported the meetings. Such a provision had been included in the Five-Mile Act, and had proved to be effective – or at least seemed to be so to the bishops – so now it was added here in 1670. The king again applied to the Lords requesting that a clause be inserted in the measure granting him the power to suspend the penalties of the act in certain cases. His suggestion was proposed as an amendment but was beaten down by a group of peers led by Sheldon's friend, Lord Finch. The archbishop and most of the other members of the bench were also firmly in opposition.[31] However, the House of Lords did add a provision which stated that neither this act, "nor anything contained therein, should extend to invalidate his Majesty's supremacy in

---

[28] Add. Mss. C. 308, Sheldon to the bishop of London, no date, 1669.
[29] Lords Journals, XII, 287.
[30] *Works of Andrew Marvell* (London, 1836), II, 316.
[31] See Feiling, p. 144, for this incident.

ecclesiastical affairs."³² Charles would have preferred the suspensive power, but the weaker provision appeared better than nothing. Perhaps he could make use of it later.

The archbishop and his colleagues were delighted with the new law. In commending it to his bishops, Sheldon became almost lyrical in its praise.

> Yet, my lord, [he wrote] I have this confidence under God, that if we do our parts now at first seriously, by God's help and the assistance of the civil power... we shall in a few months see so great an alteration in this kingdom... it will be the glory of God, the welfare of the Church, the praise of his Majesty and government, and the happiness of the whole kingdom.³³

He was sure that at last they would see "the seduced people returning from their seditious and self-serving teachers to the unity of the Church," and he urged his bishops to exert themselves to the utmost to break up conventicles wherever they existed.³⁴

Nor was assistance from the civil government lacking. For the first time since 1660, Charles put the full power of the government behind his primate's program of repression. He ordered all justices everywhere to prosecute every offender. He placed troops of soldiers at the disposal of the authorities wherever they were needed, and as a result, conventicles in London and elsewhere throughout the country – some of which had never been touched before – now found their meetings ruthlessly broken up, and their leaders hustled off to jail. In London alone, Sheldon had "several meeting houses used illegally by nonconformists for years" delivered into his hands, and he forthwith appointed orthodox and loyal Anglicans to their pulpits.³⁵

There is little question but that this was the most effective persecution of dissenters in the whole period. In June when the above meeting houses were ordered seized, the duke of York gathered troops and awaited the riots which everyone was sure would immediately ensue.³⁶ For over a year the government continued energetically to apply itself to the suppression of dissent. Sheldon was delighted. He was suspicious of this sudden reversal of royal policy, not sure at all what it portended, but he took full advantage of the new power which the Church had at its command, and nonconformists filled the jails everywhere. The prosecution was only halted after parliament's prorogation on April 22, 1671. But even this brief period had been effective. The archbishop felt sure

---

[32] Bate, p. 67.
[33] Neal, historian of the Puritans, repeats this letter, II, 674.
[34] Cardwell, II, 276.
[35] Harl. Mss. 7377, Sheldon to Mr. John Bradshaw, June 27, 1670.
[36] Stoughton, III, 387.

that with another year or two of this kind of wholehearted assistance on the part of the secular power, he could have reduced all of England to complete religious conformity.[37] Chaplain Parker noted happily that all over the country the effect had been the same, "it drove the Schismaticks to quiet for the time being." [38]

Yet in no sense had Charles abandoned his project for achieving ultimate toleration. His assistance to the bishops was merely a tactic in a long-range plan which he was developing in this year. It was obvious that his hopes of winning parliament over to a kindlier attitude toward the dissenters were now blasted. Sheldon and his cohorts in both houses were too strong and too stubbornly determined upon persecution ever to change. Nor could the king dispense with the legislature. He was hopelessly in debt and only parliament could offer financial assistance. Still parliament had specifically declared his power in religious matters in the 1670 act, and if he could find a source of income large enough to permit him to leave the members in recess for a year or two, then he intended boldly to apply that power. But his plan had one more facet. In his dealings with the Presbyterians in 1667-68, he had found them extremely reluctant to admit the Roman Catholics to a share in any toleration that might be granted. But the king was determined to include the Catholics, and he sent Orlando Bridgman to them to put the matter frankly. If they expected it for themselves, Bridgman pointed out, then they must accept toleration for Papists and Independents also.[39] However, Bridgman found that he could not budge them on this issue. They boggled at the prospect of tolerating Papists. It was far too dangerous. Now Charles was giving them a bitter taste of what legal prosecution and persecution, backed by the full strength of the government's power, could mean for themselves. When the next opportunity for toleration presented itself, he fully expected that they would be much more amenable to the inclusion of the Romanists. Or as Colbert is supposed to have expressed it in June, 1670, the determined prosecution of dissenters

---

[37] See a letter from Sheldon to Bishop Piers, June 14, 1669, Add. Mss. C. 308, where Sheldon has great hopes for the 1670 Conventicles Act.

[38] Parker, p. 134. There can be no question of the effectiveness of this period of intense persecution. The bitter invective employed in all Puritan writings for this period, indicates that they were being severely hurt. They directed most of their attacks at the archbishop whom they assumed was the originator and director of this brutal persecution. See an anonymous pamphlet, *The Act of Parliament Against Religious Meetings* (London, 1670), where on p. 6 the author ascribes this whole program of oppression to "Gilbert, Archbishop of Canterbury, who being not a creature of God's making nor any part of divine ordinance, must answer the darkness of his original."

[39] Bate, p. 59.

"will give him [Charles] the easier means of increasing the force of his troops and coming speedily to the end he proposes." [40]

But Charles' distaste for the ugly business of persecution was signaled clearly by one event in the fall of 1670. In the midst of this vicious program of legal harassment, he summoned one of the Presbyterian leaders to him and, giving him 1000 guineas, ordered him to use it to assist in any way possible those dissenting ministers whom his own government had so recently hustled into prison.[41]

The 2,000,000 livres that came to him from the treaty of Dover, signed in late December, 1670, plus an £800,000 subsidy from a more compliant parliament in the spring of 1671, gave Charles the freedom of action he had been seeking. He prorogued parliament successively for almost two full years and set his plan in motion. On March 15, 1672, he issued his Declaration of Indulgence, and two days later, fulfilling one requirement of the Dover treaty, he declared war on Holland.

The indulgence affected both recusants and dissenters. All Catholics were granted the freedom to attend mass as long as the services took place in the privacy of their own homes. Dissenters could worship publicly providing they applied for and received a license from the government. At one stroke Charles utterly destroyed the Anglican monopoly which the Sheldonians had created against great odds and had successfully protected for twelve difficult years.

Over 1500 licenses were issued during the next year – 848 to Presbyterians, 368 to Independents, and 201 to Baptists – and dissenting congregations sprang up in every part of the kingdom.[42] The country had religious toleration at last, and the Puritans went wild with joy. After all the years of royal promises and official backing and filling, the king had finally moved to fulfill their fondest dreams. It was almost too good to be true. One Presbyterian poet caught the dissenters' mood accurately when he wrote:

> So Great, so Universal, and so Free!
> This was too much (Great Charles) except for Thee,
> For any king to grant or subject hope! [43]

The Anglicans were equally cast down. Morley wrote bitterly to the archbishop, "I consider the whole fabrick of my scheme is ruined." [44]

---

[40] Stoughton reproduces this letter, III, 388.
[41] Bate, p. 90.
[42] *Ibid.*, p. 98.
[43] *Dr. Wilde's Humble Thanks for his Majesty's Gracious Declaration for Freedom of Conscience* (London, 1672).
[44] Tanner Mss. 43, Morley to Sheldon, Sept. 9, 1672.

Sparrow, bishop of Exeter, wailed, "I see daily to my heart's grief the poor sheep committed to my trust snatch out of the fold by cunning wolves, and I know not how to bring them back." The justices, he reported to Sheldon, were all resolved to sit still. Many of them expressed satisfaction with the new religious arrangements, while the remainder felt it not wise "to disturb the disturbers." [45] Another bishop reported grimly that Presbyterians, Anabaptists, and Quakers had sprung up in his diocese in such numbers that "if there be not a sudden stop put to their daring growth, I dislike to write the consequences." [46] All looked to the archbishop for advice.

Sitting at Lambeth watching the destruction of the religious system which he had struggled so valiantly for so many years to create, Sheldon surely must, at least mentally, have cursed the monarch who was the cause of all his troubles. How was he ever to make the Church secure against such high-placed opposition? But the doughty old prelate was not one to give way to despair for long. He quickly moved to counteract the royal indulgence as best he could.

He had, he knew, several allies in this struggle. One was the widespread fear of Catholicism which was infecting an ever-increasing proportion of the population. To many it seemed that the royal indulgence and the war against Holland were but two parts of a single plan. The war would destroy a bastion of Protestantism abroad while the indulgence was only the first step in a plan to re-impose the Roman ritual at home. Fortunately, from Sheldon's point of view, as 1672 wore on anti-Catholic fears were significantly heightened by rumors which began to circulate concerning a secret treaty made at Dover – one which called for Charles' open conversion to Rome. What else might have been agreed upon there could only be conjectured; fear, ominous and irrational, began to pervade the country.

A second sure ally was parliament. That body had demonstrated its undeviating support for the established church many times in the past, and the archbishop was sure that with some careful fence-mending and preparation, he could get it to reverse the royal indulgence. Thus one aspect of his advice to the bishops was that they bide their time, "and what can be done to heal that sore," he wrote, "we shall be able to give some guess when Parl't meets." [47]

[45] Add. Mss. C. 305, Sparrow to Sheldon, no date, but written in March or April, 1672.
[46] Tanner Mss. 43, bishop of Lincoln to Sheldon, Aug. 29, 1672.
[47] Harl. Mss. 7377, Sheldon to a cleric in Ireland, no date, but in the midst of the indulgence crisis. He wrote essentially the same thing to Bishop Fuller of Lincoln on Aug. 29, 1672. See letter in Tanner Ms. 43.

The archbishop was aware too that, regardless of their attitude toward the indulgence, many people, including some loyal cavaliers attached to the court, were worried about the constitutional issue. If the king could use his prerogative to flout the laws of the land in this fashion, might he not go on to establish a more absolute monarchy than that of his father from 1629 to 1640? For what had they fought the Civil War? In small groups this point was frequently discussed, and there was no doubt that it agitated the country greatly.[48]

In order to take advantage of these feelings and fears, orders went out from Lambeth Palace instructing all the clergy throughout the land to preach often and long on the dangers of the Catholic power, and to lay out clearly for all their hearers the doctrinal differences between the Church of England and the Church of Rome. At the same time Sheldon urged his clerics to magnify the powers of parliament in matters of religion. At this critical juncture there was to be no thought of passive obedience.[49] Most of the Anglican clergy responded enthusiastically. Pulpits resounded with cries of "No Popery! No Popery!", and parliament was exalted over the throne as the proper body to deal with the country's religious practices.

Nor can there be any doubt of the effectiveness of the archbishop's campaign. Anti-Catholic sentiment rose to a fever pitch, and Charles himself finally summoned Sheldon to him and ordered a halt to this constant preaching on controversial issues. It was only done, he charged, to alienate the hearts of the people from their rightful loyalties to him and to his government, and he angrily ordered the primate to see that it was stopped.[50]

Sheldon was loath to obey the order. The clerical propaganda program was going well, and the times were so dangerous that he thought that once more he should disobey the Church's supreme governor. But rather than act alone, he called a meeting at Lambeth of several bishops and leading clergy and put the question up to them. They agreed with their chief. The only record we have of the meeting shows John Tillotson, lowchurch in sympathy and future archbishop, bellicosely suggesting that Sheldon inform his Majesty, "that it was more than strange for a professedly Protestant monarch to forbid his clergy to preach in defense of Protestantism." [51] This may very likely have been Sheldon's answer. No more is heard of that particular royal command.

---

[48] Bate discusses the impact of this fear, p. 84.
[49] *Ibid.*
[50] *Ibid.*
[51] *Ibid.*

There remained one further avenue by which the Church could strike at its triumphant foes. That was through the justices and the courts. While it was true that nothing could be done against the dissenting congregations, providing they secured a royal license for their meetings, still there was such a freedom exercised throughout the nation that many ignored the requirement for the license and held their meetings anyway. Sheldon urged his bishops to ascertain what groups in their dioceses had obtained licenses and to find out to what specific locations they applied. Any group, he instructed them, who met without a license, or anyone who attempted to preach in a place other than the one named in his permit, was breaking the law and should be proceeded against in the usual way.[52] As a group, all Quakers refused to apply for the licenses, but in their stubborn, wilful fashion met openly anyway, and in many places they were ignored by the justices. These at least, the archbishop felt, should and could be stopped. Numbers of complaints were instituted along the lines Sheldon suggested by the more determined prelates, and in some cases they were able to halt the growth of conventicles. Bishop Carleton of Bristol ignored the royal licenses completely. Denouncing them as mere pieces of paper good for nothing but to introduce popery and countenance the breach of the laws, he fined everyone who claimed the royal permission, and imperiously drove the justices to their task as though the king had issued no indulgence at all.[53]

But Carleton was an exceptional case. Most persecution and prosecution came to an end, the jail doors swung open, albeit reluctantly, for those who were imprisoned by reason of their consciences. John Bunyan was released after twelve years in Bedford jail, and many others were freed too. Whitehead petitioned the king that 470 Quakers be released, and he was received so favorably that the relatives of a number of other jailed dissenters sought his aid on their behalf also. Sheldon was at the privy council meetings when these two pleas for clemency were accepted by that body.[54]

As 1672 drew to a close, it became apparent that parliament would have to be called early in 1673. There was a war on, and once more money and supplies were in short supply, the Dover grant having long

---

[52] See Sheldon's instructions to the Bishop of Lincoln on these points, Harl. Mss. 7377, Sheldon to Lincoln, Sept. 7, 1672.

[53] Bate repeats this story, p. 103. Most of the bishops, however, respected the king's licenses. Peter Mewes, shortly to be bishop of Bath and Wells, got up out of his sickbed at Oxford, to halt the lynching of some dissenters by some university students. He detested the whole business, however, and would have preferred to let them suffer. See Add. Mss. C. 302, Mewes to Sheldon, June 26, 1672.

[54] Stoughton, III, 405.

since been spent. The bishops looked forward to the meeting with eager anticipation as indeed did most of the country. As Morley wrote to his old friend, the question was "will Parl't hold, and what will be done if it do hold?" [55] How determined was the king? Would he resort to force to have his way on the religious issue? Sheldon was at court regularly throughout 1672 and the king's attitude toward him had taken a sudden turn for the better. He was more friendly, and he followed Sheldon's advice on the nominees for three vacant bishoprics – Chester, Gloucester, and Bath and Wells – during that year.[56] However, he procrastinated on Durham which, to the great scandal of the Church, had been left vacant for two years and was apparently reluctant to translate Sheldon's nephew, Dolben, from Rochester to that richer see. Even here, however, the king did not reject Sheldon's favorite out of hand, and the archbishop wrote to Morley that he was very hopeful for his nephew. Things, he thought, were looking significantly better for the Church. Morley responded:

> Your Grace's last gives me hopes that there may be an alteration of the present posture of things for the better; pray God it proves so: I am sure I should be very glad, not for his sake [Dolben's] only but for the churches and your Grace's also. For then I shall begin to hope that you Grace is or will be shortly returned to the same place you had and ought to have in the king's trust and favour.[57]

However, the archbishop watched the Stuart monarch's activities warily. On maturer thought, he took the king's sudden show of friendliness as a tactical maneuver designed by the slippery monarch to lessen his primate's opposition to the indulgence. Sheldon considered the king to be determined indeed on the issue of the indulgence. Troops were being assembled, ostensibly to fight on the continent as the Dover treaty stipulated, but the archbishop was not sure. To him it seemed entirely possible that the king intended to use them at home to force his indulgence upon the country. He certainly would not put it past Charles, as he stated gloomily in a letter to Morley in September.[58] Thus to his way of thinking the important questions were still: "Would Parliament hold? And what would happen if it did hold?"

When the order finally went out for parliament to assemble, Sheldon was overjoyed. He immediately wrote to the bishops informing them of the fact and, with great urgency, demanded that every prelate physically

---

[55] Tanner Ms. 43, Morley to Sheldon, Sept. 23, 1672.
[56] *Ibid*. Morley here is elated "that the bishoprics are disposed of so well," and wishes Durham were too.
[57] Tanner Ms. 43, Morley to Sheldon, Oct. 14, 1672.
[58] See Morley's answer, *ibid.*, Morley to Sheldon, Sept. 9, 1672.

able be in his place when the session opened.⁵⁹ Anyone who could not attend, he expected to dispatch his proxy so that it would arrive in ample time. The necessity of "raising all the force we can make," as he wrote to the bishop of Banger, was evident in the importunate tone of all of these letters.⁶⁰ This might well be the most important parliament of the reign from Church's standpoint, for the archbishop was determined to put an end to the iniquitous system of licensed dissent.

When Charles met parliament on February 5, 1673, he boldly went over to the attack on the religious issue. After informing the members of the course of the war and of his need for money and supplies to prosecute it properly, he continued

> Some days before I declared the war I put forth my declaration for indulgence to dissenters.... There is one part of it that is subject to misconstruction, which is that concerning the Papists, as if more liberty were granted them than to the other recusants, when it is plain there is less.... In the whole course of this indulgence I do not intend it shall in any way prejudice the church; but I will support its rights and it, in its full power. Having said this, I shall take it very, very ill to receive contradiction in what I have done: and I will deal plainly with you, I am resolved to stick to my Declaration.⁶¹

Parliament, however, was not to be bullied, even by the king. Ignoring the war, supply, and all other problems, the members immediately turned to a consideration of the indulgence. On February 14, the legislature read its master a lecture on the constitution, the main point of which was that "the penal laws in matters ecclesiastical cannot be suspended but by Act of Parliament." Therefore it requested that those "said laws may have their free course" until legislature changed them.⁶² Ten days later Charles returned a message to the Lower House in which he flatly rejected their views of the English constitution. He and his ancestors, he declared, had always had the right to suspend laws in ecclesiastical matters – after all neither property rights nor liberties of the subject were involved, and he specifically disclaimed the right of royal suspension in those areas. He ended by pointing out that he was only taking off the penalties for *loyal* dissenters, something which he believed they themselves were very willing to do.

Two days later, February 24, Commons answered. Charles was, they said, very much mistaken. He had no suspensive power in ecclesiastical affairs and no such powers have ever been claimed "by any of your

---

⁵⁹ Tanner Ms. 43, Sheldon to all bishops, no date, but mention of the indulgence makes it 1673.
⁶⁰ Harl. Mss. 7377, Sheldon to the bishop of Bangor, Dec. 28, 1672.
⁶¹ Lords Journals, XII, 525, gives this speech.
⁶² Bate, p. 109.

Majesty's predecessors." Such a power, they felt, would alter the constitution in a revolutionary fashion, and they politely requested that Charles give them "a better answer to their said petition and address." [63]

So the legislature and executive were at an impasse – one potentially as serious as that between Charles I and his parliament in 1642. Apparently at this critical point Buckingham and Lauderdale suggested that military force be resorted to. They elected to go the way of Charles I. But this Charles Stuart was no fool. It wasn't that he lacked courage – Sheldon had assessed him accurately on that point – but he was not foolhardy. If he chose to fight, it would be only when the odds were more favorable than they appeared at the moment. Charles had badly underestimated the strength of the country's anti-Catholic phobia. Whipped up by the Anglican clergy, it had united almost all groups in opposition to the indulgence. To the average Englishman it appeared far too dangerous to permit the king to succeed in his tolerationist project, and Charles now recognized the almost complete unanimity which prevailed throughout the country on this point. After a feeble attempt to enlist the House of Lords on his side, the king surrendered. He tore up the indulgence in council on March 7 and publicly renounced it the following day in the presence of the Peers. It was a humiliating surrender, but one that was absolutely necessary.

So parliament had held after all, and the indulgence was no more. Furthermore, although Sheldon could not have known it at the time, this victory was the decisive one. The king was at last convinced. The ignominious defeat he had suffered left a deep wound, and Charles would never again attempt to use the royal prerogative in ecclesiastical matters.

If Sheldon and the bishops rejoiced over their victory, it could only have been a celebration of short duration, for the 1673 House of Commons suddenly displayed a distressing shift in its religious thinking. Indeed by their demagogic preaching against the dangers of Catholicism, Sheldon's clergy may have been instrumental in creating this new outlook. Fear of Rome and Roman Catholic France now took precedence over all other religious problems, and many members of the lower house had now come to the conclusion that Protestants should not be fighting one another in the presence of this more dangerous foe. Even Morley, Ward, and Dolben, Sheldon's collaborators and long-time friends, took this view. Apparently in 1673 and 1674 they were engaged in conversations with some of the Presbyterian leaders, looking to some agreement

---

[63] *Ibid.*, p. 117.

which would comprehend them within the Church, or at least ameliorate the penalties against them.[64]

In line with this shift, a bill was introduced in the House of Commons "for the ease of Protestant dissenters from the Church of England." It proposed to take away all penalties for non-attendance at church, to eliminate the assent and consent clause in the Act of Uniformity, and would permit the dissenter to subscribe before the Quarter Sessions to his belief in the Thirty-Nine Articles, and take there the oaths of allegiance and supremacy to the throne.[65] As long as they met those requirements and then preached only in the place prescribed in their licenses, the nonconformist ministers would not be further disturbed for their activities. In essence this act would have replaced Charles' indulgence in every respect except that it provided no relief for Catholic recusants. For them Commons only proposed harsher legal penalties.[66]

Although he applied all the power at his disposal, Sheldon was unable to block this bill in the lower house. His support there for the moment had dissolved, and for the first time in the reign a majority of the members voted for toleration. However, when the measure came before the Lords there was very little time left to prorogation, and Sheldon, along with some of his friends in the upper house, labored assiduously to defeat it there. Their method was to tack numerous amendments to the bill, amendments which they knew full well the Commons would never accept and which could only result in time-consuming conferences between the two houses. In their determination to block the bill, they even proposed an amendment which would have granted to the king the suspending power in religious affairs. This they knew the Commons would never stand for.[67]

Many of the Lords did agree with the purpose of the easement bill. These members felt that some abatement of the penalties against nonconformists ought to be enacted. Three different times a majority of the peers agreed upon the principle involved but always ended by disagreeing about the extent of the abatement. On one occasion one lord decried the fact that they were using up their time so lavishly that the poor dissenters

[64] See Tanner Ms. 43, Sept. 9, 1672, a long letter from Morley to Sheldon where he warns the archbishop that he is going to go his own way in religious matters when parliament meets. Also Stoughton reports this same development, III, 428 and 466. I find nothing to indicate that Sheldon shared their fears. To him the papist hysteria was a convenient tool which he could exploit in order to bend parliament to his will.
[65] See Bate's description of this bill, p. 125.
[66] Lords Journals, XII, 547, 549, 555, where actions are proposed against recusants.
[67] Bate discusses this amendment, p. 127.

were very probably going to be denied any relief at all. In answer Sheldon rose to his feet and agreed that it was a shame. Even he, he said with tongue in cheek, was in favor of some amelioration of the lot of the loyal dissenters. All that he desired was that they be required to acknowledge that the war against Charles I was unlawful and traitorous. If they would make that single acknowledgment, then he was willing to grant them some relief.[68] The chamber grew quiet. Everyone knew that what the archbishop asked was totally unacceptable to the Puritans. Sheldon had the last word. Time ran out, and the Toleration Act of 1673 was lost.

However, the Test Act of 1673 – a measure which Sheldon wholeheartedly approved – was passed by both houses. It required all officeholders, civilian and military, to take communion in the Anglican form and to subscribe to various oaths, one of which denied the doctrine of transubstantiation. Among others, this measure smoked out both Clifford and the duke of York. Both admitted their Romanist loyalties and resigned their posts. By their act the anti-Catholic hysteria was fanned even higher.

Also the Test Act helped the Cabal toward its breakup. Clifford was out of office, Buckingham was temporarily out of favor, and Ashley was in the process of veering over to the country party. As a result the king began to rely more and more upon Thomas Osborne, shortly to be created earl of Danby. In September of 1674, Danby succeeded in replacing Arlington as Secretary of State with his own loyal assistant, Sir Joseph Williamson, and from that date to his impeachment, says one of his biographers, Danby was Charles' chief minister.[69]

A main element in the new favorite's policy was to reunite the Anglicans and old cavaliers behind the throne, where by rights, in his opinion, they should be anyway. Then with their assistance he proposed to build a majority party in both houses which would give the king some financial independence. To accomplish these ends, first and foremost he had to placate Sheldon and the bishops and win their confidence.

Thus on October, 1674, Williamson sent out letters to the prelates ordering them "to repair to London with all possible speed" to advise the king concerning important matters relating to religion and the Church.[70] This move signalled a reversal of royal policy, and for the old archbishop it came not a moment too soon. Since Clarendon's fall in 1667, he had maintained the Church's privileged position in the English

[68] Parker, p. 314.
[69] A. Browning, *Thomas Osborne* (Glasgow, 1951), I, 135.
[70] Bate, p. 140.

system only with the assistance of the House of Commons. However, the abortive Toleration Act of 1673 proved that the lower house was no longer a reliable ally. If the archbishop could now be sure that the king was sincere in his new acceptance of the Anglican monopoly, then he would gladly, willingly, switch alliances and perhaps in the process secure the Church for all future time. Thus he eagerly sent his own letters re-enforcing those of Williamson and especially urged certain of his most trusted subordinates to be present.[71]

When the meeting convened, besides Sheldon, there were present Morley, Ward, Dolben, Pearson of Chester – all Sheldon men – and Crewe of Durham, Henshaw of Peterborough, and Brideoak of Chichester. They formulated their recommendations in January, 1675, and the price of their support for the new policy was high indeed. They demanded the diligent suppression of popery throughout the country, but more important, "that his Majesty be pleased to take effectual care for the suppression of conventicles." They pointed out that many of these illegal religious groups were still meeting openly and were defending themselves by the licenses they had lately procured from the king. They now asked that Charles unequivocally and publicly declare "that the licenses were... recalled and that they had no authority or encouragement from him." [72] Further the bishops apparently requested a test act on the order of the 1673 measure, but applicable this time to members of the lower house of parliament. The previous one had reduced the Church's enemies in the government, they wanted one now that would do the same for the legislature.

A month after the council of prelates had presented its demands, the king acted to implement the first part of their program. On February 3, 1675, an order in council was issued in which Charles declared:

that he found it necessary that the laws which were made for the preservation of both church and state should be put in execution with more care and diligence than of late they have been; and that having long since commanded his judges to do their duty herein, he had also lately advised with several of his bishops and upon due consideration of the whole matter had resolved and doth therefore order... that effectual care be taken for the suppression of conventicles; and whereas divers pretend licenses from his Majesty and would support themselves by that pretense, his Majesty declares that all his licenses were long since recalled, and that no conventicle hath any authority, allowance or encouragement from his Majesty.[73]

[71] *Ibid.*
[72] *Ibid.*
[73] *Ibid.*

A public declaration to the same effect followed on February 10, and the king's humiliation and subordination to the Church was complete.

Furthermore the machinery of government began to turn again on behalf of the Anglican monopoly. Nor was it, as so often in the past, a half-hearted effort. To Sheldon's great relief and joy, Danby's administration put its full strength into the suppression of dissent. The nonconformist position had been at best an ambiguous one since the king had rescinded his declaration in March of 1673. Now with the February 10 declaration against them, most dissenting congregations either ceased to meet altogether or went underground once more. However, it apparently proved impossible to suppress all of them ever again. A number of Presbyterian congregations in England today date their continuous existence from Charles' 1672 indulgence.[74]

In April 1675, the Test Bill was introduced in the House of Lords and supported tirelessly there by the bishops and friends and supporters of the government. The main speakers for it, we are told, were Morley, Seth Ward, bishop of Salisbury, Lauderdale, and Heneage Finch.[75] To show his wholehearted support of the measure, the king came in person almost every day to the house to listen to the debates, and Danby strenuously exerted the government's power to the full to secure its passage. Once it was accepted, he felt certain that the Cavaliers and Anglicans in parliament would then vote a liberal supply, and for the first time in the reign, Charles and parliament would be united in policy and objectives. To further demonstrate the government's firm adherence to its new policies, the king re-appointed George Morley to the privy council, along with Ward of Salisbury and Colonel Strangways from the lower house – a tower of strength to the Anglican cause there. With their appointment Sheldon's isolation in council came to an end. As in the good old days under Clarendon's ministry, the archbishop and his friends were once again respectfully consulted in all matters pertaining to religious policy.

But the Test Act was not destined to pass in 1675, no matter how diligently pushed by Danby and the bishops. Shaftesbury fomented a quarrel between the two houses, and it became necessary to prorogue them before the Commons had acted on the measure.[76] During the recess, Danby pressed his church policy resolutely forward, however. He was determined to provide the king an adequate financial base, and

---

[74] Bate is explicit on this point and Firth, in his introduction to Bate's book, is equally certain. Bate, introduction, and p. 142.
[75] Feiling, p. 160-161.
[76] Browning, I, 161.

he could do so, he was certain, only with the assistance of the royalist Anglican majority in the country. Therefore the bishops and the Church had to be propitiated.

Unfortunately with the failure of the Test Bill and with the storm of controversy which was aroused in both houses by it, the king once more began to waver in his support of Danby's policies. In late 1675, the Puritan-leaning noblemen at court were again throwing their influence against the new favorite and his schemes, and their most telling argument concerned the supposedly great numbers of nonconformists across the country. Was it right or even feasible, they asked, to proceed legally against such a large proportion of the population? Was it not a case of one-half the country persecuting the other half? [77] Although Danby was writing in the fall, hopefully, that the king "was every day more fixed to show his steadiness to the Church of England," still he recognized that the arguments of his enemies were eroding Charles' determination. Therefore he consulted with the archbishop, and the two agreed that factual data was the only adequate answer to such assertions.[78] As a result, Sheldon dispatched letters to all his bishops, in both provinces, ordering a complete census of the population of England and Wales. He proposed to lay this calumny once and for all.[79]

Every bishop was required to answer three questions about his diocese:

1st. What persons are there by common account and estimation inhabiting within each parish subject unto your jurisdiction. 2ndly. What numbers of popish recusants, or suspect for such recusancy, are there resident among the inhabitants aforesaid. 3rdly. What number of other dissenters are in each parish (of what sect soever) which either obstinately refuse or wholly absent themselves from the Communion of the Church of England.[80]

Later, at the request of the bishop of Norwich, he clarified his orders further. He wanted, he stated, every male and female included – all in fact who were old enough to communicate.

---

[77] That these were the arguments urged at court is shown conclusively by a letter from Sheldon to archbishop of York, Cardwell, I, 290, where the primate wrote: "The consideration of the numbers of dissenters hath been an argument much insisted upon, as if their party were too formidable to be suppressed, or that the combination of the ... factions being infinite, it were but lost labour to reenforce the censure and the execution of the laws against them."

[78] See a letter from Sheldon to the archbishop of York, Jan. 22, 1675/6, where discussing the census, Sheldon writes, "not that I am immediately commanded by his Majesty so to do, but from the assurances I have from a person near unto him [Danby] that it will be no less for his Majesty's particular satisfaction than for the general good." Harl. Mss. 7377.

[79] *Ibid.*, Sheldon to all bishops, Jan. 25, 1675/6.

[80] *Ibid.*

As the statistics began to flow into Lambeth Palace, where they were assembled into orderly ranks by the archbishop's clerks, they demonstrated, as Sheldon was sure they would, that dissenters were such a small group relative to Anglicans that they could be no serious threat to the country's security. The bishops reported only 108,676 nonconformists, and 13,856 Roman Catholics, compared to 2,477,254 Anglicans.[81] Politically their small numbers proved the nonconformists insignificant, and in Sheldon's words, their suppression was now "a work very practicable."

All the returns were not in nor fully tabulated until the end of the year 1676. This was Sheldon's last significant act on behalf of his beloved Church – he died in November of the next year – and yet it was perhaps as important as anything he had accomplished in the whole reign. Apparently Charles was finally and fully convinced by the census. The country was overwhelmingly Anglican, and he never again for the remainder of his life attempted to alter in any way the Anglican monopoly. Furthermore, although the Test Act failed of passage and was not enacted in Sheldon's lifetime, yet it was passed the year following his death during the Titus Oates craze. It did for parliament what the Act of 1673 had done for the administrative departments of the government – it eliminated papists and many dissenters from their seats in the legislature. Thus future attacks from that important quarter were stopped, and by this act the Church of England was finally secure in its position as the only legally permissible religious institution in the country. From the world beyond the grave the archbishop must have smiled and finally relaxed. He could feel a great sense of personal accomplishment.[82]

---

[81] Cardwell, Annals, I, 290. The validity of the Sheldon census has been attacked frequently. T. Richards in "The Sheldon Census," *The Transactions of the Society Cymmrodorion,* (1925-26), Supp., pp. 1-19, maintains that Sheldon dictated the returns he wanted in the letter to the bishops ordering the count. Thus he considers Sheldon's figures unreliable. However, S. A. Peyton in an article in the *English Historical Review,* Vol. 48, pp. 99-104, compared Sheldon's figures for Lincolnshire with the records of the Quarter Sessions and the Archdiaconal courts of the same county and came to the conclusion that "the Compton return [the Sheldon census] covering the portion of Lincoln under review ... gives a reasonably correct account of the prevalence of active dissent in both its varieties." When one compares the number of licenses issued to dissenting congregations by the government in 1672 – some 1500 – with the total number of congregations in England – some 8568 – it becomes apparent that Sheldon's census was probably a fairly accurate count. (For the latter figure see statistics Sheldon assembled on all holdings in the Church, Add. Mss. C. 302.)

[82] Of course occasional conformity became a general practice within a very few years. Yet to Sheldon laws were to be obeyed, and he would have looked upon the 1678 Test Act as a great victory for the Church.

CHAPTER VII

SHELDON AND PARLIAMENT

Sheldon's success in protecting the Church's monopoly against the king and that segment of the court and gentry who favored a lower, more comprehensive religious arrangement did not come easy. It could only have been achieved by a leader who was thoroughly familiar with the workings of parliament, in both its houses; who recognized the importance of, and knew how to mold, public opinion; and who was a shrewd, penetrating judge of people and their motives. Sheldon possessed all of these characteristics, plus an absolute dedication to the Church's cause. This latter attribute permitted the archbishop a certain latitude in his selection of means – as long as the end was properly served – and resulted also in a ceaseless vigilance when it came to legislation, or any other action, which might affect his beloved Church of England.

During the whole period of his primacy, however, it was to parliament that he devoted most of his attention and thought. It was only through its agency that the Church could be preserved from the profane hands of the compromisers. Both houses of the national legislature were important, since a battle lost in one could still be retrieved in the other; therefore, the archbishop carefully counted and marshalled his votes among both Lords and Commoners.

To the upper house, he and his loyal supporters had immediate access; consequently, here his methods were direct. One of them was to be himself involved in every aspect of the Peers' deliberations. Thus he would know all the leaders, be able to gauge their strengths and weaknesses, and ready his defenses against them. To accomplish these ends, Sheldon became one of the most politically-oriented, and also perhaps the most politically astute, of all of England's primates.

The most casual survey of the journals of the House of Lords for the period of the 1660's reveals the archbishop as the most active prelate in the house as well as one of its most energetic leaders. As usual his forte was not public speaking nor debate. Although he did on occasion take the floor, he possessed subordinates such as Bishops Morley, Ward, Gunning, and Henchman, men with great oratorical abilities, who could very ably defend the Church from the rostrum. Sheldon's gifts were for person-to-person dealings, and he vastly preferred the give-and-take of committee work where, even as today, most of the important decisions were made. The number of committees Sheldon served on in the decade of the sixties was astounding; indeed he could have had time for nothing else when parliament was meeting. In the first two sessions of the Cavalier Parliament alone Sheldon served on committees to consider a bill of Lord Scudamore's for endowing several churches in Ireland, to consider a bill establishing tithes where none had existed before, to provide competent allowances for curates where the incumbent chose not to reside, to consider the Bill for Uniformity – Cosin, Skinner, Henchman, Morley, Reynolds, and Gauden joined him on this important matter – and to discuss a bill to punish Quakers who refused to take oaths. Moreover, he, Clarendon, and Bridgewater represented the upper house in the compromise conference which composed the differences between the two houses on the Bill for Uniformity. In addition, Sheldon was appointed to a committee in 1663 to draw up a petition requesting that the king issue a proclamation ordering the eviction of Jesuits and other Catholic priests from the country. When Charles agreed, the archbishop joined Morley, Albermarle, and Berkeley in conveying to him the gratitude of the House of Lords for that act. Further, Sheldon was appointed to a committee to consider his own bill for the better observation of the Lord's Day, and on another in July of 1663 to amend the Act of Uniformity to forgive those clergymen who had been unable to take the St. Bartholomew's Day oath because of illness or other disability. So it went. Sheldon was seldom omitted from any committee considering church or religious affairs for this whole period.

However, while important, religious matters were only a part – and not the greatest part either – of the activities of the archbishop in the upper house. Because of his acknowledged business acumen, Sheldon was also in great demand for service on committees considering secular problems, and he accepted appointment to a number of these positions. In the same two sessions noted above the archbishop served on committees to examine the following matters: A proposed act for limiting the number of hackney coaches in London, one to consider a legal case between Sir Henry and Sir James Thrynne, one to examine a case between the earl of Derby and his creditors, another to consider reversing Strafford's Bill of Attainder, and still others to grant temporary relief to collectors of public monies, to settle the jurisdiction of the Court of Admiralty, to govern the declaration of bankruptcies, to consider an act for the better relief and employment of the poor in certain cities, to make certain rivers navigable, to govern the importation of madder-pure and unmixed, to confirm an agreement between some Somerset miners and Sir Thomas Bushell, to settle a mansion house on Viscount Campden and his heirs, to consider private bills in behalf of the duke of Albemarle, Lord Derham, Sir John Pakington, Anna Ferrers, George Morley, and others, to confirm patents for an invention dealing with glass manufacture, and another for the Marquis of Worcester who had invented a water commanding [sic] machine. He served on committees to improve highways, to settle lands claimed by both Lord Lucas and the earl of Kent, to encourage trade, to examine bills for the better collection of the excise and hearth taxes, and a number of others of the same nature. Thus it went at every session.[1] It would seem that the archbishop was deliberately immersing himself in the house's business. He was determined to know the peers and to have a hand in their problems and deliberations in order to secure leverage which could be used on behalf of the Church.

Nor was the archbishop alone in this effort. There were twenty-seven bishoprics in England and Wales and thus twenty-seven seats were reserved for the Church's representatives in the upper house. While not all were as capable or as dedicated as their primate, still many served the House of Lords in various capacities, and thus increased greatly that reservoir of influence and good will which could be tapped for the Church's benefit in an emergency.

Sheldon was well aware too of the voting strength which he possessed in the members of the episcopal bench. The twenty-seven prelates comprised approximately seventeen per cent of the membership of the upper house.[2] Since absenteeism on the part of the peers was endemic, Sheldon's subordinates often of course represented a far higher percentage of actual members present and voting. However the twenty-seven were not all prepared to accept the archbishop's leadership in legislative matters. There were some two or three bishops who espoused the doctrine of nonresistance to the will of the monarch and who, as a result, voted regularly with the throne even when to do so meant to

---

[1] See Lords' Journals, XI, 354-587, for these numerous committee assignments.
[2] Walter Simon, *The Restoration Episcopate* (New York, 1965), p. 69. It should be noted that episcopal votes were actually twenty-six. Sodor and Man sat in the Lords without a vote.

vote to dismantle their own church.³ In addition, there were always a few – like Reynolds, Gauden, and Wilkinson – whose low church opinions often led them to support measures which were anathema to Sheldon and his followers. But disregarding these four or five bishops, Sheldon could count upon twenty to twenty-two votes which would be cast as a block in the Church's interest – no mean total for a clever parliamentarian to wield.

That the archbishop fully recognized the political potential inherent in this group is shown by the great emphasis he placed on the matter of prompt and regular attendance at every session of parliament. He first mentioned this matter in November of 1661 while he was yet bishop of London. At that time in a letter to Cosin, he mentioned some business which the two were to transact when they met which, he said, "must be at the beginning of the Parliament; for the king expects it from all of our order, and when his great business for his revenue and that of the Church is over, any [bishop] may have liberty to return to his diocese." ⁴ And, Sheldon concluded his letter, the importance of the business to come before the session demanded personal attendance on the part of every bishop. He would not accept a proxy, except in the most urgent of emergencies.

From this point on, parliamentary attendance runs like a recurrent theme through Sheldon's administrative correspondence. At every crisis in his struggle against the king and the comprehensionists, the primate sent letters to his subordinates, sternly ordering them to be in London immediately the legislative session opened and that without fail. To the elderly bishops the prospect of a grueling trip up to the capital in the heat of the summer or the frost of the winter was almost more than they could face, and the plaintiveness of their letters begging to be excused from this arduous duty exhibits as well as anything can, the cruel pressure Sheldon was applying to assemble his voting strength. Typical of these is a letter written to Sheldon by Bishop Nicholson of Gloucester in September of 1666. He pleaded age, expense, and illness as reasons for not making the trip to parliament and continued:

I know that those truant bishops that are farther off are fatter and much better able in body and purse, and if they will eat the provender 'tis reason they do the work, and not lay the load upon a poor old jade that can scarce stand on his

---

³ *Ibid.*, p. 80, where Cosin is the chief speaker in favor of the Roos' Divorce bill which the Sheldonians in a body voted against. There were one or two others, like Nathaniel Crewe later, who took the nonresistance doctrine seriously and voted against the Church interest in support of the throne.
⁴ Cosin, *Correspondence,* II, 26, Sheldon to Cosin, Nov. 16, 1661.

legs. My Lord [he pleaded] I was never absent before; I beseech Your Grace therefore I may be excused this once.[5]

Sheldon was not impervious to such pleas, and in those cases where he was convinced the trip would be detrimental to a prelate's health, he did excuse attendance. However, when malingering seemed clearly indicated, the archbishop's reproof could be savage indeed, as John Hacket, bishop of Lichfield, found in 1667. Presuming upon his closeness to the archbishop, Hacket wrote casually in September of that year to inform Sheldon that while he had not yet experienced his usual seasonal attack of fall illness, still he expected that it would be much more acute this year since he had been forced to travel to parliament in the unusually severe heat of the previous summer. Therefore, he informed his chief, he would be to town later just as soon as the expected malady had run its course. At that moment Sheldon's temper was on edge anyway as he saw Clarendon toppling from power, and the Church and his friend in great danger as a result. Some of this was evidenced in the curt, biting letter he fired off to Hacket, mercilessly dressing down that surprised prelate and ordering him to be in his seat the opening day of parliament without fail. Petulantly Hacket replied:

I never did, I never will, draw back from anything your Grace commands. If I am not to be suffered to cherish myself when never failing recurrent maladies afflict me, God's will be done. I will prepare for a most distasteful journey.[6]

The bishop ended his letter with a sad prayer for "poor unfinished Lichfield Church" which now, he was certain, would probably never be completed. But Hacket was in his seat when parliament opened.

Under the impetus of Sheldon's imperious orders, it was not uncommon in those sessions where the Church was under dangerous attack, to find twenty-two or twenty-three of the episcopal peers in attendance, and considering the advanced ages of most of them, this could only have resulted from powerful pressure, rigorously applied by the archbishop.

In the general letters in which he periodically memorialized his bishops on the subject of parliamentary attendance, Sheldon invariably insisted that any bishop who could not make the trip send his proxy in ample time. He also made this a condition for any absence he permitted. The house's rules required a new proxy for each session and one member was permitted to vote only one proxy.[7] Usually, as the northern bishops

[5] Add. Mss. C. 302, bishop of Gloucester to Sheldon, Sept. 22, 1666.
[6] Tanner Ms. 45, Lichfield to Sheldon, Sept. 21, 1667.
[7] See Add. Mss. C. 308, Sheldon to Cosin, no date, where the archbishop excuses Cosin from attendance but discusses the necessity of a new proxy.

did in the plague year of 1665,[8] the excused member left the proxy blank, thus enabling the archbishop to intrust it to a dependable subordinate who would vote it as he directed. Every vote counted, and as parliament's opening day approached, Sheldon was never satisfied until all proxies were safe in his own possession. In 1665, for instance, when striving to secure the passage of the Five-Mile Act, he wrote anxiously to Clarendon, who was in Oxford arranging for parliament's sitting there, inquiring about his bishops' proxies. The Lord Chancellor answered him reassuringly that "most proxies are sent up with clarkes [sic] . . . so you need have no worries of receiving them into your hands." [9]

The influence and power which the episcopal bench wielded in the upper house is a matter of record. Sheldon's mustering of the Church's votes and the effectiveness of the bishops in debate, along with the influence and friends which the Church naturally possessed in that house, helped save Clarendon's life and property in 1667, helped secure the Conventicles Act of 1670, helped hold the house steady in its opposition to the royal indulgence in 1673, and the bishops fought a skillful delaying action which scuttled the Toleration Bill in that same year. As has been noted, on several occasions Charles' threats to the bishops who opposed him clearly indicated that he considered their power in the Lords to be of significant proportions.

They did not of course always carry their colleagues in the upper house with them. They failed for instance to defeat the Irish Cattle Bill in 1666; [10] they failed also to block Lord Roos' divorce in 1670; [11] and they failed to secure passage of the 1675 Test Act which they ardently desired as the capstone to their legal program.

In the lower house, since there were no churchmen present, the problems were different, the means were of necessity indirect, and the pressures exerted had perforce to be much more subtle. Yet Sheldon's successes here too have been noted.[12]

Because of its enthusiastic Anglicanism in the early years of the Cavalier Parliament, the House of Commons was a much more reliable ally for the Church than the House of Lords. In many cases, it was enough simply to fan that inherent Anglican sentiment to secure the desired result. We have noted above Sheldon's careful preparation of

---

[8] Cosin, *Correspondence,* II, 137, Archbishop Sterne to Cosin, Sept. 18, 1665.
[9] Add. Mss. C. 303, Clarendon to Sheldon, Sept. 18, 1665.
[10] Simon, p. 73.
[11] Lords' Journals, XII, 311.
[12] See Chapters V and VI.

the lower house in the case of the Toleration Bill of 1667.[13] His letters to the members detailing the riotous actions of the Puritans in that period, while no doubt exaggerated, had the desired effect. Commons gave the proposed act a decisive and resounding negative. To secure the Conventicles Act of 1670 – without which the Church's monopoly might have been effectively destroyed – we are told that the archbishop wrote over 300 letters to the members urging them, with many logical reasons, to support the impending legislation. Because of these diligent efforts, his enemies even accused him of using bribery to secure the law's passage.[14]

Bribery was probably too strong a term – although Sheldon would no doubt have entertained that as a possibility – to describe the archbishop's methods. He was merely lobbying, with all of the power and influence at his command, to create majorities in favor of the Church in the lower house. He approached this problem with all the politician's traditional array of ploys. One of the most important was the use of the vast patronage at the disposal of the Church hierarchy. Another was his own personal influence with the law courts, the privy council, the court itself – at times – and through the Church and its friends, with government offices at home, in Ireland, and the colonies. Add. Mss. C. 308, housed at the Bodleian Library, is a letter-book of Sheldon's containing carefully preserved copies of over 200 letters written by the archbishop on behalf of personal projects of numerous gentry and their relatives in the early 1660's. Other manuscript letters contain numerous instances of the same kind of assistance. For instance, in 1673 Sheldon wrote to the lord lieutenant of Ireland to secure a place for a Mr. Murray who was to have been made bishop of Virginia, but since that plan had been cancelled, Sheldon wanted a place for Murray in Ireland. He was particularly interested in the case because the man was a relative of Sir Robert Murray, a great friend of the Church.[15] On another occasion he wrote to Sparrow at Exeter urging him to forward a project of Sir John Arundell. Sir John, he said, "is a very worthy person for whom I have a great esteem and kindness and should be loth any suit of his should fall to the ground." [16] When the Toleration Bill of 1667 was under discussion, we find a number of such letters being written. One was to Sir Martin Lister, member of Commons,[17] another to the lord

---

[13] *Ibid.*
[14] W. D. Whitley, repeats this charge in *A History of British Baptists* (London, 1923), p. 119.
[15] Harl. Mss. 7377, Sheldon to the lord lieutenant of Ireland, April, 1667.
[16] *Ibid.*, Sheldon to Sparrow, Aug. 7, 1671.
[17] Add. Mss. C. 308, Sheldon to Sir Martin Lister, Oct. 21, 1667.

chancellor of Ireland on behalf of "a person of quality whom I could not refuse;"[18] a third for a pensioners' place in charterhouse for a poor relative of Sir Thomas Master, Esq.;[19] and still another for Lord Maynard on some business he was conducting for that nobleman at court.[20] And for this same period, although he hated enclosures, we find Sheldon assisting in arranging a number of them for certain knights.[21] In the case of enclosures the economic consequences, which Sheldon deplored, would simply have to take second place to the Church's urgent needs in the legislative arena. Copies of scores of letters dealing with favors of this sort were not preserved by accident. The archbishop knew perfectly well how to collect his *quid pro quo* from the recipients on the floor of the national legislature.

Sheldon's influence extended also to hundreds of scholars' places at the two universities. Here too his recommendation was eagerly sought by the gentry for their sons and relatives. And more often than not, the letters were written for the very people whose connections were highly-placed in the counties and who often sat in the House of Commons. Although the archbishop demanded punctilious fairness in the administration of the elections for scholars' places,[22] still he wrote many a recommendation, and in the event of a close competition, the archbishop's stamp of approval could be of great value.[23] There are large numbers of these letters of recommendation extant in the Sheldon correspondence, and they most certainly provided the archbishop a great amount of leverage in his dealings with the members of the lower house.

With 8-9000 benefices in all of England and Wales, with several hundred scholars' berths at the universities, and with a powerful influence in the Church and secular courts and in the government itself, Sheldon, in effect, headed a vast patronage system which, used shrewdly, could immensely increase his power in parliamentary affairs.

Some people of course were impervious to this kind of lobbying pressure. For these the wily, old archbishop developed still other, more refined techniques. One of these was the institution of the "Sheldon dinners." The archbishop spent a great amount of money on his table at Lambeth Palace. He also employed excellent chefs and possessed a

[18] *Ibid.*, Sheldon to the lord chancellor of Ireland, April 1, 1667.
[19] *Ibid.*, Sheldon to Sir Thomas Master, Esq., Nov. 5, 1667.
[20] *Ibid.*, Sheldon to Lord Maynard, March 15, 1666/7.
[21] For one of these, see *ibid.*, Sheldon to Dr. Bayley, president of St. Johns College, Dec. 10, 1666.
[22] *Ibid.*, Sheldon to Ralph Bathurst, April 18, 1664.
[23] See *ibid.*, and also Harl. Mss. 7377, Sheldon to warden of All Souls, Nov. 7, 1674.

well-stocked wine cellar. As a result dining with the archbishop was considered a rare treat, and an invitation to attend a banquet at Lambeth was a social prize of considerable consequence. The gaiety, wit, and rapier-sharp repartee which one was sure to meet there added greatly to the enjoyment of the visit. In addition the archbishop kept the conversation on a high moral plane that was instructive as well as entertaining. So much was this known to be true that many noblemen deliberately encouraged their sons to seek out his company, and we are told that "a great many flocked to him." [24] The fact that numbers of young noblemen resorted again and again to Lambeth Palace to hear the old archbishop discourse wittily and pungently about life and religion, and what they were all about, reveals certainly another aspect of the character of Charles II's primate.

What these young men heard was no brief for the private, pious monkish kind of religious life. This Sheldon scorned. Rather, he said,

Take care to be good and virtuous in the first place, and then be as pious and as much devoted to religion as you will. No piety can bring any advantage to you or anyone without probity of life and morals; For God gives no rewards to idol-worshipers, neither can any benefit arise from a barren piety. But if men sincerely resolve themselves first to lay the foundations of Religion in a good life, that will cause them to delight in the worship of God and their duty to man.[25]

The archbishop summed all this up in the saying, delivered with a peculiar pungency: "Do well and be merry."

The kind of religion Sheldon was advocating had nothing to do with the mystical, enthusiastic, soul-searching, conversion-seeking, personally-vital experience of God which occupied so much of the thought and time of so many of his contemporaries. Apparently such mystical experience was wholly alien to his own nature, and besides his experience with the Presbyterians, Congregationalists, Quakers, and Baptists had conditioned him to look upon these people as utter hypocrites. "Next to Atheists and Fanatics, he despised that disdainful sort of men," says Parker, "who would have all the duty of man placed in the ceremonies and offices of worship, and because perhaps they are oftener at prayers than others, therefore think themselves better." [26] He had not, said Sheldon, known more than three or four of these who had not attempted, like thieves, to carry off the best preferments of the Church "under a cowl of religion." As far as the primate could see in his own lifetime, such religious fervor and enthusiasm had brought nothing but trouble and turmoil to church and state. It was an error of the past which had

[24] Parker, p. 44.
[25] *Ibid.*
[26] *Ibid.*, p. 43.

ensnared many an otherwise honest man, and it should be stamped out. What he was advocating was a cool, rational, thoughtful approach to religion wherein the emphasis was on an upright life, service to man and God, and a loyal observance of the Church's forms and ceremonies. Fiery preaching and loud and ostentatious praying were to be abhorred. Sheldon here was deliberately attempting to mold the Anglican Church into the institution it was to become in the eighteenth century. His teachings clearly foreshadowed the future.

But the Sheldon dinners were not only planned for the gentry's sons who came to be taught; they also were a favorite resort of many of their elders – men influential in the legislature and in government offices. Often these were sought out by the archbishop and invited to Lambeth Palace. One favorite way he found to attract them there was to celebrate their birthdays at his dinners. The number of celebrants honored in this fashion must have been several score, since almost every memoirist of the period who could have been useful to the Church – and a number of these were members of the House of Commons – records a birthday celebrated or a special dinner he attended at Lambeth Palace.[27] Most were honored and pleased by the event, and by the archbishop's flattering attention. Few of these people are ever mentioned in Sheldon's correspondence, indicating clearly that they were neither friends nor personal acquaintances but simply individuals with whom the archbishop was attempting to curry favor.

As Clarendon's influence and power in the royal counsels waned markedly in 1665 and 1666, the archbishop and the lord chancellor spent many an anxious hour considering the future of the Church and how it might be safeguarded. If Charles and the Comprehensionists around him ever dominated the government, it was obvious that the Anglican monopoly was apt to be shortlived. How could they cement their alliance with the lower house which seemed to be the only safe ground to which the Church might retreat? One fear which seemed to dominate the Commons' membership, even among the loyal Anglicans there, was the Church's independent taxing power. In the event of a deadlock between the king and parliament, might not the monarch attempt to finance an

---

[27] Evelyn reports dining with the archbishop in April of 1669 and noted gratefully that the primate "was infinitely civil to me." See *Diary*, p. 528. Hooke was present at a Sheldon dinner on August 20, 1673, and he reported that Sheldon "made much of me." See *The Diary of Robert Hooke 1672-1680* (London, 1935), for that date. Pepys dined there on more than one occasion. See Pepys' *Diary*, II, 1679, where he describes Sheldon's table as the greatest cheer he had ever seen and "the Bishop mighty kind to me." For John Milward, who was given a surprise birthday party at Lambeth, see *The Diary of John Milward* (Cambridge University Press, 1938), p. 33. Milward was vastly pleased at the honor.

independent policy by drawing upon the Church's wealth? This very thing, of course, had been attempted by Charles I in 1640 when convocation was kept in session after parliament was dismissed, and the clerical house had then pliantly voted the king a sizeable subsidy. The fear of an overly powerful king was still omnipresent among members of the lower house. They fully intended to keep the whip-hand in finances in the future as they had in the past. It was their strongest weapon. The Church's great danger from the government now drove Sheldon and Hyde to a momentous decision – a step which has been called "the greatest alteration in the constitution ever made without an express law." [28] By mere verbal agreement between themselves and some of the leaders of the House of Commons, they conceded the Church's right of taxing itself in convocation and agreed instead that in the future clerical property and incomes would be included in the money bills of the House of Commons.

Throughout his life Sheldon had a great respect for precedent and tradition. Prescriptive right in his mind was divine right, and he never surrendered a single prerogative as archbishop that had the sanctity of time behind it – except in this one instance. The Church's great danger, however, was over-riding; in the archbishop's mind it had to marry itself to the lower house.

The agreement was concluded in the summer of 1665, although the primate had been discussing it with his suffragans for several months prior to that.[29] The timing of this move resulted from other considerations. For one, the bishops and clergy had always paid more taxes in terms of their wealth than had the laity. Partly this was because they were more subject to the court and thus were expected to contribute more from their means to support the king and government, and partly it was because so many of the convocation divines were royal chaplains and seekers after court favor and promotion, and hence were prone to further their own careers at the expense of their colleagues. Yet no matter how generously they gave, the members of the lower house always suspected that the Church was not taxed to an extent that was commensurate with its great wealth.[30] Now in 1665 the need for additional revenues was so great that the members of parliament were once more

---

[28] Opinion of Bishop Gibson, quoted in T. Lathbury *History of Convocations*, (London, 1836), p. 260.

[29] See a letter to John Hacket and Hacket's reply on this subject in Tanner Ms. 47, October, 1664.

[30] *Ibid*. Much of the material in this paragraph follows Hacket's line of reasoning.

critically eyeing the clerical holdings as a source from which some of this new revenue might be raised.

As a result, there was a move on foot to revalue the Church subsidy. Bishop Hacket freely admitted that this had been, eighty years previously, a significant amount, but now, as a result of steady inflation, it actually amounted to very little. But the Church came out of the Civil Wars much impoverished. Hacket maintained that in a diocese which contained over 500 benefices, there were not fifty in Lichfield and Coventry which would adequately support a scholar "with a competent maintenance and a tolerable library" after the Restoration. His statement is supported by similar statements from other dioceses. To have revalued the subsidy and then to have required the same number of them as before, as would certainly have occurred, would have been disastrous for the Church. It was infinitely preferable, as Hacket pointed out to the archbishop, to accept a tax on land at the same rate as the lay landholder. "For let us name what we will," snorted the bishop of Lichfield, "some ill-willers will think it not enough, but if we submit to that which is demanded, the mouth of detraction is stopt, since we do as much as demanded." [31]

So, late in 1665, the agreement was concluded, and Church property became subject to taxation by parliamentary act at the same rate as private property. In any event, we know that in the spring of 1666 when the assessors appeared at Worcester to evaluate the diocesan properties, Bishop Skinner, apparently unaware of the new arrangement, angrily refused them entrance to his property. Sheldon had to order the indignant bishop to comply with the lay assessors' demands. Soothingly, the archbishop wrote, "As for the distinction between us and the laity which you speak of, it is now at an end and I hope to our advantage, of which, when we meet, we shall discourse more at large." [32]

In the long run the Church did lose considerable influence because of the new arrangement. When convocation could no longer use its subsidies as a lever to extract from the government measures which it desired, then convocation ceased to be important, and later ceased even to meet regularly.[33] Thus the Church's influence upon the civil government was considerably diminished. It has been charged that through this action Sheldon betrayed the Church, that he struck an unnessarily bad bargain.[34] Yet one must remember the context of the period in which he

[31] *Ibid.*
[32] Add. Mss. C. 308, Sheldon to Skinner, March 15, 1665/6.
[33] N. Sykes, *Sheldon to Secker* (Cambridge, 1959), p. 43, describes this effect.
[34] Stoughton, III, 324.

acted. The archbishop of Canterbury was involved in a relentless struggle to preserve the Church's existence. If he were unsuccessful, there would be no long term for the Anglicans. The sacrifice simply had to be accepted. He did attempt to preserve the Church's traditional rights by seeing to it that in the first money bill which levied taxes upon the clerical establishment, a clause was inserted which read: "Provided always that nothing herein contained shall be drawn into example to the prejudice of the ancient rights belonging to the Lords spiritual and temporal, or the clergy of the realm." [35]

The immediate effect upon convocation appeared to be nil. Throughout Sheldon's primacy that body was called into session regularly whenever parliament met. Partly no doubt this was the mere force of tradition. Convocation had always convened along with parliament, so it was called to London as usual. Yet there is more to it than that. Sheldon was insistent in every crisis of the Church's legislative affairs that the delegates to convocation be present in their places when the legislative session opened. In 1666 we find him writing to Bishop Blandford of Oxford urging the absolute necessity of having deacons, archdeacons, and procurators in London for the parliamentary session.[36] In his letter of 1669 to all bishops, admonishing them to be present for the opening day of the session, he also ordered them to see to it that the members of the convocation attended the meeting without fail, "at which time," he added, "there may be much occasion to make use of yours and their assistance." [37] Again in 1672, in his general letter on parliamentary attendance, he included the clerical representatives in his orders to be present.[38] And in 1673, we note him writing to the bishop of Bangor to insure that new elections of the lower house of convocation were held so that "your Lordship and the clergy concerned in the Convocation will give us your assistance here this Parliament." [39] And so it went at every crisis of the Church.

Since there was very little real business conducted in convocation and few formal sessions were even convened after 1665, one can only conclude that Sheldon was "making all the force possible" by using the bishops and the clerical representatives as an organized corps of lobbyists. Many of the clergy would have friends and acquaintances in both houses of parliament. They could talk freely with those legislators and

---

[35] Lathbury, p. 260.
[36] Add. Mss. C. 308, Sheldon to the bishop of Oxford, March 15, 1665/6.
[37] Harl. Mss. 7377, Sheldon to all bishops, August, 1669.
[38] Tanner Ms. 43, Sheldon to all bishops, no date, 1672.
[39] Harl. Mss. 7377, Sheldon to the bishop of Bangor, Dec. 28, 1672.

exert some measure of influence upon them when Church legislation was under consideration. In this, as in other matters, Sheldon missed no opportunities to protect the Church throughout the period of his primacy.

With all this assiduous pressuring, indefatigable maneuvering, and ingenious lobbying, what did Sheldon accomplish? We have already noted his success in preserving the Anglican monopoly when it might have gone down before the onslaughts of a determined monarch assisted by enthusiastically tolerationist ministers.[40] This success was mainly a result of Sheldon's carefully nurtured Anglican majority in the House of Commons. This was his primary achievement.

However, because of their persistent politicking, the Sheldonians were equally successful in securing a considerable body of repressive legislation which greatly aided them in stamping out dissent. These legislative acts, generally termed "the Clarendon Code," consist of the following: The Act of Uniformity passed in 1662; the Corporations Act – requiring all corporation officials to take communion in the Anglican form – passed during the same year; the First Conventicles Act – establishing penalties for those who persisted in holding illegal religious services – passed in 1664; and in 1665, the Five Mile Act which prohibited a dissenting minister or teacher from residing within five miles of a parish where he had previously taught or preached, unless he took an oath accepting the religious arrangements of the country as established by the Act of Uniformity. The first two of these seem to have been driven through parliament by the Cavaliers in the first flush of enthusiasm which followed the Restoration. Although both encouraged the passage of these bills, neither Sheldon nor Clarendon were primarily responsible for their enactment. There was very little opposition to them. The latter two acts, however, resulted from the difficulties encountered by the bishops as they attempted to stamp out dissent within their dioceses. The Act of Uniformity proved unenforceable without assisting legislation. The swelling tide of complaints flowing in from all parts of the country concerning the difficulties of dispersing conventicles, and the additional problems engendered by the dissenting leader who remained in his home community where he became a focal point of resistance to the bishop's Anglicanizing efforts will be dealt with shortly.[41] The correspondence of the bishops were full of these kinds of complaints, however, and it was as a result of these that the latter two bills were enacted.

Although both were introduced in the lower house first, Clarendon

[40] See Chapter V.
[41] See below, p. 145.

was intimately involved in securing their passage. He maneuvered the government's delegation in the House of Commons in their favor, and in the House of Lords he actively advocated both measures. In his opening speech to parliament in 1665, he begged the members to pass the Five Mile Act which was designed, he said, "to suppress your enemies at home that your enemies abroad [the Dutch] may be less exalted." [42] But despite this expert advocacy by the lord chancellor, the problem remains: Is the Code appropriately entitled? Was it Clarendon's code? Did the chancellor take the complaints which Sheldon and the bishops enumerated and fashion laws to assist the Church? Or did Sheldon himself formulate the necessary measures and, with Clarendon's help, see them through both houses? The key to this problem would seem to lie, partly at least, in the relationship between the two men.

As has been noted, both before and after the Restoration the two worked closely together. Despite some disagreement at times over tactics, they had similar views of both Church and state and generally agreed on what they wished those institutions to be. More than that, however, the two were close personal friends. Sheldon married the Hyde children and counselled them concerning their religious beliefs and problems. On the occasion in 1665 when Sheldon remained in the plague-stricken capital city while Hyde travelled to Oxford to arrange for the parliamentary session which was to be held there, the two friends exchanged letters about every third day.[43] This interesting series of letters reveals two men who had known one another for years, who knew the same friends and acquaintances, and who could, as a consequence, skip freely and easily over a wide range of subjects, the details of which were automatically understood by both. Clarendon freely offered advice regarding Church affairs and appeared deeply interested in them. He discussed problems of various livings, the appointment of some bishops, and wished to increase the incomes for Gloucester and Oxford dioceses so that a prelate might more nearly be able to afford to reside in those sees. He wanted Blandford to be bishop of Oxford; Sheldon was opposed. In one case he gave Sheldon's word on a living to be exchanged and seemed perfectly confident that the primate would approve.

However, when the Chancellor strongly disagreed with the archbishop over the appointment of Robert Morgan to be bishop of Bangor, and proceeded to criticize that appointment with some heat, he drew a fiery reply from Lambeth Palace, and it was effective. In his next two letters

---

[42] Lords' Journals, XI, 689.
[43] See Add. Mss. C. 303, for this interesting series of twelve to fifteen consecutive letters.

Clarendon humbly begged forgiveness for interfering to too great a degree in the archbishop's affairs. In the second of the two, he wrote, "Your Grace's favour of the 26th obliges me again to ask your pardon for all I said in my last concerning Bangor." [44] The lord chancellor seemed to have a great respect for Sheldon's opinions, and this, coupled with, and perhaps as a result of the latter's successful opposition to Clarendon in August, 1662, would seem to indicate that the archbishop was the dominant partner where Church matters were concerned.

In addition Sheldon was drawing up legislation for the Church throughout this period. Among his papers there is a draft of a bill – apparently in Sheldon's own hand – which would limit the number of pluralities one clergyman could possess and, additionally, providing for a minimum salary to be paid to a curate by an incumbent who chose not to reside in his parish.[45] Such a measure was introduced in the House of Lords on May 14, 1664.[46] From its title it would seem to have been drawn in essentially the same terms as the draft in Sheldon's papers. A year later Ward, writing from Exeter, discoursed at length to Sheldon on the difficulties he was experiencing in arranging for adequate incomes for the ministers in his city parishes. In one case, he reported, a congregation had provided an income of 100 pounds per year for a deserving minister through the device of a free-will offering. He continued:

> But, my Lord, it will never be well till such men shall cease to depend upon voluntary contributions, to which purpose the late act for union of churches signifies nothing at all in this city, where the legal dues for all the parishes [combined] will hardly raise a good maintenance for one good man. If your Grace would be pleased to think of something to be ready against the next Parliament, it may be it may pass at the beginning of the session.[47]

Subsequently, acts were passed by parliament arranging for tithes where none had existed before. Ward's appeal to the archbishop had produced action.

At a somewhat later date we find the primate writing to Peter Mewes, bishop of Bath and Wells, taking him to task for the dearth of catechizing in his diocese. Sheldon reminded him of the great importance of this duty, along with the absolute necessity of gathering all the young people of every parish into the catechism classes. "But," he added, "I conceive it is not so proper to reinforce these duties by way of J. P.'s, but rather to procure an act (the next session of Parliament) for confir-

---

[44] *Ibid.,* Clarendon to Sheldon, Aug. 29, 1665.
[45] For Sheldon's draft of this act, see Add. Mss. C. 307.
[46] Lord's Journals, XI, 616.
[47] Add. Mss. C. 305, Ward to Sheldon, Feb. 24 1665/6.

mation of the Church's power in that behalf." [48] With the aid of the episcopal bench, he felt certain that such an act could be secured. Furthermore, he asked Mewes to draw up the necessary legislation and have it ready when he came to town, along with the reasons and arguments he thought most pertinent in its behalf.

Finally there is proof that Sheldon wrote the Five Mile Act. Numerous references to this bill were made by the lord chancellor in the series of letters which he wrote to Sheldon during the late summer of 1665. The archbishop had sent the bill to him by messenger and on Sept. 16, he wrote to Sheldon, "I have not yet seen the bill, but I am full of hope for it." [49] On another occasion, "I suppose those Bishops who cannot make the journey to Oxford (and it is a pity they should all be put to it) will send their proxies, and thus *our business* may go on at will." [50] By Sept. 26, the draft measure had still to arrive at Oxford, although Sheldon had been describing it in his letters, and the chancellor remarked, "We long all to see this good bill, of which you prophesy so well." [51] The only important Church legislation introduced that fall was the Five Mile Act, and it can only have been to this that Clarendon was referring.

From this evidence it appears that Sheldon was regularly creating legislation during this period. The Five Mile Act came from his pen, and the fact that other legislation concerning the Church was authored by him in 1664, the year of the First Conventicles Act, would tend to support the view that he drew up the latter also. In addition, he has been given the sole credit for the Second Conventicles Act of 1670,[52] and we know that he was working hand in glove with Danby to secure the passage of the Test Act of 1675. If not the actual author, he no doubt helped dictate the terms of that measure. When one couples these facts with Sheldon's ascendancy over his friend in religious matters, it becomes apparent that the "Clarendon Code" should more appropriately be entitled the "Sheldon Code." The Archbishop and his suffragans produced it; the chancellor assisted in its passage. For good or ill, Gilbert Sheldon must bear the onus for having created the majority of the oppressive legislation of his day.

This view coincides perfectly with that of the harassed and persecuted Puritans who suffered from the effects of the Sheldon persecution. In

[48] Harl. Mss. 7377, Sheldon to Peter Mewes, July 15, 1674.
[49] Add. Mss. C. 303, Hyde to Sheldon, Sept. 16, 1665.
[50] *Ibid.*, Sept. 5, 1665.
[51] *Ibid.*, Sept. 26, 1665.
[52] Whitley, p. 119, ascribes the Second Conventicles Act solely to Sheldon's determined advocacy.

almost every year of his primacy, hundreds, nay at times thousands, were persecuted and prosecuted under the terms of this repressive body of legislation. Their houses were broken into, their meetings were broken up, they were arrested, fined, jailed, transported, all because they wished to worship in accordance with their own beliefs. Many died from the treatment they received; many more migrated to the New World or became exiles in the old. And quite correctly they ascribed most of their troubles to "Gilbert of Canterbury, that proud prelate," and his episcopal subordinates. These, they were sure, were responsible for contriving "that Act of violence" (the Conventicles Act) which was

executed against them, in so precipitate and furious a manner, that ... their common rights as Englishmen and Free-born are forcibly taken away, and they, in their persons and estates, are exposed to the utmost of rapine and malice of all that are willing to destroy and devour them.[53]

And they were right. Sheldon's correspondence is full of angry letters, furiously driving his bishops and the J. P.'s on to a fuller execution of the laws against all dissenters.

---

[53] *The Act of Parliament* (London, 1670), p. 5, – an anonymously published pamphlet.

CHAPTER VIII

SHELDON, PASTOR AND HIS PEOPLE

As Sheldon saw it, his task as archbishop was three-fold. He must (1) defend the Anglican monopoly, (2) suppress all dissent, and (3) restore the Church of England to a preeminent position in the minds and hearts of the English people. By their nature the first two took precedence, but the third area was in no sense insignificant. Indeed it was an essential part of his total program, and in terms of time and attention required it probably occupied a greater number of the archbishop's waking hours than any other topic.

After twenty years of virtual anarchy in religious matters, it would be no mean task to restore order and unity to the nation's religious life. Yet this was the task the indomitable, old prelate set himself, and "order" and "unity" became his watchwords.[1] The Church of England as he envisioned it would be one in which the decorous and orderly service prescribed in the Book of Common Prayer would be celebrated in beautiful, well-appointed cathedrals and churches, by learned, pious, and properly attired divines, before solemnly devout and reverent congregations in every parish in England and Wales.

By 1662 the Book of Common Prayer with its prescribed order of service, was completed and was accepted by parliament, and its stately cadences were so well and beautifully phrased that they were to remain virtually unchanged for 270 years. But of his entire program, that proved the easiest element for Sheldon to achieve.

For one thing cathedrals and churches throughout the country were in a lamentable state of decay and disrepair. St. Paul's had been used as a stable. Durham had housed prisoners of war who ripped out all of

---

[1] Sheldon's emphasis on a properly enforced order and unity of belief is implicit in every instruction he wrote to his bishops. He stated his belief in the efficacy of these two doctrines most plainly, however, in a letter to William Piers, bishop of Bath and Wells, June 14, 1669, Add. Mss. C. 308.

the cathedral's beautiful woodwork and burned it in a desperate effort to keep warm. Lichfield had no windows, or spires, or very little roof remaining. St. Asaph's was in such disrepair that services could no longer be held there, and Exeter had been defaced by wooden partitions, so that both Presbyterian and Congregational could hold simultaneous services in its sanctuary. Some churches were in better condition than these, many were worse.

Throughout his primacy Sheldon pushed a vigorous program of church building and restoration. The subjects of spires, lead, windows, bells, and organs reoccur again and again in his correspondence. He gave vast amounts to many of these projects from his own purse, and he assisted in collections for many others. He warmly encouraged John Hacket, an indefatigable church-builder who was determined to make Lichfield Cathedral "the most handsome in all England." [2] When Thomas Wood, Hacket's obstreperous dean, refused to pay £50, a sum which represented his fair share of the building program, it was Sheldon who intervened and pressured Wood into paying.[3] He did the same for the duke of York when that notable forgot his £100 pledge to Lichfield. When the bishop and chapter at St. Asaph's became embroiled in a bitter squabble over which of them was responsible for the cathedral's repair — so that for several years nothing was accomplished in the matter — Sheldon vigorously intervened and ordered both sides to place the issue before an arbitrator. In the meantime, that very spring, he demanded that they begin the rehabilitation of the cathedral "to prevent the utter ruin of it." [4] It was in this manner that Sheldon prodded and encouraged his clergy to rebuild and restore all churches to their old level of beauty and munificence. He was sure that beautiful, well-kept houses of worship would do much to provide the proper atmosphere for the dignified services established by the new Prayer Book, and in addition would induce a more respectful, reverential attitude on the part of the worshipers.

But is was not only the sanctuaries which were in disrepair at the Restoration. Bishops' mansions, clerical residences, chapter houses, and attendant out-buildings — all were in a ruinous state upon the Church's return. Because of this, and because, in his opinion, all must be rebuilt and restored to their proper functions, Sheldon fought tenaciously to prevent any redistribution, or any curtailment of, episcopal and other church incomes at the Restoration. He has been criticized for this

[2] Tanner Letters 43, Lichfield to Sheldon, Sept. 11, 1669.
[3] Add. Mss. C. 308, Sheldon to the dean of Lichfield, Oct. 24, 1667.
[4] Harl. Mss. 7377, Sheldon to the dean of St. Asaph, March 30, 1671.

attitude.⁵ Income might well have been redistributed from some of the wealthier sees so as to equalize episcopal incomes, or so that poverty-stricken curates might have received a more adequate recompense for their labors. But bishops were great lords in their dioceses, and Sheldon wanted them to regain all of their old dignity and power, and that, along with the vast amount of rebuilding necessary, took money. So he stubbornly resisted all moves aimed at the reduction of episcopal incomes.

This policy left many disgruntled persons, particularly among the dissenters, and they publicly leveled criticism after criticism at the bishops' luxurious mode of living when so many of their parish priests, and so many other good Christians, were suffering want. To answer these clamorous critics, in December of 1666 and again in July of 1670 the archbishop required all bishops and deans to submit to himself at Lambeth a complete list of properties, and the incomes derived therefrom, for every diocese in England and for every cathedral chapter. On both these occasions he demanded also that all bishops, deans, and other wealthy Anglican clergymen remit to Lambeth Palace a complete list of monies they had dispensed since the Restoration upon public and pious works. Among these, besides gifts to the king, sums expended for the redemption of English captives at Algiers, and other charitable gifts, he asked them to list specifically what they had spent on "restoration of their churches, utensils, and ornaments thereof, and upon their own houses." ⁶ He reminded the clerics "with what an evil eye some men look upon the possessions of the church," and he promised to use the information they submitted only for the purpose of defending the religious establishment from "scurrilous" attacks.⁷ Both returns show large amounts spent in every diocese for repair and restoration of buildings.⁸

But the archbishop was not only instrumental in encouraging and

---

⁵ See Chapter IV.
⁶ Harl. Mss. 7377, Sheldon to all deans, July 29, 1670.
⁷ *Ibid.*
⁸ Most of these returns are available in Add. Mss. C. 302, the Bodleian Library. As an example, William Piers, bishop of Bath and Wells, listed the following charitable donations in 1666:

Repayment of Interregnum Debts	£ 1,000
Law Suits to Recover Episcopal Lands	300
Repair of Bishop's Palace at Wells	4,000
Repair of Mansion House at Barnwell	800
Augmentation of Poor Vicarages	140
Ornaments for Wells Cathedral	450
Redemption of Captives at Algiers	100
Monies to the King	1,100
Total Disbursed in Six Years	£ 7,890

prodding others to improve and beautify the church's physical plant. He himself was a passionate builder, and he left his mark both upon his beloved university at Oxford and upon the city of London.

Sheldon had long planned a theatre at Oxford – a building which could accomodate academic convocations and could be used for the various secular activities engaged in by the students and faculty there. Among these latter was an especially offensive annual production by the students called "The Act," which apparently had its antecedents back in the Middle Ages. Part scholarly display and part bawdy, ribald humor, "The Act" required one student, known as the *Terrae Filius*, to give a speech in which he lampooned in the coarsest and most vulgar terms possible every scholar and college president in the university along with most of their wives. As one outraged victim described it, "all, or most of the heads of houses and eminent persons in the University, with their relations, being represented as a company of whoremasters, whores, and dunces" – all of course in the most perfect Latin scholarship.[9]

It was a desire to remove such profane activities from St. Mary's Church that prompted Sheldon, shortly after his elevation to Canterbury, to set Christopher Wren the task of designing a theater for the university. Constructed at a cost of £25,000, the building was completed and presented to the university officials in 1669.[10] Sheldon provided another £2,000 endowment for maintenance purposes, and the classically proportioned Sheldonian Theatre has been a landmark of the Oxford scene ever since.

This was the first significant building which the youthful Wren – he was only twenty-nine years old when it was finished – designed. But long before the theatre was completed, Sheldon had set the young architect upon his life's work. Following the London fire of 1666, Inigo Jones had been assigned the task of rebuilding St. Paul's on its old foundations. Wren had predicted that the old foundations were too weakened to support the new edifice and had opposed the rebuilding. When sudden and total collapse of one of Jones' new walls proved him absolutely correct, Sheldon summoned Wren from Oxford and gave the

---

[9] Neal, *History of the Puritans*, II, 669, taken from a letter from John Wallis to Robert Boyle.

[10] Perhaps because of his secular surroundings – Sheldon's new theatre – the *Terrae Filius* in 1669 outdid all previous performances in scurrility. The speech was so outrageously vulgar that John Evelyn, one of the hearers, vigorously protested to the vice-chancellor of the university and urged him to ban such disgusting drivel from all future convocations. See Evelyn's *Diary*, p. 531, and Burrows, *Worthies*, p. 228.

young mathematician complete responsibility for the new cathedral.[11] When Wren sought guidelines concerning the amount of money the new edifice should cost, Sheldon suggested only that he design a cathedral worthy of the capital city of a great kingdom. They would assume that the money would somehow be forthcoming.[12] The result of course was the magnificent St. Paul's of today.

This lucky choice of the archbishop did more perhaps than any other act of his career to bring England's churches to the level of beauty and munificence which the primate had envisioned. Before he laid his burden down decades later, Wren had not only created St. Paul's, he had designed and constructed fifty-one other churches within the capital's environs.

Sheldon was also responsible for the present Lambeth Palace library. During the Civil Wars that building was completely destroyed and its books and manuscripts carried off. A start at the rebuilding process had been made under Juxon, but the library's design was revised by Sheldon who carried the project to completion. He then instituted a search at Cambridge and elsewhere for all the volumes which had previously lodged there. Ultimately he saw most of these returned once more to Lambeth where, according to Sheldon's plan, they were to be joined at his death by his own books and personal and public papers.

All told, Sheldon's primacy saw an immense amount of construction accomplished, construction which repaired and re-embellished the church's physical plant and which went far to eliminate the scars left by the Civil Wars and the Interregnum period. To find a sufficient number of learned, dedicated, and pious divines to make proper use of these refurbished buildings was another matter.

A cursory survey of Sheldon's immense correspondence as archbishop can only lead the reader to conclude that never was a church leader beset by a more stubborn, self-seeking, litigious, insubordinate corps of clergymen. Examples abound: The avaricious vicar at Croydon, William Carver, who ruthlessly coerced his poor parishioners into increasing their

---

[11] H. H. Milman, *Annals of St. Paul's* (London, 1869), pp. 387-391, discusses Sheldon's part in calling Wren from Oxford after the building collapsed, as well as Sheldon's role in planning the new St. Paul's. He himself gave £ 2000 towards the new building. In addition, he ordered that in the future when bishops were consecrated to their office, instead of the usual gift of expensive gloves to all of their episcopal colleagues, they subscribe £ 50 to the St. Paul's building fund. The greatest amount of the expense of rebuilding was drawn from the new duty on coal which was imported into the capital, passed in 1670. Sheldon ushered the measure through the upper house, and indeed it may have been his original proposal which became law. See Lords' Journals, XII, 350.

[12] Rawlins Mss. Q. C. 11, Bodleian Library.

Church contributions far beyond all legal requirements; some he had ordered arrested, others threatened, a few he had utterly impoverished, and some were forced to flee the parish to avoid financial ruin. Appointed in response to the parish's bitter complaints, Sheldon's investigating committee scaled all of the grasping cleric's demands downward by a twentieth, a twelfth, a sixth, or, in some cases, to only a fourth of what he had demanded.[13] Another was Rice Wynne, a notoriously drunken and debauched curate, whose life became such a public scandal that Bishop Griffith of St. Asaph's moved to expel him from his living despite the outcries of his high-placed patrons.[14] The cases of Daniel Evans and John Bargrave, members of the chapter at Canterbury, was especially serious. They engaged in a savage fist fight in the chapter house at Canterbury.[15] This same Evans was later accused of mercilessly beating another clergyman during a church service at Bristol.[16] Equally damaging to the Church's prestige was the notorious case of a priest whom a young blacksmith brained with a pair of bellows because the vicar would not desist from his pursuit of the smith's shapely wife.[17] Another source of constant trouble and complaint was the scandalous quarreling of chapters and their deans – such as occurred between Dean Robert Creighton and the chapter at Wells when Creighton offered to resign the deanship providing his colleagues inserted his own son in his place.[18] Nor did bishops and deans seem to get along any better. They entertained bitter quarrels such as those between Bishop Piers and Dean Robert Creighton at Wells and Bishop Cosin and Dean John Sudbury at Durham. (Both bishops were leasing Church lands for three lives rather than twenty-one years – against Sheldon's express orders – in order to appropriate the higher fees which the longer leases brought into their coffers; both deans refused to concur in the leases.[19]

Perhaps the most serious problem relating to the clergy was that of

[13] Add. Ms. C. 302, Adam Browne to Sheldon, Sept. 11, 1673.
[14] Add. Ms. C. 304b, bishop of St. Asaph's to Sheldon, Jan. 25, 1666/7.
[15] Add. Ms. C. 307, John Bargrave to Myles Smith, April 7, 1669.
[16] Add. Ms. C. 302, George Williamson to Sheldon, July 22, 1669.
[17] For a description of this scandalous incident, see Add. Ms. C. 307, Wm. Somers to Myles Smith, May 23, 1666.
[18] For this illegal attempt of Creighton to insert his son in the deanship, see Add. Ms. C. 308, Sheldon to Grindall Sheafe, May 11, 1667.
[19] For the Creighton-Piers quarrel, see Add. Ms. C. 305 where there is a paper prepared by the dean and chapter at Wells describing this sordid affair. For the Cosin-Sudbury clash, see Add. Mss. C. 305 and 308 where there are a series of letters between Sheldon and Cosin and Sheldon and Sudbury, written between 1665 and 1667, concerning this unhappy business. In addition, Cosin was accused by the dean of giving Church leases and benefices as dowries for his daughters. Sheldon generally supported Sudbury, a close friend, against Cosin, much to the disgust of the latter.

non-residence. To get the Anglican clergy to remain in their parishes and render the prescribed services to their people seemed very nearly impossible. Canons who refused to perform services in their cathedrals, nor even live in their canonical houses, vicars who would not serve their parishes nor provide a substitute, diocesan officers who drew their incomes but who never appeared in their diocese – it was glaring examples such as these, often held up to public ridicule by the Church's enemies, which gave the Anglican establishment such a bad reputation in the years after 1660.

The cathedral chapter at Wells was a prime example. When he became bishop there in 1670, Robert Creighton reported that almost half the canons were regular absentees. What was worse, as he wrote to Sheldon, many of these non-residents had been given dispensations by the archbishop's Court of Arches or by the primate's own officers to be absent. One of these – a Mr. Tynt – had not been seen in Wells for seven years and was living in Salisbury Plain, ostensibly for his health, although, reported the bishop indignantly, he was "a great, fat man, succulent and full of juice – no Benedictine or Popish priest fatter." [20] Another who drew Creighton's ire was his own son-in-law and son of his predecessor, William Piers. Piers had moved in with a fellow canon and rented out his own canonical residence for ten years to a victualler, a tailor, and a coachman – all of whom were defacing the property and remodelling it to serve their own needs. Furthermore, Piers defied Creighton to do anything about the matter.[21] In an attempt to get these wayward churchmen to resume their residence and their duties, Creighton encouraged the resident canons to deny the absentees their annual dividends. This drastic step raised an outcry that reverberated from one end of the kingdom to the other, and the non-residents descended upon Wells determined not only to regain their fees but also to secure control of the commissary's position and thus "make the residents sweat for their dividends the next year." And they very nearly succeeded in this nefarious scheme, much to the amusement of both the court and country.[22]

Perhaps the greatest Church scandal of Sheldon's whole primacy occurred in the ranks of the bishops themselves. This was the case of Thomas Wood, bishop of Lichfield and Coventry.

Sheldon knew Wood well, and nothing about the man recommended him for elevation to episcopal rank. He was rich, had high connections

---

[20] Tanner Ms. 140, bishop of Bath and Wells to Sheldon, Aug. 16, 1672.
[21] There are several letters between Creighton and Sheldon on this incident. See Add. Mss. C. 305 and Harl. Mss. 7377.
[22] Add. Mss. C. 305, Robert Creighton to Sheldon, Dec. 17, 1669.

at court, and was exceedingly proud and stubborn. As John Hacket's dean at Lichfield, he had caused that poor prelate untold amounts of distress and grief. He was a non-resident dean – preferring to spend his time in the capital – defied his bishop on every issue, refused to bear his share of the rebuilding expense at Lichfield, and spread dissension and turmoil throughout the diocese. On one occasion Hacket begged the archbishop to summon his obstreperous dean to Lambeth and impose some discipline upon him. Please, the distraught bishop wrote to Sheldon, "call unto you this wand'ring sheep, or rather stubborn ram, to make him obedient to his despised bishop's authority." [23]

Prior to Hacket's death in 1671, Wood arranged a marriage between his niece, a wealthy heiress, and the duchess of Cleveland's son. In return the duchess used her considerable influence with the king to secure Wood's appointment to succeed Hacket as bishop of Lichfield and Coventry. Thus the non-resident dean became a non-resident bishop. Two years after his consecration, despite many urgent messages and letters from Sheldon on the subject, Wood had not yet set foot in his diocese. The Church was under fire anyway – Sheldon was at that moment desperately struggling to muster sufficient political power to insure the defeat of the king's 1672 indulgence – and this scandal only added substance to the denunciations of the Church's critics. In addition Sheldon was ill, afflicted by some kind of epileptic seizures.[24] All of this illness, frustration, worry, and anger was poured out upon the hapless Wood in a letter which Sheldon personally penned to the miscreant bishop.

I have [he said] by so many messages intreated your company out of the respect I bear to your person and the ancient friendship between us, otherwise I should not have troubled myself to desire what the authority of my place can compel, nor have made it my business to persuade what I am sufficiently enabled to require. I would not have reminded you of your faults had I been as forgetful of kindness and civility to you as you are pleased to be of your duty, and been as unwilling to let the scandal increase which through your means is grown too great already.[25]

In short, thundered the archbishop, "the matter concerns the reiterated and continued complaints I receive of your absence from your diocese." [26] And Sheldon itemized the complaints. The laity needed a bishop – many sought his advice and desired confirmation; the clergy

[23] Tanner Ms. 45, Lichfield to Sheldon, Jan. 27, 1667/8.
[24] See later this chapter.
[25] Harl. Ms. 7377, Sheldon to Thomas Wood, June, 1673.
[26] *Ibid.*

needed guidance and instruction; and many persons sought ordination which at present required a lengthy, expensive, and often futile, trip to the capital to seek their bishop out. He ordered Wood to make immediate preparations to depart for his diocese.

If advice will not do you [grimly warned the archbishop] you must give me leave with all the power and interest I have to enforce it. If I do not, it must at last reflect upon me.[27]

Since there are no subsequent letters regarding this matter, one can only conclude that, however reluctantly, Wood departed for Lichfield.

Certainly the Thomas Woods, the Rice Wynnes, the Daniel Evanses were in the minority. There were without a doubt hundreds of loyal, pious, dedicated Anglican divines in this period who were quietly, humbly, going about their duties. But the sheer weight of numbers of contrary cases which appear in Sheldon's official correspondence would seem to indicate clearly that standards of morality and dedication among the Restoration clergy were deplorably low.

To remedy this situation Sheldon urged his bishops to make frequent and regular visitations throughout their diocese. He drew up articles of visitation for them, charging them not only to take action against nonconforming clerics but also to censure and discipline those ministers whose lives and performance were not up to the high standards he demanded.[28] Where there were honest differences of opinion, he invariably urged arbitration so that the matter might be settled fairly and justly, and above all quietly, so that there would be no public furor.[29] At times he exerted his own considerable influence upon some erring divine to bring him to a realization of his duties.[30] At other times, he authorized a bishop to proceed against a clergyman in the courts of law, although always reluctantly, since he hated "to give advantage and make sport for those who will be glad to see us engaged one against another." [31] In 1668 when at Sheldon's orders many bishops were going on visitation and were to proceed forcefully against all scandalous clergy, Sheldon summoned Giles Sweit, dean of the Court of Arches, into his presence and cautioned him against being too hasty and liberal in granting in-

---

[27] *Ibid.*

[28] *Ibid.*, Sheldon to several bishops asking about their visitations, Sept. 1, 1674.

[29] For an example where Sheldon strongly urged arbitration upon squabbling clerics, see the St. Asaph's cathedral restoration quarrel mentioned above. Sheldon himself served as arbitrator in some of these cases.

[30] Add. Mss. C. 308, contains a letter from Sheldon to Dr. Jones, Chancellor of Bristol Diocese, written Nov. 7, 1667, in which Sheldon personally intervened to discipline an erring cleric. There are numerous similar incidents.

[31] Harl. Mss. 7377, Sheldon to Creighton, Oct. 20, 1669.

hibitions and absolutions in the case of any erring cleric. He wanted miscreants punished as summarily as possible and demanded that Sweit confer with himself before taking action in such cases.[32]

Many of these "scandalous" clergymen were the product of overly hasty ordinations. Charges were constantly being brought to Lambeth that bishops were ordaining unfit persons into the ministry. It seems that officers of some of the older bishops particularly were promoting ordinations simply for the fees which accrued to themselves. As a result, persons of inferior education, of immoral life, or of inferior birth – or all three – would travel from all parts of England to obtain these easy ordinations.[33] Probably in response to the celebrated Robert Hammond affair – Bishop Piers had ordained Hammond, although he was of low birth, had very little education, and even though he had been for some time a weaver's apprentice – the archbishop in 1665 dispatched a primatial letter to all bishops ordering them to see to it that all canons "concerning ordaining" were carefully and fully observed in the future. No one was to be admitted to holy orders unless he possessed letters dimissory, and no bishop "not being in his own proper diocese" was to ordain anyone without a license from the archbishop himself.[34]

Sheldon adverted to this subject on numerous occasions throughout his primacy. He was determined to improve the quality of the Anglican clergy, and he had very definite ideas as to the caliber of man who should be recruited to that holy office. In a letter to Reynolds of Norwich, written in 1670, he described the ideal cleric as one that

will be very tender of the credit of religion, of the dignity of their function, and of the success of their ministry; and endeavour by their sober, pious, and prudent conversations, to stop the mouths of any that watch of their halting, to bear witness to the truth of that doctrine which they preach, to be guides and examples of holiness to the people over whom they are set, and to lay up for themselves a comfortable account against the time we shall appear before the Great Shepherd.[35]

As he was only too well aware, in the 1660's and 1670's the reality often was a far cry from this ideal.

The emphasis given this topic throughout Sheldon's primacy was not only to "stop the mouths" of the Church's detractors. The clergyman

[32] Add. Mss. C. 308, Sheldon to the dean of the Court of Arches, Aug. 4, 1668.
[33] William Piers of Bath and Wells acquired a reputation for performing these irregular ordinations. His sons were his subordinate officers, and they were apparently grasping for all the fees they could possibly accumulate before their aging father died, and they were dispossessed from their lucrative offices. See Add. Mss. C. 302, bishop of Bath and Wells to Sheldon, St. Innocent's Day, 1665.
[34] Add. Mss. C. 308, archepiscopal letter to the bishop of London for all bishops, no date, but from internal evidence, written in July, 1665.
[35] Quoted in Stoughton, III, 474.

was the kingpin in Sheldon's plan for remoulding the religious life of the kingdom back into traditional Anglican channels. The conformable, pious, and dutiful clerics which he sought would, he was sure, help produce equally conformable, pious, and dutiful congregations. Since the vicar had great influence and power in his parish, and since he imposed discipline upon his own services, the right kind of priest would create the outwardly dignified kind of church service which Sheldon so urgently demanded. Given the supervision of a godly, determined clergyman, people would attend church regularly, they would take off their hats within the sanctuary, bow reverently at the name of Jesus, and conduct themselves in general in an orderly, respectful manner. On this point Sheldon was much like Queen Elizabeth. He would not "make windows into men's souls," but he doggedly insisted upon outward conformity.

But the archbishop was ever thinking in long range terms. The Church firmly established and secure for future generations was his ultimate goal. To achieve that aim he must win the younger generation over to a wholehearted allegiance to the Church of England. And here again the clergy were cast in the key role. Two institutions affected a young person's outlook and thinking – his school and his church, his teacher and his clergyman. In Sheldon's view the two should work hand in hand to achieve the desired end, and since the religious hierarchy was the licensing agency for schools and teachers, it appeared that support from the classroom should be relatively easy for the Church to secure.

In all of his articles of visitation Sheldon urged his subordinates to check carefully on these two things: that every school teacher be loyal and conformable to the Church of England, and that all clerics be careful to hold their catechism classes every Sunday afternoon.[36] In writing to Peter Mewes, bishop of Bath and Wells, on this topic in 1674, Sheldon pointed out emphatically that catechizing and the regulation of schools which "have always been hitherto pressed ... are the best expedients for the preservation of unity both in church and commonwealth." [37] He was sure, as he wrote to another friend, that one could do much more good through faithful catechizing than he could through "many sermons." [38] When the king accused the Anglican clergy of neglecting this important function, Sheldon reacted immediately by circularizing all bishops in both provinces requiring them to report to Lambeth the amount of catechizing going on in their dioceses. He pointed out that

[36] See two letters from Sparrow to Sheldon, June 15 and July 28, 1668, Add. Mss. C. 305, where Sparrow is carrying out the archbishop's orders on these points.
[37] Harl. Mss. 7377, Sheldon to the bishop of Bath and Wells, July 15, 1674.
[38] Harl. Mss. 7377, Sheldon to Sparrow, June 10, 1671.

"his Majesty is pleased . . . to impute the increase of the now prevailing sects and disorders amongst us [the time was 1672, just after Charles had issued his indulgence] for the most part to this neglect." [39] Sheldon indignantly rejected the imputation, but he desired some firm documentation from each diocese on the subject and promised to make "good use of it in due time and place." [40] At the same time he reiterated his order that "in the future all school teachers take such oaths and declarations as necessary to make sure they are loyal persons." [41] The archbishop was positive that school and church, working together, could rear a loyal, disciplined generation of Anglican laity.

In a letter to his friend and favorite, Seth Ward, bishop of Salisbury, Sheldon summarized the advice which he had been showering upon his bishops for fourteen years. These, he said, are the goals which every bishop should set for himself in administering his diocese:

> That the clergy [be] kept up to an unblamable conversation and regular conformity to the doctrine and discipline of the Church; that Divine services and public prayer be performed with that duty and exactness which the Rubrick requires; and lastly that the duty of catechising be reinforced as the most effectual means to prevent the further increase of . . . sects and disorders amongst us.[42]

The old archbishop was certain that discipline and order, firmly enforced, would ultimately bring unity and peace to the Church and the nation.

The primate's methods as an administrator matched the sternness and rigor of his program. After 1660 one hears very little of the famed Sheldon wit and humor, characteristics which made him such a delightful companion in his earlier life. While still ordinarily soft-spoken and gentle towards close friends and members of his official family, there was now a note of impatience and asperity in much of his administrative correspondence. Reading his letters, his subordinates must have pictured the writer as a grim, foreboding, father-figure, all-seeing, impatient of every shortcoming, one whose anger was ever loosely chained, just below the threshold of his terse, pointed messages. At times, indeed, as has been noted already, that suppressed rage and frustration could blaze forth in flashing anger or biting sarcasm.

"If he were in my province I know well enough how to deal with him presently," Sheldon grimly finished a letter to John Wilkins, bishop of Chester, about a man who had possessed himself of a benefice illegally.[43]

[39] *Ibid.*, Sheldon to the archbishop of York, Jan. 27, 1672/3.
[40] *Ibid.*
[41] *Ibid.*, Sheldon to the bishop of London, Feb. 6, 1672/3.
[42] *Ibid.*, Sheldon to the bishop of Salisbury, Sept. 1, 1674.
[43] Harl. Mss. 7377, Sheldon to the bishop of Chester, Aug. 28, 1671.

In another to the officials of the city of Dover who had highhandedly seized some disputed property and leased it out, he promised immediate legal prosecution of the mayor and the corporation and continued ominously, "I doubt not but I shall have my suit tried where you shall not be both parties and judges, which I have some reason to believe is the greatest strength you have in your cause." [44]

To Joseph Henshaw, bishop of Peterborough, whose diocese seemed to be a hotbed of nonconformist activity, the archbishop took an even stronger tack. Furiously, he itemized one minister's deficiencies:

> He renders not the common prayers ... but in parts and parcels according as the present humor takes him, never wears the surplice, takes no notice of holy days or fasting days, discourages those that like and observe the prayers and ceremonies of the church ... and falls into disputes against them. I am sufficiently convinced of the naughtiness of the man, as I am sure you would be too, if you would only properly investigate.[45]

Angrily Sheldon ordered Henshaw to take some action against the offender "either by making him conformable or his place too hot for him." [46] To Dr. Wake, Peterborough chancellor, who, the archbishop believed, was conniving at keeping the miscreant in his benefice, Sheldon ended a merciless wigging with the words, "In short, do what is your office justly and legally against him, or I shall exercise mine upon you and let you see that I will have no trifling in matters so scandalous to the church." [47]

The doughty old archbishop's gaze probed into and attempted to bring order and a proper formality to every aspect of the country's religious life. He wanted the sabbath properly observed – as Pepys found when he was stopped from "crossing the water" on the Lord's Day because Sheldon had banned pleasure boating on Sunday.[48] He attempted to augment poor livings wherever he could, and he encouraged others to follow his example in this matter.[49] He issued strict

---

[44] Add. Mss. C. 308, Sheldon to the mayor of Dover, March 28, 1668.
[45] *Ibid.*, Sheldon to the bishop of Peterborough, Nov. 10, 1666.
[46] *Ibid.*, Same to Same, Dec. 22, 1666.
[47] *Ibid.*, Sheldon to the chancellor of Peterborough, Dec. 22, 1666.
[48] Pepys *Diary*, I, 326.
[49] Sheldon was well aware of the extreme poverty of many poor vicars, and he pushed the augmentation of their incomes in many ways. He gave money himself to increase many parish incomes, he obtained letters from the king recommending such augmentations to the nobility, and he received many gifts from various persons which he used for this purpose. He also was the author of numerous enabling acts making such augmentations possible. See Add. Mss. C. 308, Sheldon to the dean of Wells, June 2, 1668 and June 15, 1668, where he discusses some very necessary steps which must be taken to increase the incomes for some poor vicarages.

orders that plural livings be allowed only to exceptionally talented persons and then only if the benefices were located in close proximity to one another so that they could be properly supervised.[50] He ordered all Church lands to be leased under contracts for twenty-one years rather than three lives as some clerics were prone to do.[51] He was interested and active in supervising the two universities, demanding that favoritism be put aside and that the best men be chosen for fellowships and other scholar's places.[52] And his interest and influence reached overseas to the Church in Ireland, in America, and to the English factories in Portugal and elsewhere.[53]

From the scope of his interests and activities, and from the vigor with which he applied himself to the task of administering the Church, it seems apparent that the determined, old prelate was attempting with all the power of his personality to extirpate wrongdoing from the religious establishment and by applying unrelenting pressure upon clergy and parishioners alike to bring a universal acceptance of the formal and dignified services prescribed in the Book of Common Prayer. "There is nothing but discipline that keeps societies in order, and good order is that which makes them continue and stand."[54] From Lambeth one could hear the words intoned like a litany.

Yet the demanding imperiousness of his official style often overshadowed other facets of the primate's complex nature. He possessed an innate sense of fairness in human relations which prevented his being quite as overbearing as he sometimes sounded. It showed for instance in his dealings with the universities and their college heads. As archbishop Sheldon possessed great influence at both institutions of higher learning, and might well have forced upon those bodies his own favorites or the sons of politicians whose favor he was currying in order to protect the Church. Yet he himself had bitterly resented Laud's action in this respect when he had earlier been warden of All Soul's, and he never forgot.[55]

---

[50] Add. Mss. C. 308, Myles Smith to the bishop of Gloucester, April 1, 1667, where Smith discusses the archbishop's orders upon this point.

[51] See footnote number 19 above.

[52] Harl. Mss. 7377 and Add. Mss. C. 308, contain dozens of letters written to the college heads of both universities on this subject.

[53] For letters relating to the Portugese factories, see Harl. Mss. 7377, Sheldon to a businessman, Nov. 26, 1669; for Sheldon's interest in America, see Harl. Mss. 7377, Sheldon to the lord lieutenant of Ireland, April 1, 1667, where Sheldon was considering appointing a bishop for Virginia; as far as his Irish interests were concerned, Sheldon had many friends there, including the duke of Ormonde, the lord lieutenant in the 1660's, and he took an active part in directing and advising the Church there.

[54] Add. Mss. C. 308, Sheldon to William Piers, June 14, 1669.

[55] See Chapter I for this incident.

He not only refused to follow that mode of procedure himself, he also fought to preserve the colleges' freedom of action from interference by the king and other governing officials. Until his fall from favor in 1667, he was invariably successful in protecting the colleges from this kind of high placed interference, and even afterwards he himself seldom exerted pressure on behalf of anyone.[56] Although he wrote several hundreds of recommendations for scholar's places while primate, he almost always left the final determination in the matter in the hands of the college itself. "If upon competition," he wrote to Ralph Bathurst, president of Trinity College in 1664, "the youth shall appear himself of as good abilities and desert as any other that shall stand with him, I shall take it kindly from yourself if you prefer him; but if you find him unfit or not too deserving, you cannot do me a greater kindness than to refuse him." [57] He made this a regular charge in almost every letter of recommendation which he sent to the universities, and one can be sure that here too Sheldon was not only protecting the college heads. He was thinking of the future as well. He wanted people promoted on merit and ability; future leadership in Church and nation depended upon the quality of the graduates which Oxford and Cambridge produced.

Moreover, this characteristic of thoughtfulness for the rights of others often showed through in his routine dealings with the lower clergy. In a letter to the dean of Worcester who was loath to send in his cathedral charter for revision – something which Sheldon was demanding of all chapters in the early sixties – he wrote sympathetically:

I assure you you shall not be surprised for want of concern here for your consideration. If you have anything to object [in the new charter's terms] let them [sic] be set down and sent in. If they are reasonable, they will be allowed; if not, you will have to submit to the king.[58]

The chancellor of Bristol diocese, who had been accused of licensing schools simply for the fees involved, found the same fairness and consideration when he defended himself before the archbishop. "If there is a design to discredit you," Sheldon reassured the man, "you shall not be condemned without very just and good proof." [59]

In an age of intensely personal human relations, when vindictiveness

---

[56] Lambeth Mss. SR-138, Sheldon to the warden of All Souls, Feb. 2, 1666/7.
[57] Add. Mss. C. 308, Sheldon to Ralph Bathurst, April 18, 1664. In dozens of letters of recommendation to college heads, Sheldon is on record as only once insisting upon an election. This was the case of the son of Sir Dudley Digges who sought a fellowship at All Souls. See Sheldon to the warden of All Souls, Nov. 10, 1673, Harl. Mss. 7377.
[58] Add. Mss. C. 308, Sheldon to the dean of Worcester, April 13, 1665.
[59] *Ibid.*, Sheldon to Dr. Jones, Nov. 7, 1667.

and pique actuated many an ill-founded accusation. Sheldon, in most cases, held his judgment in abeyance until he had what he thought were accurate facts. Only then did he move with his customary vigor and dispatch to chastise the culprit.

Indeed far from being the crude, unfeeling tyrant which his enemies have sometimes described, the archbishop displayed a sensitivity to genuine suffering and the needs of others which is often surprising and frequently moving in its depth and sincerity. At the time of the 1665 plague outbreak, Sheldon remained at his post in London all during the months of greatest danger, and he labored mightily to keep the churches open and religious services available to those frightened people confined to the city.[60] He himself composed a special prayer for the fast days promulgated throughout the land to seek divine relief from the terrible visitation.

For there is wrath gone out against us. That dreadful arrow of thine sticks fast in our flesh,[61]

prayed the archbishop, in full regalia, from the choir of St. Paul's.

The genuine distress of the poor in the capital city in this period moved Sheldon deeply. He was on the scene, and he daily saw terrible suffering and misery, and he wrote moving letters to all the bishops pleading, begging, commanding, that they take up offerings to aid the beleaguered poor who were confined to the dangerous city. In ordering the collections, Sheldon described the situation for Henchman, bishop of London. Large amounts of money, he said, were absolutely necessary to succor

the miserably distressed in and about this great city, ... whose calamity is far more to be pitied than any elsewhere, not only by the raging of the infection, but even for the very want of necessaries for life, many perishing that way, which otherwise might have escaped the danger, and many thousands of poor artisans being ready to starve for lack of means to be employed in their callings, all trading being dangerous and laid aside by reason of the plague.[62]

The urgency in this letter and others on the same subject is that of a man writing while surrounded on every side by terrible suffering. The archbishop was deeply affected by what he was daily witnessing. He himself gave thousands of pounds to alleviate the distressed conditions in the capital. But more importantly, in response to his primatial orders, many thousands more were collected from parishes throughout the

[60] Walter G. Bell, *The Great Plague in London in 1665* (London, 1951), p. 224.
[61] *Ibid.*
[62] Lambeth Mss. SR-138, Sheldon to the bishop of London, no month, 1665.

kingdom and relayed to the capital for the benefit of the London poor.⁶³

Hardly had the plague begun to abate than the London fire broke out. Raging unchecked over three days, it destroyed a good part of the capital, and thousands of citizens were rendered homeless and destitute and were literally reduced to starvation. Again Sheldon sent out urgent letters stirring the clergy to extend themselves to meet this new visitation of God's wrath. "The case is so miserable in itself," he wrote to the bishops, "that it will need no other argument but the bare relation to move pity." ⁶⁴ Again the clergy stirred their parishioners on behalf of the indigent, suffering Londoners, and again thousands of pounds poured in to Lambeth to be disbursed to the destitute citizens.

Nor were these charitable activities merely sporadic, occasional interests of the archbishop. Sheldon took an active interest in the ransoming of Englishmen held in slavery by the Moslem pirates of Algiers and Tunis, and he vigorously pushed the charitable drives which brought in further thousands for this purpose.⁶⁵ In the case of a terrible fire in Shropshire in 1667 which caused great loss of property and suffering in that county, he again was instrumental in activating the parish clergy to assist the victims of that tragedy.⁶⁶ He also took more than a merely official interest in the plight of wounded and crippled sailors from the Dutch wars – as has already been noted – and hospital places for these and others who were old, ill, or incapacitated, were regular subjects of consideration in his letters.⁶⁷ Not only did the archbishop feel that the Church must provide charitable aid for those who were indigent, sick, or otherwise unable to care for themselves, he himself displayed great personal compassion and concern for such people all of his life.

Curiously, Sheldon's humanity did not extend to the dissenters. He displayed a callous contempt for those poor unfortunates, and as far as is known he never suggested the abatement of one jot of any law to ease the condition of those who were enduring terrible hardships as a result of his own policies. Yet this is only a seeming paradox. Sheldon

---

⁶³ Ward alone collected over £ 2000 in Exeter diocese for this charity in August and September of 1665. See a letter, Add. Mss. C. 305, Ward to Sheldon, Sept. 30, 1665.

⁶⁴ Add. Mss. C. 308, Sheldon to all bishops, Nov. 9, 1666.

⁶⁵ Every cleric who reported on his ten years' charitable contributions included a figure for ransoming slaves at Algiers, indicating that Sheldon had placed this collection in a position of high priority. See Add. Mss. C. 308, where the returns of each of the bishops and deans are carefully recorded.

⁶⁶ Lambeth Mss. SR-138, Sheldon to all bishops, May 23, 1666.

⁶⁷ For Sheldon's interest in the subject of hospital places – In-Brothers and In-Sisters, or Out-Brothers and Out-Sisters, as they were called in those days – see letters from Wm. Somers to Sheldon, Nov. 21, 1665, and Dec. 11, 1665, Add. Mss. C. 302.

was no Jekyll-Hyde character. In his eyes, the poor Londoners were enduring hardships which were the result of an act of God — something they themselves could in no way help. The nonconformists, on the other hand, were really suffering only from their own wilfulness and stubbornness. All the latter group needed to do to enjoy peace and security was to attend Anglican services as the law demanded and refrain from their illegal conventicling. They were causing their own pain and suffering; it was not he who was to blame.

Sheldon's charitable giving both as cleric and later as archbishop amounted to a great sum. Samuel Parker, his chaplain, estimated that his charitable contributions as archbishop amounted to some £ 73,000 excluding the 18,000 which he laid out upon the construction of his theatre. Archbishop Dolben, his executor, estimated the total amount as closer to 80,000 pounds.[68] When one adds the Sheldonian theatre expenditure, the total must have been the equivalent of $ 5-7,000,000 in modern purchasing power.[69] Since he gave away immense amounts also during the Civil Wars and the Interregnum period, the total of his lifetime charitable contributions must have been as great as any English bishop has ever given. It appears as though the archbishop valued money and wealth simply as tools to be employed for useful and charitable purposes.

Throughout the period of the 1670's, Sheldon had frequent bouts of illness, some of which were seriously incapacitating. During the spring of 1673 the worn-out, old prelate suffered from seizures — on the order of epilepsy — which brought on frequent faintings and kept him from his work for months on end. As the decade wore on, these periods of illness became ever more frequent, and by the spring of 1677 it became evident that he had not long to live.

The court buzzed with speculation regarding his successor. Some thought Henry Compton, newly-made bishop of London and a powerful, fearless churchman in his own right, was the natural choice. Sheldon himself at one time had favored his friend and protegé, Seth Ward, bishop of Salisbury. But Sheldon's views were not apt to be effectual, and Compton had alienated the duke of York by insisting boldly that York's motherless daughters be reared as Anglicans. Nathaniel Crewe, bishop of Durham, and a York favorite, was rumored as a possible

---

[68] Parker, p. 53.
[69] £ 100,000 × 5 = $ 500,000 × 12 for depreciation to 1960 = $ 6,000,000. These figures are, of course, very, very rough estimates.

choice, and he hurried to London to be on the scene where he could take advantage of whatever opportunities arose.

Sheldon's painful illness dragged on into November, and when he finally gasped his last breath, word went out that William Sancroft, gentle, scholarly dean of St. Paul's had received the nomination. Charles II sought a more pliant primate to replace the intrepid, old archbishop who had so successfully thwarted the royal will on so many past occasions.

On a dreary, rainy, November day the archbishop's remains were carried in state from Lambeth chapel, where the funeral services were conducted, to the village of Croydon. There, as archbishop, Sheldon had possessed a summer home where he spent many delightful hours and which he came to love above all his other residences. Thus in Croydon Church he was interred, and his tomb still occupies a prominent place there today. A friend – perhaps George Morley or Seth Ward – penned an epitaph:

A man equal to very station, superior to every title, constant in adversity, virtuous in prosperity, superior to either event; father of the poor, patron of the learned, guardian of the church, it is not right to say so little of so great a man, to say much would be useless; his contemporaries knew his excellence, and posterity will believe it.

Sheldon's contemporaries did indeed know his excellence; his tragedy was that posterity soon forgot.

CONCLUSIONS

Who and what was Sheldon? Perhaps about no other personage in history have judgments rendered by both contemporaries and historians been so much at variance. Baxter felt that under no conditions was he fit for the office of bishop and certainly never for that of archbishop of Canterbury. On the other hand Sir Francis Wenman was often heard to declare that Sheldon was "made for Canterbury." Stoughton concluded that his courtier-like manners, geniality, and easy hospitality fitted him for the position of a county nobleman but never for the service of the Church, while dissenters from Anglican doctrine found in him no sign of geniality whatsoever. Burnet was sure that Sheldon had no deep sense of religion, if any at all, while Samuel Parker considered him totally dedicated to the Church and to his religion. Bosher sees him as a great primate in the medieval tradition of Langton and Becket; Molesworth charges that he came out of the Civil Wars a complete debauchee.

Much of this disparity of course comes as a result of the individual author being either a friend and admirer of the archbishop or an enemy who disliked him, his views, and his actions. This too, of course, says much about Sheldon. He was no neutral figure. Either one approved of him heartily or he despised him intensely.

However, there are certain aspects of Sheldon's character about which both friends and enemies are agreed. He was not, for instance, a great preacher. The fact that only three of his sermons are extant, considering his eminence in his own day, supplies firm testimony on that point. Nor was he a debauchee as Molesworth has charged and as Pepys has intimated. The one was writing from his low church prejudices, while the other was repeating loose gossip heard in the streets. For a debauched cleric to have denied a debauched king access to the communion table would have been a laughable act at best. But there is no record that anyone laughed; and the fact that his enemies, who have been his main biographers, have chosen to ignore this incident is of course quite understandable. In any event the archbishop possessed many staunch friends and allies of unimpeachable moral character who confidently, unquestioningly, accepted his advice and direction on religious and moral issues. These would certainly seem, once and for all, to give the lie to any such charge. Neither was the archbishop a scholar. He had the training, titles, and credentials; he tried on more than one occasion to write something significant, but none – not even unpublished manuscripts – of these efforts has been saved for posterity. He read widely and avidly, was the friend and advisor to many eminent scholars, appreciated their work, often encouraged them monetarily and verbally, but he himself did not possess those gifts.[1]

He was, on the other hand, an administrator of exceptional capacity. Even Bishop Burnet, who had little good to say of him in other respects, admitted that he possessed a penetrating judgment in practical affairs that was far beyond the ordinary. Sheldon was a shrewd judge of character and human motivation; he was long-headed and could think deeply, intensely, and logically about practical problems; furthermore, he possessed the energy, determination, and dedicated application that enabled him to see his plans carried through to fruition. To these points both his contemporaries and his own accomplishments bear testimony.

Finally, few would quarrel with Keith Feiling's description of Sheldon as a man with a will of iron. He was strong. He knew what he wanted, and he would drive imperiously toward his goal, would oppose friend, foe, the king, the privy council, Cromwell's army, the devil himself, were he convinced of the rightness of his action. Here again the facts of his life testify for themselves.

But from whence came this great strength? It would seem that his very lack of imagination aided him immensely here. He could never see the other person's point of view, could never put himself sympathetically in his enemy's place. Consequently, he always ascribed evil, self-seeking motives to those who opposed him. Moreover, Sheldon was simply and totally unaffected by the perception and discovery of intellectual truth, no matter what the realm of investigation. As has been noted, he was attracted by neither of the main theological doctrines of his day –

---

[1] Partly, no doubt, Sheldon's lack of success as a preacher was a result of a lack of imagination. The sermons which have come down to us, show a plodding, logical mind, grimly setting down example after example from the bible and the Church fathers to re-enforce his point. It was probably a case of over-kill. In addition, his sermons show little wit, or humor, and no imaginative flair at all. See Sheldon's sermon before the king at his return, Gilbert Sheldon, *A Sermon Preached Before the King* (London, 1660).

Calvinism or Arminianism. He was a member of the Royal Society, but, we are told, he seldom attended its meetings and did not much approve of the outlook or the work being conducted there. New discoveries, new truths, did not excite him; for him there was no high adventure in pushing back the frontiers of knowledge. Thus it might be said that Sheldon *received* his opinions. He grew up with them. Once received, however, he loved them, cherished them, clung to them, and valiantly defended them. In fact, the most striking thing about Sheldon's life is the consistency and continuity of his religious and political opinions. From early adulthood until his death, his views on these topics remained virtually unchanged. To the archbishop, what had been received from the past was God's will, and hence he would stand firmly, determinedly for those beliefs. In other words, Sheldon was a thoroughgoing conservative who never doubted the wisdom of the past.

What did this iron-willed primate accomplish? He was, first of all, the architect of the Anglican restoration in 1662. And contrary to popularly accepted belief, this was no Laudian restoration. Sheldon had early rejected Arminianism, the chief English proponent of which in the twenties and thirties was Laud, and therefore he had never favored the Laudian church reforms. Nor was he close to any of Laud's supporters or the other chief Arminians. Both Morley and Sanderson leaned toward Calvinism; both were his closest friends. Wren, Laud's good right hand, could not even recognize Sheldon's initials in the 1650's, and although Wren was restored to his bishopric of Ely in 1660 and lived there until 1667, there is no single exchange of letters extant between Sheldon and himself. Cosin, another enthusiastic Laudian, was not in touch with Sheldon during the Interregnum, although many others on the continent were, and he and Sheldon had numerous and bitter disagreements after the Restoration. Neither Peter Heylin, Laud's friend, supporter, and favorite chaplain, nor Herbert Thorndike, the outstanding Arminian scholar, were promoted to episcopal rank after 1660. As for Jeremy Taylor, another of Laud's favorites, Sheldon appreciated some of his writings but distrusted the man. He became a bishop only in the exile of Ireland.

The Prayer Book revision of 1662 shows the same disregard for the Laudians and their ideas. The Laudian members of the bench – among whom were Cosin and Wren – made their suggested revisions in what has been termed the "Durham Book." However, the Durham Book changes were rejected by the 1662 Convocation.[2] Thorndike, strongly Anglo-Catholic in outlook, drew up a new Prayer Book which was also

[2] Stoughton, III, 219 on.

in the Laudian tradition; it too was decisively rejected in 1662.[3] The Laudians drew up a service for Charles' martyrdom which contained references to saints in heaven praying for the "church militant" here on earth; but another service was adopted which omitted this reference.[4] They also wished to include in the new Prayer Book an injunction forbidding extemporaneous praying – "extinguishing one of the last hopes of the Puritan party" – but this design too was frustrated.[5] Neither was anything said about the placing of the communion table – that great bone of contention under Laud. Nor did that matter ever become an issue during the seventeen years of Sheldon's primacy.

It has generally been agreed that Sheldon's voice was the dominant one at the Restoration, and his conservative inclinations were never more in evidence. He simply returned the Church of England to the doctrinal position it had held since the Elizabethan settlement in 1559. A great opportunity certainly existed after 1660 to redefine the Church's doctrine, but no such redefinition took place. The Thirty-Nine Articles were retained even though "they have always been considered as representing the more thoroughly Protestant or Evangelical side of the Church formularies" [6] and even though three of them at least could be interpreted as supporting Calvinist theology – another doctrine which Sheldon had decisively rejected. Sheldon held the Church firmly to the old Elizabethan mean.

What he did, however, was to resolve finally and for all time the questions and problems which had been provoked by the Reformation a century earlier but which the Church's leaders had never been able, to that time, to settle. Although he did not define the Church's doctrinal position in any more precise terms, Sheldon now implacably demanded that that imprecise definition be finally accepted by all who chose to remain within the Church. There were to be no more attacks upon the religious establishment by Catholicizers on the right or Puritans on the left. Sheldon received from every minister who remained within the fold an oath of "assent and consent" to everything contained in the Book of Common Prayer. The dissenters who would not take the oath left the establishment forever, and they could now only attack the Church from without, no longer from within.

Then the archbishop spent the remainder of his life removing from beneath the opposers all bases of power – either within the government

---

[3] *Ibid.*
[4] *Ibid.*, p. 217.
[5] *Ibid.*
[6] *Ibid.*, p. 220.

or the society itself – from which they might mount a successful attack upon the Church. The Corporations Act placed Anglicans in control of the towns. The Test Act of 1673 eliminated Catholics and convinced Presbyterians from the executive branches of the government. But the archbishop would never rest easy until they were eliminated also from the national legislature. Here was the real threat. Although he failed to purge parliament of Catholics and Presbyterians in his proposed act of 1675, still that act did become law during the Titus Oates hysteria in 1678, less than a year after Sheldon's death. Then was the legislature pure Anglican in make-up, and then was Sheldon's dream finally achieved. The Church of England was safe from its enemies. They were now a despised remnant, powerless to cause more trouble.

Sheldon's second great achievement had to do with the determined program of re-Anglicanization of the country, a program which he steadfastly pursued from 1660 on. There is no certain way to ascertain the relative strengths of Presbyterian, Independent, and Anglican adherents within the English population at the Restoration. Certainly after two decades of religious anarchy and official opposition to all Church of England doctrine, loyal supporters of the latter faith must have been a minority group.[7] This did not deter the iron-willed prelate. He set himself the task of remolding Englishmen back into the form of faithful Anglicans. Through penal laws, legal prosecution, official persecution, all backed by a strong propaganda campaign on behalf of the Church, while still bishop of London, Sheldon began the process of coercing the population into attending Anglican services and accepting Anglican practice and belief. He applied himself determinedly to the task of extirpating the heresy of Puritanical dissent in all of its forms.

Just how successful was he in this venture? The best evidence we have on this point comes from Exeter diocese. Containing the coastal trading cities of Exeter and Plymouth, Devonshire had been a hotbed of Puritan sentiment throughout the Civil Wars. Cornwall was little better. Beginning in 1661 with the election of Seth Ward to that see, for the next fifteen years Sheldon had loyal and energetic suffragans at Exeter who would enforce his policies with all of the power at their command. When Ward was translated to Salisbury in 1667, Anthony Sparrow, whose

[7] This is, of course, a debatable point and one that probably can never be conclusively resolved. My own feeling is that Anglicans, by 1660, were a minority group in the total English population. However, there is no question but that by 1660, as Christopher Hill has stated in his *The Century of Revolution* (Edinburgh, 1961), p. 189, the majority of nobles and gentry, driven by a fear of social revolution, had again become enthusiastic supporters of the established Church. This of course accounts for the Cavalier Parliament.

name belied his spirit, replaced him. Sparrow was a fearless, determined, dedicated Anglican and a great favorite of the archbishop. Both of these men kept Sheldon regularly informed of all that went on in the Exeter area. Consequently, the record for that diocese is more complete than for any other in Sheldon's province.[8]

When Ward arrived in Exeter to take up his duties in 1661, he was appalled to find there were no Anglican services being held in the city at all. Presbyterians and Independents had partitioned the cathedral down the middle and were each using half for their services. They generously offered to divide the building three ways, so that Anglican services might also be conducted there, but the outraged bishop ordered both groups out, had the partition torn down, and inaugurated regular Church of England services there. This action made him such an unpopular figure within the city that, as he reported to Sheldon, his very life was endangered, and he could not have remained there had it not been for the mayor who, almost alone, came to his support.[9] When he applied to the justices for their assistance, Ward found to his dismay that fourteen in Exeter and even more, he was told, in Cornwall were "arrant Presbyterians."[10]

Despite this discouraging beginning, Ward energetically applied himself to his work. He wrote to the judges, expostulated with the justices, upbraided the city magistrates, and solicited aid from the deputy-lieutenant. By the time he finished his first visitation in 1665, he could report that conditions were vastly improved. There were, at least for the moment, no more conventicles in Cornwall, the justices were acting against dissenters, and he had confirmed over 6000 people in that one county.[11] Only Exeter and Plymouth remained stubbornly Presbyterian in outlook, and Ward ascribed that to the nonconformist ministers who, remaining in residence there, encouraged their former parishioners to hold fast to their old faith.[12]

When Sparrow took over the diocese in 1667, he vigorously seconded all measures which Ward had put into effect. In addition, he immediately called all the ministers of both Exeter and Plymouth to meetings where he spoke urgently to them of their duties and ordered them to begin

[8] Nearly all of this correspondence is contained in Add. Mss. C. 305, the Bodleian Library.
[9] *Ibid.*, Ward to Sheldon, no date, but in 1661 shortly after Ward arrived in Exeter.
[10] *Ibid.*, Same to Same, Dec. 19, 1663.
[11] *Ibid.*, Same to Same, Sept. 1, 1665.
[12] It was largely because of several letters from Ward and other bishops describing the impact of these resident nonconformist ministers that Sheldon determined to push for the Five-Mile Act.

holding regular catechism classes in all their parishes. This they solemnly promised to do, and, he reported to his chief, the mayors and their councils seemed pleased with this action.[13]

Over the next several years Sparrow's correspondence shows steady progress in his program of suppression of dissent and of rewinning the people of Exeter diocese over to the Church of England. He suffered only two serious setbacks – one when the Conventicles Act lapsed in 1669, and the other during the period of the king's indulgence in 1672-73. Otherwise progress at Exeter was almost continuous. By 1675, shortly before his translation to Norwich, the good bishop could report great satisfaction with conditions in all parishes under his jurisdiction. "Even at Burford," he wrote to Sheldon, "which we reckon to be the worst since the Proclamation [the 1672 Indulgence], the Conventicles are down, and the greatest part of the conventiclers come to church to their prayers, and not a man puts on his hat at sermon." [14] Furthermore, he concluded, scandalous clergy had practically disappeared and almost all magistrates were doing their utmost to enforce the laws.[15] It would appear that in fifteen years, Exeter diocese, once notorious for its non-conformity, had been Anglicanized.

Nor must we rely solely upon Ward's and Sparrow's reports to reach this conclusion. The historian of nonconformity in Exeter, after examining the records of the Exeter City Sessions from 1673 to 1678, found these figures:

1673 — 8 cases involving conventiclers were tried in that Court.[16]
1674 — 4 ,, ,, ,, ,, ,, ,, ,, ,,
1675 — 2 ,, ,, ,, ,, ,, ,, ,, ,,
1676 — 2 ,, ,, ,, ,, ,, ,, ,, ,,
1677 — 1 ,, ,, ,, ,, ,, ,, ,, ,,
1678 — 0 ,, ,, ,, ,, ,, ,, ,, ,,

Following 1678 there were three to four cases each year which came up before the City Sessions – probably encouraged by the Titus Oates affair. All told, there were only thirty cases involving nonconformist activity tried in Exeter between 1673 and 1687, and a number of these were repeaters.[17] Certainly this would seem to support the optimistic picture we receive from Ward and Sparrow.

---

[13] Add. Mss. C. 305, Sparrow to Sheldon, June 15, 1668.
[14] *Ibid.*, Same to Same, March 20, 1674/5.
[15] *Ibid.*
[16] A. Brockett, *Nonconformity in Exeter* (Manchester Univ. Press, 1962), p. 39.
[17] *Ibid.*

Furthermore, Sheldon's own census for 1676 demonstrates the same trend for the whole of England and Wales. According to the census figures, active dissent within the realm had been reduced to less than five per cent of the total population. By relentless execution of the laws, by persecution and prosecution of all dissent, Sheldon and his loyal subordinates had coerced the great majority of the islanders into renewing their allegiance to the Church of England – and this within a span of only sixteen to eighteen years. After a period of excessive liberty – at times bordering on chaos – driven by Sheldon, "order and unity" once again prevailed in English society.

Contrary to popular belief, such wholesale transformations of a people's religious and political beliefs through the agency of force and violence are hardly a rarity in history. In the seventeenth century Bohemia was converted from a predominantly Protestant country to a Catholic one, also in one generation; Protestantism was similarly stamped out in Poland earlier; and the Soviet transformation of Russian opinions and beliefs in the twentieth century is an even more obvious example.

Of course the price of such enforced conformity is always great, both in terms of the human suffering imposed at the time and also of the ultimate impact upon the country and its institutions. England was no exception to the rule. The Sheldon repression excluded from the Church some of its finest scholars and most saintly and devout leaders. As a result in the next generation there was a marked decline of intellectual vigor, a lowering of spiritual tone, and by mid-eighteenth century a general stultification ensued which affected every aspect of the country's religious life. This too must be traced, to some extent at least, to Sheldon's policies.

In sum, Sheldon's life accounted to a large extent for the following: It was because of his and Hammond's outstanding leadership that the Anglican organization survived the Interregnum as well as it did. He and his followers were, as has been shown, the architects of the Restoration religious settlement. Because of them the Church was re-established, doctrinally at least, in its Elizabethan form, much as it had been before the Civil Wars began. In addition, Sheldon was the key figure who saw to it that, once re-established, the Anglican monopoly was maintained over the next two decades. He guarded it against onslaughts from the Puritans, the king and his advisors, and parliament in turn, and succeeded in preserving it in what, in his opinion, was its proper form. As a result of his skillful defense and his determined repression of all dissent, most Englishmen came once more to accept the Anglican Prayer Book forms as their own.

In light of these accomplishments, it might be said that Sheldon influenced English development in the seventeenth century as much as any man living in that period with the possible exception of John Pym. As Pym could be considered the instrument which destroyed the social and religious system that was old England, so Sheldon was the instrument which restored that part of it which again entered English life and thought.

BIBLIOGRAPHY

PRIMARY SOURCES

A. Unpublished Manuscript Sources

British Museum Manuscripts
Add. MSS. 4162
Add. MSS. 5831
Egerton MSS. 2618
Harleian MSS. 3784
Harleian MSS. 3785
Harleian MSS. 6942
    This is a basic source for this work. There are some 150 letters, addressed to Sheldon during the period of the Interregnum, available in this manuscript.
Harleian MSS. 7377
    There are over 100 letters addressed to Sheldon in this manuscript, all of them from the latter part of his primacy.

Bodleian Library Manuscripts
Add. MSS. C. 302 and 303
    These manuscripts are the Dolben papers which contain a number of Sheldon's letters as well as many of his official records.
Add. MSS. C. 304a
Add. MSS. C. 304b
Add. MSS. C. 305
    There are numerous of letters from Sheldon to his bishops here.
Add MSS. C. 307
Add. MSS. C. 308
    This manuscript is Sheldon's private letter-book and contains numbers of letters which he wrote during the early years of his primacy.
MS. Bib. Eng. 1648, d. 3
    Seldon's personal bible.
Rawl. MSS. Q.C. 11
    Sheldon's will case.
Tanner MSS. 43, 45, 47, 49, 140
    There are a great number of letters to Sheldon available here, all written while he was archbishop.

Clarendon MSS. C. 70
Wood MSS. f. 35

Lambeth Palace Manuscripts
Lambeth MSS. No. 943
Lambeth MSS. SR-138
Cartes Miscellany, Vol. VI

B. *Published Primary Source Materials*

The Act of Parliament Against Religious Meetings. Anonymous Pamphlet. London, 1670.

Baillie, Robert. *The Journals of Robert Baillie*. 2 vols. London, 1842.

Baxter, Richard. *Savoy Conference*. London, 1661.

Birch, T. (ed.). *Familiar Letters of William Sancroft*. London, 1710.

Burnet, G. *History of His Own Times*. 2 vols. ed. by O. Airy. Oxford, 1897.

Burrows, Montagu (ed.). "The Register of the Visitors of the University of Oxford from A.D. 1647 to A.D. 1658." *The Camden Society Publications*. New Series, Vol. 29 (1881).

Calamy, E. *An Historical Account of My Life*. 2 vols. ed. by J. T. Rutt. London, 1830.

Cardwell, Edward. *Documentary Annals of the Reformed Church of England*. Oxford, 1839.

Clarendon, Edward, Earl of. *Life and Continuation of His Life*. 3 vols. Oxford, 1761.

— *History of the Rebellion and the Civil Wars*. 3 vols. Oxford, 1849.

— *Calendar of State Papers, Clarendon*. 4 vols. ed. by F. J. Routledge, et. al. Oxford, 1872–1928.

— *Calendar of State Papers, Clarendon*. Vol. 5. ed. by F. J. Routledge. Unpublished manuscript in typed form at the Bodleian library.

Clarke, W. N. "Illustrations of the State of the Church During the Great Rebellion." *The Theologian and Ecclesiastic*. Vols. VI through XV (1848–1853).

Cobbet, Wm. *Parliamentary History of England*. Vol. IV. London, 1808.

Cosin, J. *Works of John Cosin*. 4 vols. Oxford, 1845.

— "Correspondence of John Cosin." *Publications of the Surtees Society*, LII (1868). London, 1869.

Crewe, N. *The Memoirs of Nathaniel Crewe*, ed. by A. Clarke. Camden Society. New Series, LIII. London, 1895.

De Beer, E. S. (ed.). *The Diary of John Evelyn*. 6 vols. Oxford, 1955.

Dering, Edward. *Parliamentary Diary of Sir Edward Dering, 1670–73*. New Haven, 1940.

Gee, Henry, and Hardy, Wm. (eds.). *Documents Illustrative of English Church History*. London, 1914.

Great Britain. *Journals of the House of Lords*. Vols. VIII, IX, and X.

— *Journals of the House of Commons*. Vols. II, VIII, IX, and X.

— *Calendar of State Papers, Domestic*. For the years 1660–1680.

G. S. *The Dignity of Kingship Asserted*. For the Facsimile Text Society, Publication No 54, New York, 1942. (originally published in London, 1660).

Hamper, William (ed.). *The Life, Diary, and Correspondence of Sir William Dugdale*. London, 1827.

Heber, Reginald. *The Works of Jeremy Taylor*. Vol. I. London, 1828.

Historical Manuscripts Commission Reports.
Hockliffe, E. (ed.). *Diary of Ralph Josselin, 1616–83.* Camden Society Publications, 3rd Series, XV. London, 1908.
Hooke, Robert. *The Diary of Robert Hooke.* London, 1935.
Hughes, P. L. and Fries, R. F. (eds.). *Crown and Parliament in Tudor-Stuart England.* New York, 1959.
Isham, Sir Giles (ed.). *The Correspondence of Bishop Brian Duppa and Sir Justinian Isham, 1650–1660.* Northhamptonshire Record Society, Vol. XVII (1956).
Jacobson, W. (ed.). *The Works of Robert Sanderson.* 6 vols. Oxford, 1854.
Laud, Wm. *The Works of Archbishop William Laud.* 7 vols. Oxford, 1840.
Marah, W. H. (ed.). *Memoirs of Archbishop Juxon and His Times.* London, 1869.
Marvell, Andrew. *The Works of Andrew Marvell.* London, 1836.
McNeill, Charles (ed.). *The Tanner Letters.* Dublin, 1943.
Morley, G. *A Modest Advertisement Concerning the Protestant Controversy about Church Government.* London, 1661.
— *Several Treaties.* London, 1683.
Parker, Samuel. *History of His Own Time.* London, 1777.
Pepys, Samuel. *Diary and Correspondence of Samuel Pepys, FRS.* ed. by H. B. Wheatley. New York, 1955.
Todd, H. J. (ed.). *Memoirs of the Life and Times of the Rt. Reverend Brian Walton.* London, 1821.
Sheldon, Gilbert. *A Sermon Preached Before the King.* London, 1660.
Sudbury, John. *A Sermon Preached at the Consecration of the Right Reverend Father in God, Gilbert, Lord Bishop of London.* London, 1660.
Sylvester, M. (ed.). *Reliquiae Baxterianae.* London, 1696.
Walton, I. *The Complete Angler and Lives.* London, 1678.
Whiteman, E. A. O. *Calendar of the Letter Book of Archbishop Sheldon.* Unpublished summary of Add. MSS. C. 308. The Bodleian library.
Wilkins, David. *Concilia Magnae Britanniae et Hiberniae.* Vol. IV. London, 1737.
Womock, Laurence. *Pulpit-Conceptions, Popular-Deceptions.* London, 1662.

SECONDARY SOURCES

Barwick, Peter. *Life of John Barwick.* London, 1724.
Bate, F. *The Declaration of Indulgence, 1672.* London, 1908.
Bell, Walter G. *The Great Plague in London.* London, 1951.
Belloc, Hilaire. *Charles I, King of England.* Philadelphia, 1933.
Bloxam, M. H. *Monumental Effigies of Croydon Church.* London, no date.
Bosher, R. *The Making of the Restoration Settlement, 1649–1660.* London, rev. ed. 1957.
Bowles, W. L. *Life of Thomas Ken and Fortunes of George Morley.* 2 vols. London, 1830.
Brockett, A. *Nonconformity in Exeter.* Manchester, 1962.
Brown, L. F. "Religious Factors in the Convention Parliament," *English Historical Review*, XXII (1907), 51–63.
Browning, A. *Thomas Osborne.* 3 vols. Glasgow, 1944–51.
Bryant, A. *King Charles II.* London, 1931.
Cardwell, Edward. *History of Conferences.* Oxford, 1840.
Clarke, J. S. *Life of James II.* London, 1816.
Clarke, S. *Lives of Ten Eminent Divines.* London, 1862.

BIBLIOGRAPHY

Coltman, I. *Private Men and Public Causes, Philosophy and Politics in the English Civil War.* London, 1962.
Dictionary of National Biography.
D'Oyly, G. *Life of William Sancroft.* London, 1821.
Duncan-Jones, A. S. *Archbishop Laud.* London, 1927.
Echard, L. *The History of England.* Vol. III. London, 1718.
Every, George. *The High Church Party, 1688–1718.* London, 1956.
Feiling, K. *History of the Tory Party, 1640–1714.* Oxford, 1924.
Fell, John. *Life of Henry Hammond.* Oxford, 1847.
Fuller, T. *Church History of Britain to 1668.* London, 1868.
Gwatkin, H. M. *Church and State in England to the Death of Queen Anne.* London, 1917.
Hook, W. *Lives of the Archbishops of Canterbury.* Vols. XI and XII. London, 1875.
Hutton, W. H. *A History of the English Church.* New York, 1903.
Jordan, W. K. *The Development of Religious Toleration in England.* Vol. III. Cambridge, Mass., 1938.
Keith, C. P. *Henry Compton, Bishop of London.* Philadelphia, 1920.
Kennett, W. *A Complete History of England.* London, 1706.
Lathbury, T. *History of the English Episcopacy.* London, 1836.
— *History of Convocation.* London, 1842.
Lewis, George. *Robert Sanderson.* London, 1924.
Makower, Felix. *Constitutional History of the Church of England.* London, 1895.
Mathews, A. G. *Walker Revised.* Oxford, 1948.
Milman, H. H. *Annals of St. Paul's.* London, 1869.
Molesworth, Wm. *History of the Church of England from 1660.* London, 1882.
Morrah, Patrick. *1660, The Year of Restoration.* London, 1960.
Neal, Daniel. *History of the English Puritans.* London, 1754.
Ogg, David. *England in the Reign of Charles II.* 2 vols. Oxford, 1955.
Osmond, P. H. *Life of John Cosin.* London, 1913.
Pearson, Hesketh, *Merry Monarch.* New York, 1960.
Peyton, S. A. "The Religious Census of 1676," *English Historical Review*, XLVIII (1933), 99–104.
Plumptre, E. H. *Life of Thomas Ken.* 2 vols. London, 1890.
Pope, W. *Life of Seth Ward.* London, 1697.
Powicke, F. *Life of Richard Baxter.* London, 1924.
Pugh, P. H. *A Study of the Court of Arches from Michaelmas Term, 1668, to Michaelmas Term, 1670.* Unpublished B. Litt. thesis, Oxford University, Bodleian library.
Richards, T. "The Sheldon Census," *Transactions of the Society Cymmrodorion, 1925–26.* Published by the Society, 1926.
Salmon, N. *Lives of the English Bishops.* London, 1731.
— *Life of Bishop Compton.* London, 1718.
Shaw, W. A. *A History of the English Church, 1640–1660.* 2 vols. London, 1900.
Simon, W. G. *The Restoration Episcopate.* New York, 1965.
Southey, Robert. *The Book of the Church.* London, 1824.
Staley, V. *The Life and Times of Gilbert Sheldon.* London, 1913.
Stoughton, J. *History of Religion in England.* Vol. III. London, 1908.
Strickland, A. *Lives of the Seven Bishops.* London, 1866.
Sykes, N. *From Sheldon to Secker.* Cambridge, 1959.
Thoroton, J. *History of Nottinghamshire.* London, 1839.

Trevor-Roper, H. R. "The Restoration of the Church, 1660," *History Today*, II (Aug., 1952), 539–43.
Turberville, A. S. "The House of Lords Under Charles II," *English Historical Review*, XLIV (1929), 405–27.
Underdown, David. *Royalist Conspiracies in England, 1649–1660*. New Haven, 1960.
Usher, R. G. *Rise and Fall of High Commission*. Oxford, 1913.
Vernon, G. *Life of Peter Heylin*. London, 1862.
Walker, John. *Sufferings of the Clergy*. London, 1714.
Wedgwood, C. V. *The King's Peace*. New York, 1955.
— *The King's War*. London, 1958.
Whiteman, Anne. "The Re-establishment of the Church of England," *Transactions* of the *Royal Historical Society*, 5th Series (1955), 166–183.
Whiting, C. E. *Nathaniel, Lord Crewe*. London, 1940.
Whitley, W. T. *History of British Baptists*. London, 1923.
Williamson, H. R. *Jeremy Taylor*. London, 1951.
Wood, Anthony. *Athenae Oxoniensis*. 5 vols. London, 1820.
Wormold, B. H. *Clarendon: politics, history, and religion*. Cambridge, 1951.
— "The Earl of Clarendon and the Reformation of the English Church," *Cambridge Historical Journal*, V (1935), 14–15.
Wright-Henderson, P. A. *Life and Times of John Wilkins*. London, 1910.

INDEX

Act of Uniformity, 84–85, 92, 107, 143
Ailsbury, William, 43
Albemarle, duke of, see *Monk*, George
Allestree, Richard, 39, 57, 59
Anabaptists, 77, 118
Anglican Clergy, in Interregnum, 38
Anglicans, effects of Charles I's execution 34–35
Arlington, earl of, see *Bennet*, Henry
Arminianism, 5–6
Arundell, John, 136
Baillie, Robert, 64, 67
Bargrave, John, 153
Barlow, Thomas, bishop of Lincoln, 28–30, 51
Barrow, Isaac, bishop of Sodor and Man, 39
Barwick, John, 39, 43, 49–50, 52, 57, 61, 68, 72
Bates, William, 64
Bathurst, Ralph, 162
Baxter, Richard, 64, 66, 68, 72, 75, 78–80, 82, 89, 112
"Belleau", 37
Bennet, Henry, earl of Arlington, 96–98, 106, 125
Blandford, Walter, bishop of Oxford, 142
Book of Common Prayer and church discipline during the Interregnum, 49–50, 70, revision of, 83–84, 169–170, 148, 161
Breda, Declaration of, 62, 67
Bridgman, Orlando, 107, 116

Buckingham, George Villiers, 2d duke of, 99, 106, 123
Burnet, Gilbert, bishop of Salisbury, 80, 167–168
"Cabinet Council" at Canterbury, 64
Cabal, 125
Calamy, Edward, 64, 73, 75, 82
Cambridge University, contributes to Charles I's war finances, 14
Carleton, Guy, bishop of Bristol, 120
Carver, William, 152
Cary, Lucius, viscount Falkland, 7, 9, 47
Castlemaine, Lady, see Barbara *Palmer*, Duchess of Cleveland
Catherine of Braganza, Queen of England, 65
Cavalier Parliament, 81, 93
Charitable Uses Fund 41–42, 58
Charles I, King, 9, 13, 15, vow to restore Church of England, 16, 17, character of, 19, imprisoned at Carisbrooke Castle, 21, conversations with Sheldon, 23, 34, 71
Charles II, King, 9, 41, 48, 53, 63, 64, on religious settlement, 68–69, character of, 91, sympathetic to dissenters, 94, 103, 104, threatens Sheldon and the bishops, 105, and schemes of Comprehension, 112, Royal Proclamation against dissenters, 113, 116, asssits dissenters, 117, 119, 122, recall of Royal Licenses, 126, 159
Chillingworth, William, 5, 11

INDEX

Church of England, 36, restoration, reasons for, 88–90, 94, 119, 129
Church of Rome, 119
Clarendon, earl of, see *Hyde*, Edward
Cleveland, duchess of, see *Palmer*, Babara
Clifford, Thomas, Lord Treasurer, 106, 125
Comprehension, schemes of, 1667–68, 107
Compton, Henry, bishop of London, 165
Conventicles Act, 1664, 95, 143, proposed act 1668, 112, new act 1670, 114, 136, 146
Convention Parliament, 61, 70, 75, 76, 82
Convocation, 82
Cooper, Anthony Ashley, earl of Shaftesbury, 96, 98, 106
Corporations Act, 143
Cosin, John, bishop of Durham, 53, 83, 133, 153, 169
Council of Bishops, 1675, 126
Coventry, Thomas, 2, 3
Creighton, Robert, bishop of Bath and Wells, 153, 154
Crewe, Nathaniel, bishop of Durham, 165
Crofts, Herbert, bishop of Hereford, 18
Croydon Church, 166
Danby, Thomas Osborne, earl of, 125, 127
Declaration of Indulgence, 1672, 117
Declaration on Religion, 1661, 76
Dolben, John, bishop of Rochester, 105
Dover, Treaty of, 117, 118
Duncan, Eleazor, 39, 55, 59
Duppa, Brian, bishop of Salisbury, 17, 20–21, 38, 46, 48, 49, 51, 55, 61, 70
Durham Book, 83, 169–170
Dutch War, 1672, 117
Earle, John, bishop of Worcester, 5, 71
Elizabeth, Queen, 53
Episcopal Consecrations, 1660, 1661, 72
Evans, Daniel, 153
Evelyn, John, 41, 72
Exeter City Sessions, court of, 173
Exeter Diocese, its Puritanism, 171
Fell, Samuel, vice-chancellor of Oxford University, 24, 27
Fell, Mrs. Samuel, 30
Ferne, Henry, bishop of Chester, 37

Fifth Monarchy Men, 77
Finch, Heneage, Baron, 127
Five-Mile Act, 95, 112, 143–44, 146
Frewen, Accepted, archbishop of York, 78
Garthwaite, Timothy, 46
Gauden, John, bishop of Exeter, 72
Great Tew, 47
Great Tew Circle, 5
Griffith, George, bishop of St. Asaph, 72
Gunning, Peter, bishop of Chichester, 46, 131
Hacket, John, bishop of Lichfield and Coventry, 110–11, 134, 141, 149, 155
Hale, Mathew, 107
Hales, John, 5, 11
Hammond, Henry, activities during war, 14–15, joins king at Holmby Castle, 18, Leads Oxford Resistance Movement, 24, imprisoned at Oxford, 32, reacts to king's death, 34, 37, and correspondence network, 39, and Charitable Uses Fund, 41–42, writings, 45, guardian to young Lord Falkland, 47–48, 50, 53, 54, 57, 58
Hammond, Robert, 157
Henshaw, Joseph, bishop of Peterborough, 160
Henchman, Humphrey, bishop of London, 38, 72, 94, 113, 131, 163
Heylin, Peter, 169
Holder, Thomas 43
Hospital Census, 1665, 100
House of Commons, 18, 104, 110, 112, 122–24, 126
House of Lords, 93, 104, 105, 123, 124, 145
Hyde, Edward, earl of Clarendon, 5, and Long Parliament, 9–10, with Sheldon at All Souls, 1641–42, 13, 40, 52, 55, 56, 57, 60–63, helping Anglicans at Restoration, 66–69, 73, intercepting Puritan mails, 76, fears renewed revolt 1662, 86, 93, loses king's favor, 96–97, relations with Sheldon as archbishop, 144–45, 98, 99, fall from power, 102–4, banished from kingdom, 105
Independents, 30, 75
Indulgence, proposed, 1665, 97
Isle of Wight, Conference of, 1648, 20–21

INDEX

James, duke of York, 77, 103, 125, 149
Jenkins, Leoline, 39
Juxon, William, archbishop of Canterbury, 17, 59, 65, 72, 82, 152
Lambeth Palace Library, 152
Latitudinarians, 5
Laud, William, archbishop of Canterbury 5, 11, 93, 169
Lauderdale, John Maitland, duke of, 97, 103, 106, 123, 127
Lichfield Cathedral, 149
Lister, Martin, 136
Lucy, Henry, bishop of St. David's, 99
Manchester, Henry Montague, earl of, 68, 85, 107
Mansell, Francis, 37
Maplet, John, 47
Manton, Thomas, 64
Master, Thomas, 137
Medway, battle of, 100–101
Mewes, Peter, bishop of Bath and Wells, 145, 158
Monk, George, duke of Albemarle, 103
Morgan, Robert, bishop of Bangor, 144–45
Morley, George, bishop of Winchester, 5, with Charles I in his imprisonment, 19, leads Oxford Resistance Movement, 24, 37, 61, 71, 72, manages Savoy Conference, 80, 89, 105, 117, 121, 127, 131, 136
Nicholson, William, bishop of Gloucester 133
Non-residence in Restoration church, 154
Oates, Titus, 129, 171
Okeovers, landed family in Nottinghamshire, 35
Osborne, Thomas, see *Danby*, earl of
Oxford, surrenders to Fairfax, 23
Oxford, University of, 4, contributes to Charles war finances, 13–14, Presbyterian Visitors to, 25–31, 33, Resistance Movement, 23–31
Pakington, John, 35, 59
Palmer, Barbara, duchess of Cleveland, 63, 155
Palmer, Jeffrey, 47
Palmer, John, 33
Parker, Samuel, bishop of Oxford, 41, 60, 108–9, 111, 116, 165, 167

Parliament, Ordinance for "Reformation of Oxford University", 25, and Declaration of Indulgence, 1672, 121–22, 118
Payne, Robert, 37
Pembroke, William Herbert, earl of, 29
Pepys, Samuel, 65, 85, 86, 94, 160
Piers, William, bishop of Bath and Wells, 150, 153, 154
Plague, 1665, 163
Polyglot Bible, 45
Potter, Dr., pro-vice-chancellor of Oxford, 28
Presbyterians, 62, 116, 118
Prideaux, John, bishop of Worcestor, 6, 54
Prynne, William, 29
Pym, John, 10, 175
Quakers, 77, 118, 120
Reynolds, Edward, bishop of Norwich, 64, 72, 157
Richmond Conference on church discipline, 51
Roman Catholics, 93, 96, 116
Royal Society, 169
Rump Parliament, 34
Rupert, Prince, 100
Salisbury, bishop of, see *Duppa*, Brian
Sancroft, William, dean of St. Paul's, 72, 84, 166
Sanderson, Robert, bishop of Lincoln, 1, 5, 19, 21, 24, 28, 46, 50, 51
Savoy Conference, 78–81
Seekers, religious group in New Model Army, 25
Selden, John, 24, 45, 46
Sheldon Census, 128–29, 174
"Sheldon Dinners", 137–139
Sheldon, Gilbert, archbishop of Canterbury, early life, 1–12, and Calvinism, 6, early conservatism, 8–10, with Hyde at All Souls, 1642, 13, advises king at Oxford surrender, 15, assumes church leadership, 16, keeper of Charles I's vow, 16, joins king at Holmby Castle, 18, chief adviser to Charles during his imprisonment, 19–20, spends whole day with king at Carisbrooke Castle, 22–23, leads Oxford Resistance, 24–31, imprisoned at Oxford, 32–33, forms a correspondence net, 38, organizes Char-

itable Uses Fund, 41–44, and the problem of tutors during Interregnum, 44, and Polyglot Bible, 45, and Interregnum pamphleteering, 45–46, guardian to young Lord Falkland, 47–48, criticism of Hammond's writing, 48, and church discipline during Interregnum, 49–52, and problem of episcopal elections during Interregnum, 52–60, meets Charles II at Canterbury, 64–65, influence over Charles II, 65, livings returned at Restoration, 66, and new Anglican appointments 1660–61, 73, attempts to force Anglican discipline on London ministers, 77–78, and Savoy Conference, 79, sets strategy for Savoy Conference, 81, provides ministers for London congregations 1662, 85, leadership in securing Anglican re-establishment, 1662, 89, opposes Charles II on toleration, 92–106, becomes archbishop of Canterbury, 94, writes oppressive legislation, 95, reprimanded by king, 98, derided by court, 99, finds chaplains for the navy, 100, supervises government loans, 101, reprimands Charles II for loose living, 103, refuses king communion, 103, saves Hyde's life and estates, 105, loses influence with king, 105, and compromising bishops 1667–68, 108, influences House of Commons, 110, census of dissenters, 113, and Conventicles Act of 1670, 114–15, and Declaration of Indulgence 1672, 118–19, refuses to obey orders from king, 119, and House of Lords, 131–32, insists on bishops attendance at parliament or proxies, 133–35, politicking in House of Commons, 135–139, accused of bribery, 136, his view of religion, 138, surrenders church's right to tax itself, 140–41, author of Clarendon Code, 143, relations with Hyde as Lord Chancellor, 144, program for restored Church, 148, demands that all clerics hold catechism, 158, and ransoming Algerian captives, 164, charitable giving, 165, a thoroughgoing conservative, 169, holds Elizabethan mena, 170, restores Church of England as majority faith, 174

Sheldon, Ralph, 1
Sheldonian Theatre, 151
Shirley, Robert, 35, 59
Sion House Conference, 68–69
Skinner, Robert, bishop of Oxford, 141
Southampton, corporation of, 97–98
Sparrow, Anthony, bishop of Exeter, 118, 136, 171–73
St. Bartholomew's Day Oath, 84–86
St. Paul's Cathedral, rebuilding, 152
Steward, Richard, 15, 37
Strangways, John, Colonel, 127
Sudbury, John, dean of Durham, 153
Sweit, Giles, dean of Court of Arches, 156
Talbot, Gilbert, earl of Shrewsbury, 1
Taylor, Jeremy, 6–7, 37, 45, 51, 169
Taylor, William, 77
Test Act of 1673, 125
Test Act of 1675, 127
Test Act of 1678, 129
Thirty-nine Articles, 170
Thorndike, Herbert, 109, 169
Tillotson, John, archbishop of Canterbury, 119
Toleration Act of 1673, 124–25
Toleration Bill of 1667, 136
Tomkyns, Robert, 108
Triplett, Thomas, 46
Uxbridge, Treaty of, 15
Venner, Thomas, 77
Wallis, John, 57, 75
Walton, Brian, bishop of Chester, 45
War with Holland, 97
Ward, Seth, bishop of Salisbury, 127, 131, 145, 159, 171–72
Warwick, Philip, 33
Wenman, Francis, 5, 167
Wightwick, Henry, 27
Wilkins, John, bishop of Chester, 107–8, 159
Williamson, Joseph, 125
Wood, Anthony á, 41
Wood, Thomas, bishop of Lichfield and Coventry, 149, 154–55
Worcestor House Conference, 73–76
Wren, Christopher, 151–52
Wren, Mathew, bishop of Ely, 38, 48, 50, 54, 61, 83, 169
Wynne, Rice, 153